Tilting at Windmills

Tilting at Windmills

*How I Tried to Stop Worrying
and Love Sport*

ANDY MILLER

VIKING
an imprint of
PENGUIN BOOKS

VIKING

Published by the Penguin Group
Penguin Books Ltd, 80 Strand, London WC2R ORL, England
Penguin Putnam Inc., 375 Hudson Street, New York, New York 10014, USA
Penguin Books Australia Ltd, 250 Camberwell Road, Camberwell, Victoria 3124, Australia
Penguin Books Canada Ltd, 10 Alcorn Avenue, Toronto, Ontario, Canada M4V 3B2
Penguin Books India (P) Ltd, 11 Community Centre,
Panchsheel Park, New Delhi – 110 017, India
Penguin Books (NZ) Ltd, Cnr Rosedale and Airborne Roads,
Albany, Auckland, New Zealand
Penguin Books (South Africa) (Pty) Ltd, 24 Sturdee Avenue,
Rosebank 2196, South Africa

Penguin Books Ltd, Registered Offices: 80 Strand, London WC2R ORL, England

www.penguin.com

First published 2002

1

Set in 11.75/14.75pt Monotype Sabon
Typeset by Rowland Phototypesetting Ltd, Bury St Edmunds, Suffolk
Printed in Great Britain by Clays Ltd, St Ives plc

A CIP catalogue record for this book is available from the British Library

ISBN 0-670-89641-1

For Tina

I don't hate soccer. I hate soccer fans . . . I don't like the soccer fan, because he has a strange defect: he cannot understand why you are not a fan yourself, and he insists on talking to you as if you were . . . It isn't that he doesn't care a fig that *I* don't care a fig. It's that he can't conceive that *anyone* could exist and not care a fig. He wouldn't understand it even if I had three eyes and a pair of antennae emerging from the green scales of my nape. He has no notion of the diversity, the variety, the incomparability of the various possible worlds.

UMBERTO ECO

Whenever you get into the fanatic part of a person's personality, it's sort of ugly.

RANDY NEWMAN

Technical Note

The diagrams at the head of each chapter are designs for a tournament standard 'eternit' miniature-golf course, one of five miniature-golf systems recognized by the World Minigolf Sport Federation. Although a total of twenty-five different designs is available for 'eternit', a representative selection of eighteen has been made for this book.

Author's Note

Because *Tilting at Windmills* is a work of non-fiction, it is almost entirely mostly true. However, I have taken the liberty of sprinkling a handful of colourful lies throughout the book. To avoid confusion, where lies occur in the text, they are marked with this symbol:

I

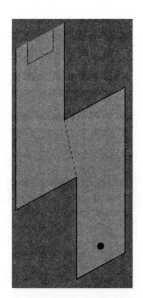

Blitz – flash of lightning

In the summer of 1984, three teenagers went to war. They did it not for their Queen or country but for themselves. Let down by nature and pretty much ignored by nurture, they allowed themselves to imagine the unimaginable, and for one summer to dream the impossible dream. It might take weeks or even months, it would require sacrifices and real strength, but through grit, determination and good old-fashioned slog (all phrases they were familiar with but never used) they would persevere and they would triumph. They would make the school hockey team. Hockey would be their game.

On the other side of the world, British athletes were in training for the Olympics. Later that summer, Daley Thompson, Sebastian Coe and a young oarsman called Steve Redgrave would all win gold for Great Britain. But that meant less than nothing to these three boys. Like most teenagers, they had been raised on football and cricket and rugby and cross-country and orienteering and swimming and climbing and tennis (optional) and athletics (100m, 200m, 1500m, hurdles, long jump, high jump, triple jump – mandatory). They had failed at all of them and therefore, some would say, they had failed at life. True, they were leading lights in the school debating society, but that had won them the approbation of almost no one – certainly no one in their peer group – except perhaps the art master who ran the society in his free time and whom the other teachers considered a weirdo.

But now a final shot at redemption had presented itself in the shape of a hockey ball. For some reason, the school was introducing hockey as the last new timetabled sport before that year's first major round of exams. The three boys would have to play it anyway, they reasoned, and nobody to their knowledge had a head start. There were no informal hockey practices, no knockabouts at break-time. Hockey was theirs for the taking. Grit, determination, good old-fashioned slog.

And so, in the first week of the summer holiday, they announced to their somewhat startled parents that they would be requiring hockey sticks, a full two months before the beginning of term. They were to begin their training as soon as possible.

Why would three infamous weeds even attempt something that a short lifetime of experience had told them was all but impossible? Aside from the ever-present expectation that, as boys, you would – should, must – like sport, the three of them shared an unspoken exasperation, a mutual disbelief, at their continued failure in the arena of physical education. All sport was apparently beyond them – theirs was a blanket incompetence. But why? They had a full complement of arms and legs, didn't they? Eyes? Only one of them needed glasses. None of them had ever actually played hockey but how hard could hockey be? It didn't look like it required too much brute force or unthinking heroics. It looked nimble, quick, conquerable, even for weeds. To master hockey would be to master sport itself, a small revenge for the playing-field humiliations they suffered on a bi-weekly basis.

On the first morning of training the three boys took a tennis ball and their new hockey sticks along to the park and warmed up by batting the ball about between them. After a while, and suitably warmed up, they realized they didn't know what to do next. Start playing a game of hockey presumably. But none of them knew the rules. So they walked to the nearest sports shop and bought a copy of *Know the Game: Hockey*, and returned to the park with it. Having scanned the first few pages and concluded that it needed serious scrutiny at a later date, they returned to knocking the ball around aimlessly. They got bored. They went home.

And so it continued for much of that summer. Their commitment to self-improvement was limited. The boys didn't change their diet or work on set pieces or start taking steroids. *Know the Game: Hockey* remained unread. All they did was take a tennis ball to the park and knock it about between them until one of them had had enough, at which point the other two would be only too happy to retire for the day and talk about The Smiths, or watch a video – an Orson Welles or an episode of *The Prisoner*. The recorder was a top-loading Ferguson that one of them had won several years previously in a competition in *Look and Learn* magazine. But they continued to practise in their own way, most days in fact, right through July and August.

One of the three – we'll call him Andy – had perhaps the least enthusiasm for this task. And, indeed, he was the most hopeless of the group. In attempting to strike the ball, he would invariably miss, skimming the top of it or hitting the ground and painfully jarring his wrists and arms. Sometimes he'd succeed in smashing the ball and it would fly straight and true. But most of the time it would curve away from its intended target, left or right, with no discernible bias that could be corrected. He never improved, he never progressed. But he tried to believe that application alone would be enough, that by turning up again and again, fairness and justice would somehow assert themselves. He played in tracksuit bottoms and top, often too hot but too embarrassed to take them off and reveal his stick-thin arms and legs. It was the summer of Frankie Says! and 'Two Tribes'. A point was all that you could score. But it would be our tribe that scored it.

The weeks ticked down and the new term arrived. In anticipation of the introduction of hockey, it was announced that there would be a training session after school on the first Tuesday for all interested parties, conducted by one of the games teachers, Dave Jackson. Mr Jackson was a hairy man with one long eyebrow who occasionally taught history badly. He couldn't spell that well and he couldn't do joined-up writing on the blackboard. Once, he had emphasized a point about the Industrial Revolution by scrawling the word **'charttism'** then underlining it for effect. His nickname was Wookie.

No one was more puzzled than Mr Jackson to see those three twits from the debating society line up on the all-weather pitch for his pre-season hockey warm-up. This session was supposed to help identify the youngsters who might make up this year's squad, not act as a nursery for no-hopers and closets. 'Miller?' said Mr Jackson, partly in disbelief but mostly because he wasn't sure that that was the boy's name.

'Sir,' replied the boy.

Wookie grunted and hoisted up his eyebrow. 'Right,' he said, 'right. Good.' He moved on to the next boy in the line, one of the rugby first-team regulars. 'Good boy, Simon,' he said.

The all-weather pitch was situated opposite the school and so-called because, whatever the weather, it was always hell to play on. No one was quite sure what it was made of. It looked like a million smashed-up bricks – the remains of a library or a hospital or something, one of the boys had said – and if you fell, it was like falling on to something harder than Tarmac. Bits of it would stick in you. But in the rain, it would haemorrhage uncontrollably, bleeding sediment all over your legs and clothes. Tiny rivers of red would flood out on to the grass and coagulate on the road.

This Tuesday, mercifully, it was dry and not too cold. If

anything coagulated today, there would at least be no confusion as to what it was.

The three boys lined up beside about a dozen of their fellows, most of whom were already members of the school's various squads. If they were as surprised as Wookie to see these outsiders, they kept it quiet, preferring simply to ignore them and to talk among themselves, which was fine with the three boys.

'Right, you lot, settle down,' said Mr Jackson, in his usual declamatory manner, although no one was doing anything except standing around waiting to start. 'Form a semi-circle.'

They did so, and Jackson stood in the middle of it, putting down the bucket of balls he had been carrying. 'Right,' he said, holding aloft a hockey stick. 'This is a hockey stick.' He paused to let them all see it. 'A stick. For playing. Hockey.'

'Yes, sir,' said somebody.

'*It wasn't a question! I know what it is!*' said Mr Jackson, unconvincingly. 'I repeat, this is a hockey stick. It is not a weapon. It is for hitting the ball, not for hitting the legs of other players. If I see anyone doing that, they are off and they will not play again. Understood?'

The boys nodded. But they were slightly taken aback. Mr Jackson was never normally so civilized. Not a weapon? It would have been marginally less surprising if he had said, 'This is a hockey stick. It is not a weapon – at least, not officially. But you may find it makes an effective cosh. A player's weak points are the eyes, the neck and the base of the spine. Understood?' But no, he had chosen the path of peacefulness and light. It was a good start. This is where it begins, thought Andy. This is going to be our game. Here we go.

'All right,' said Mr Jackson, 'let's get you hitting a few balls. Remember, don't bring the stick above waist height. That is illegal and I don't want to see it happening.' He tipped the bucket of balls out on to the ground. 'Spread out along the touchline. Start when I tell you.' And he started knocking two or three balls to each player.

Andy felt his stomach knotting up. He knew that stopping

these balls was his first major test. Stopping the ball had thus far proved to be one of the major weaknesses of his game, stopping it and also hitting it. Both were elementary hockey skills but both exposed his lack of hand–eye co-ordination. The obvious thing to do would be simply to use the hockey stick to bring the balls to rest. But he knew that was asking for trouble. So he would play it safe at this stage and use an alternative blocking technique. He braced himself to receive the first ball.

Here it was, now, rolling towards him, lazy but direct, hit one-handed by Mr Jackson. With a brief calculation, he planted his foot firmly but nonchalantly in what he hoped would be the path of the ball and waited. Andy had noticed how good players, when catching or clearing, made it look as though the result were never in doubt. They seemed to draw the ball towards them through personality alone, as though they knew there was nowhere the ball would rather be than resting at their feet or safe in their cupped hands. It just wanted to be with them. He leant, one arm extended, on his hockey stick and tried to give a smile of easy certainty that would suggest to the ball closing in on him that he, too, could be trusted, that to stop obediently at his feet would be like coming home, but even as he did so he was aware that the effect was more sinister than reassuring. With his sunken chest and over-eager grin, he looked more like Charles Hawtrey than Ian Botham. So instead he stood to attention and tried hard to look confident, hoping that that would be enough to put the ball at its ease.

It worked. The first ball rebounded gently off his right foot and cruised to a halt just by the head of the hockey stick on which he had been leaning. Perfect. The second ball followed much the same route, glancing off his toe this time, but not so fast as to send it racing away. But the third ball, dispatched again one-handed by Mr Jackson, had more spin on it, the result of being struck while the games master was turning his attention to the boy next to Andy. It was more suspicious than its partners and moved faster, more stealthily; and his foot, however firmly placed, was not enough to prevent it hopping past him, over his boot and into the long grass at the edge of the all-weather pitch.

As the ball raced out of bounds, and he turned to lunge after it, hoping his confident stance would somehow convert itself into a stylish sweep of the arm, easily plucking the ball out of the air, he knew he was going to fall over, fall over hard, clumsily and conspicuously. At that moment he hated himself, ashamed that his own ungovernable limbs were betraying him once again, in full sight of his friends and his enemies alike. His ears were burning before he hit the ground.

And yet he didn't quite fall. His right hand ploughed into the wet earth and his left slammed down right on top of the hockey ball. Pushing back as quickly as possible, he stood upright, the ball in one hand, a clump of grass in the other. He staggered back a little, muddy but unbowed. He made eye-contact with no one, just dropped the ball at his feet with its buddies and waited. There was dogshit under his fingernails, he realized. 🐾

(🐾 There wasn't. I've told this story so many times, I can't really remember which bits are true and which bits aren't. But that bit definitely isn't. There was a dog, but the rest probably appeared first in the telling about five years after the event.)

Ah, come on, he thought. But nobody had seen.

Mr Jackson had now reached the end of the line. 'OK, off you go. Waist height, remember. Let's see how you do.' And the boys began to hit the balls. Mr Jackson stood with his arms crossed, brow furrowed, assessing technique, weighing up potential, or maybe just trying to remember the guiding principles of charttism. 'Follow it through,' he said to the first boy, who was knocking balls effortlessly across the pitch, and moved on.

Andy watched his two friends. One was hitting balls ineffectually, but at the same time with an admirable lack of commitment. Matthew had long ago mastered an apparent weariness beyond his years that was all the more convincing for being completely genuine. He was now applying this to his hockey technique. He hit the ball like yawning. It was a brilliant performance, not exactly bored but demonstrably indifferent to the result.

Andy turned to his other friend Martin to point this out, but

Martin had gone, replaced by a *doppelgänger* who was striking balls with not a little skill and, worse, bright-eyed enthusiasm. The real Martin was clearly in a pod back in the changing rooms. He'd shown little of this talent during their summer practices but now, inexplicably, he was dispatching shots with aplomb. 'Good *lad*, Cowley!' said Mr Jackson, appreciatively, as he passed.

Andy looked down at the ball at his feet. He already knew, of course, that he would never make the hockey team, had known it all summer. He had neither reserves of self-confidence to draw on nor hitherto concealed ball skills with which to dazzle his comrades and impress his teachers. There would be no sudden glorious transformation for him; when the session was over, nobody would see him in a different light. But he would not be beaten today. He would keep his dignity.

He stared hard at the ball, the little bastard that had nearly caused him to tumble, and imagined with satisfaction the crack it would make as he sent it on its way, following it in his mind's eye as it flew directly upfield and out of bounds. Here we go. He drew back the stick, mustering as much control as he could, wanting to smash it hard, square, unambiguously. Here we go.

But he never made contact with the ball. Instead, at the height of its upward swing, the stick's progress was interrupted by the surprise appearance of Mr Jackson's face.

Jackson had been wandering up behind the boys monitoring their progress, but when he had reached Miller he had stopped, not to watch the useless twonk – what was the point? – but because he was thinking about something else. It was the start of term. At the end of the previous school year he had promised himself he would look around for something else. But here he was again, stuck with these hopeless specimens and trying to make men out of them. He hadn't wanted to be a games teacher, had hoped for better things from his rugby career, but it hadn't worked out. Still, there was something to be said for it. The tight little world of teams and fixtures and the company of the lads.

In fact, he'd just been contemplating Saturday's match with Trinity when – WHACK! – something struck him a glancing

8

blow on the bridge of the nose and he bawled in pain and disbelief at being knocked out of his reverie. *'MILLER!'*

Silence. All the boys froze. In the road, a woman stopped with her dog to watch the show.

Andy was stunned. Under other circumstances, the thought of giving Mr Jackson a hefty smack in the face would have been very enjoyable, but one look at Wookie's *grievously* puzzled – and bleeding – expression told him that he was in trouble.

'What did I just say, Miller?'

A ripple of anticipation passed through the group. This was going to be good.

'Hockey sticks aren't weapons, sir.'

'Aren't weapons, you PRAT!'

'It was an accident, sir. I didn't see you.' It sounded pathetic, a liar's catchphrase. But it was true.

'YOU DON'T BRING IT UP ABOVE YOUR WAIST!' roared Jackson, snatching the hockey stick from Andy's grasp. *'WERE YOU LISTENING AT ALL?'* He was getting seriously worked up now. In the road, the dog started barking.

'Come on, sir,' Andy wanted to say, 'calm down. It was just a silly mistake. There's no need for all this. I really do want to play hockey. I've been practising all summer!' But what was the point? Jackson was so angry he was practically in spasm. It would be like trying to pacify an embolism. 'No, sir,' he said. 'Sorry, sir.'

'Sorry, sir!' said Jackson, mimicking him. He shook his head and took a deep breath. 'Go on, Miller, get off. Go and get changed and then report back here to me.' He let go of the hockey stick, let it clatter on the ground. 'The rest of you, get on with it. *WELL, GO ON, MILLER!'*

All eyes were on him. He picked up the stick and his jacket and walked off the all-weather pitch, into the grass and down the slope to the road. He didn't look back, didn't make eye-contact with anyone, not Matthew, not Martin, not even the spectating woman, whose dog, he realized in a moment of sudden and unwelcome clarity, had been playing in the grass by the all-weather pitch. Still, nice to be able to put a face to it . . .

Hitting Wookie hadn't been a mistake, not really, he knew that. He hadn't meant to do it, but clearly somebody higher up had other plans. It was all too perfect, too symmetrical. Spend all summer hard at work and end up being sent off when you've barely even hit the ball, humiliated in front of your best friends, your worst enemies and a dog whose shit is all over your hand. Coincidence? No, not coincidence. There was no point in protesting because it was all part of a bigger picture. Jesus didn't want him for a hockey sunbeam. He was doomed to be an exile, condemned to wander the earth, hilariously.

And as he walked now, the unfairness of it burned like cramp. The more he thought about it, the angrier he grew. His self-pity became something else, something bigger and madder and more exhilarating.

He remembered how he had felt scrabbling about in the grass, how humiliated. He didn't want to feel like that again, and – suddenly he resolved there and then – he wasn't going to. He had been smuggled into this world and dumped, apparently alone, singularly unsuited to its particular customs and exercises. And clearly nothing he did could change that. He had tried and he had failed. He had given it – oh, yes – his best shot. So he must turn it to his advantage. He would define himself as much by what he wasn't as by what he was.

It was then that his adolescence truly began. He knew that he would get his power by saying, 'No.'

And for fifteen years he was as good as his word.

I'm sorry this book has been such a long time coming, but I honestly thought somebody else would write it first.

I hate sport.

I've always hated it.

I don't just mean one or two types of sport: I don't get any of them. I hate football. I don't understand cricket. Swimming leaves me cold. Rugby strikes fear into my heart. For something so dangerous, motor-racing is unbelievably boring. I haven't got the balls for snooker. Darts is a drag. Athletics? I've got a note from my mum. Anyone for tennis? I'd rather stick needles in my eyes.

Saturday afternoons, the beautiful game, the roar of the crowd, the euphoria of victory, the humiliation of defeat but knowing we'll be back next week, the hot pie in cold hands, the location of the hamstring, that episode of *Whatever Happened to the Likely Lads?* where they try to avoid learning the result of the big match so they can watch it on TV later, all mean *nothing* to me.

In a nutshell, and to paraphrase Public Enemy's 'Fight The Power', Sir Geoff Hurst was a hero to most but he never meant shit to me – motherfuck him, if you will, and Michael Owen too.

I don't even know why people throw Frisbees in the park on a sunny day.

Which is no mean feat when you think about it. I mean, this stuff is everywhere – if you're a man, more than everywhere. In your school, at work, on TV, on the radio, in newspapers, conversations with your mates, conversations with strangers, conversations with my mother (if the sport in question is golf), in the air, on the airwaves, in the atmosphere and stratosphere, we are all supposedly One Nation Under A Ball. The sporting life is the life of us all.

Well, not quite all. Whisper it, but many of us *aren't really bothered*. For all the thousands of people who can name the line-up of the 1966 England World Cup team, there are millions of us who can't. We have no idea what 'silly mid-on' means; we do not know the difference between rugbys 'league' and 'union'; we would be unable to name three British tennis players if you put a gun to our heads (er, Henman, Rusedski, er . . . no, you're going to have to shoot me); we do not, essentially, care What Happened Next.

The 1990s, therefore, was not a good time for us. Sport For All became an order rather than a suggestion. We watched in horror as the UK's obsession with games passed into mania, becoming unapologetically middle class in the process. 'It's in there all the time,' says Nick Hornby, in the very first line of *Fever Pitch*, referring to his love of football, 'looking for a way out.' Well, let it out, Nick, I say, let it out and be done with it. The rest of us could do with a break.

Sport started to encroach on the most sheltered of existences. Spurred on by the success of *Fever Pitch*, a weeping Gazza in Italia 90 and, post-Hillsborough, no nasty terraces, our former Walter Softy friends revealed that, actually, they liked football too but had previously been too embarrassed to admit it. Now, however, they felt free to 'come out' and celebrate their own hitherto denied fandom. Hence the unfunny fanzines and (ugh) bittersweet memoirs, the appearance of Fantasy Football in broadsheet newspapers, the phenomenon of the replica 1970s shirt – Holland, maybe, or Brazil – that showed the wearer's reverence for the classicism and flair of *futbol mondial*, the horrible rise of David Baddiel and Frank Skinner . . .

Actually *Fever Pitch* is a very good book, but I rather feel about its author the way John Lennon felt about Jesus: 'He was all right, but his disciples were thick and ordinary. It's them twisting it that ruins it for me.' Football's new converts, like many born-agains, are saucer-eyed and slightly embarrassing. In the hands of these disciples, every football victory is a rapturous celebration of being, every loss a saccharine reminder of 'thirty years of hurt'. The eerily blank David Beckham, a real-life Chauncey Gardiner, becomes an inarticulate poet of the ball, a 'noble savage' in a sarong; poor Paul Gascoigne, who started the whole thing, who beat his wife and pissed away his talent, is a genius whose fall from grace has the resonance of Greek tragedy. Or not.

But that's the top end. Mostly it's just boys making lists and sniggering.

This is my dream. If I had the money, I would spend it wisely and buy the Football League. I would then shut down every football club in the country except, say, Manchester United and Chelsea, who would be renamed the Red Team and the Blue Team. The Red Team and the Blue Team could play each other every week in a neutral and empty venue of my choosing, over and over again until people got bored with them. It might take a while but it would be worth it.

I told you I hated football.

At the same time that football was booming, thanks to the newly enthused middle class, sport in general was undergoing an unprecedented commercial upturn. Satellite and cable TV coverage multiplied; whole channels were devoted to sport, any sport. In the week I write this, British television viewers can choose between soccer, horse-racing, world pro darts, boxing, snowboarding, indoor motocross, basketball, motorsport max, two flavours of wrestling, assorted extreme sports, American football, drag racing, ice hockey, indoor bowls, rugby union, skiing and snooker. And that's just on the five terrestrial channels. Bring on the satellites and the choice explodes. And then there's the phone-ins, the quiz shows, the twice-hourly bulletins on the news networks . . .

In addition, cross-media sponsorship deals became enormous – Nike, Coca-Cola, News Corporation; the stars became bigger than the sports they represented; and ever more inventive ways were devised to part fans from their money, because now there were fans who could afford it. Three replica kits a season? Yes, please! Books, videos, videogames? Give me more! Salt and Lineker crisps? Ha ha! Brilliant! Most grisly of all, perhaps, was the rise of the high-street sportswear shops. As the country reached an arterio-sclerotic peak, we started dressing more and more like athletes. We pulled on our replica football shirts, our designer tracksuits and our expensive trainers and went nowhere. It didn't matter if you didn't take part as long as you looked like you did.

And where the money went, power followed. This boom in sport rippled through the culture. A new status quo took hold that encompassed pop, fashion, politics and literature. Call it what you like – *Loaded* culture, New Laddism, New Labour or Cool Britannia – it was everywhere, and it had its roots in the bourgeoisification, the dumbing up, of sport in the 1990s. 'Pringle?' as the *nouveau*-fan in the Arsenal shirt said on *The Fast Show*.

There is no culture of hating sport in the UK. You either love it – and it's better for you if you do – or you try to ignore it. That's not to say a working ignorance of these matters is all bad. Want to shut up a taxi driver when he asks you if you saw the match? It only takes five words – 'No' 'I' 'don't' 'like' and 'football'. Go on. Be brave. Try it.

And when, in my weaker moments, I have become interested in a particular match or an important fixture (even I've found it difficult sometimes not to be caught up in the odd international) it's the same response every time. A sort of patronizing, oh-I'm-really-glad-you-like-this-but-you're-not-a-Real-Fan-like-me sort of response. It's all about teams and gangs, cliques that number in the millions.

I have several friends – Pringles to a man – who believe in their hearts that this is a good thing, that sport is a universal language whose words and values transcend barriers of class, profession and nationality, and that the spread of sport in the last few years has brought us all closer together, healing divisions, preparing us for the challenges of the new century. To which I reply, yeah, that's lovely – if you speak the language.

Because many don't. What about those of us who don't share your enthusiasm? Where's our connection to our fellow man? What are we supposed to do? To put it in *your* terms: when it comes to sport, the world is A Game Of Two Halves – those who play and those who don't, those who believe and those who don't. It makes me Sick As A Parrot, whatever that means.

Because what it always comes down to, in the end, with sport, is this: the only reason you don't like sport, it's said, is because you're no good at it – because you were the last one to be picked for the football team.

Yes, you're right. I *was* the last one to be picked for the team. Is this an insufficient reason to bear a grudge? Eleven childhood years of institutionalized humiliation and public rejection by your peers? I don't think so.

Because, make no mistake, sport hates me too.

My sports incompetence knows no boundaries. I can't catch. I can't throw. I still don't know how to bowl over-arm. My skill with a football is about as good as Diana Ross's. You may recall her attempt on goal in the opening ceremony of the 1994 World Cup. She shot from six feet and missed. Poor Miss Ross. I know how she felt.

And the heartbreaking thing is, as a child, I was quite game. I didn't want to be bad, I just couldn't help it. I was anti-gifted. Time and again I would train or try a new sport (badminton, cross-country, three wasted summers of tennis lessons) but it was always the same story: I was useless. I can still hear Mr Wheatley as I try hopelessly to reach the football: 'Careful, Miller, you might touch it!' Mr Wheatley was all right too: he played us Neil Diamond in music lessons and made us write poems about the neutron bomb (this was the seventies), but on the sports field he was a track-suited tormentor with a whistle.

It was this lack of encouragement, this covert bullying, that gradually wore me down. I was hopeless at sport, and because sport is played mostly in terms of winners and losers, members and non-members, I stayed hopeless. Wasn't it the job of the teacher to teach me how to be better at it? Or to find a way of sustaining my flagging enthusiasm, rather than leaving me to be figuratively and literally beaten down into the ground? Apparently not.

The story I told you about the hockey practice is significant not because it happened – it did – but because it was the first time I used my uselessness at games for my own purposes. I took the raw materials of that day – embarrassment, shame, despair – and fashioned them into a shield and spear I could use in a noble crusade against sport. My failure became the first in a long line of cheerfully cynical anti-sport fables that protected me from further harm and struck back at the unfair world. Who cared if the details got embroidered here and there? The bigger truth must out.

Over the years, I have always particularly enjoyed setting about the everyday, common-sense things we think we know about sport, all that nonsense about it bringing people together and building character. I believe I have identified seven great myths of sport and established beyond all reasonable doubt their essential idiocy. I have even toyed with the idea of publishing my theories as a pamphlet and handing it out on street corners or outside football matches. It would be called *Against Sport*, or *This Sporting LIE*, or maybe just:

THE RULES

The Seven Pillars of
Received Wisdom

I • II • III • IV • V • VI • VII

I

🪁 Sport Brings People Together

Yes. People who like sport.

II

🪁 Sport Builds Character

A bit like saying, 'A hat builds character', or 'Twelve uninterrupted hours of hardcore Swedish porn build character.'

If you think it does, it does.

But WARNING: if taken to excess, hats, porn or sport will damage character beyond repair.

III

🪁 Football Is A Beautiful Game

A slogan coined by the footballer Pelé. Maybe football is a beautiful game when played by him. But not by you and not by anyone you know.

Of course, the phrase is also widely used to denote the symbolic Beauty of Football, i.e., football is a beautiful game, and so is life. By extension, therefore, the justification for nearly every bit of drivel ever written about soccer, particularly the watery self-analyses of the last ten years.

In essence, a helpful way of thinking about life if the scope of life itself is too much of a strain for you.

IV

⚔ It's Not Whether You Win Or Lose, It's How You Play The Game

I love this one. Not believed by any serious athlete, obviously, but a piece of jolly propaganda that refuses to die.

Brief history lesson: sport develops as ritualized re-enactment of man's struggle for survival. Ancient Greeks scamper about in nude and gorge themselves on red meat in pursuit of absolute glory. Generations of Britons enjoy wrestling, cudgelling, cock-fighting, etc., with no thought of self-improvement until early to mid-nineteenth century, when English public schools reinvent sport as moral instrument of education. Battle of Waterloo won on playing fields of Eton. Sub-continents oppressed and made to play cricket against their will. Together, Colonialism and Amateurism conquer the world. In 1896, sport seized upon by eccentric French aristocrat as means of reviving fortunes of French nation. Inadvertently founds Olympic movement, ushering in century of sanctimonious humbug in which bogus ideal of participation (see above) repeatedly used as front for empire-building aspirations of countries, corporations or individuals. At beginning of twenty-first century, nations enslaved to producing or consuming running shoes; Rupert Murdoch describes sport as 'battering ram' for opening up new media territories; dishonesty, drug abuse and match-fixing present at all levels of international competition.

To recap: it's not whether you win or lose, it's how you play the game. As long as you win.

V

⚔ Sport Is A Universal Language

Yes. If you learn to speak it, you can communicate on a superficial level with idiots all over the world.

A close relation of Sport Brings People Together,* and similarly non-transferable. Sport will often make a bad religious or political situation worse, e.g. foxhunting's enduring role in the class struggle, the football matches that precipitated the so-called Soccer War between Honduras and El Salvador (three thousand dead, six thousand wounded), the Troubles in Northern Ireland of the late 1960s. 'Soccer was a shared enthusiasm across the sectarian divide,' note sport historians Richard Holt and Tony Mason. 'But far from healing communal hatreds, it exacerbated them.'

We use the Universal Language of sport to distract ourselves from our routine and compulsive inhumanity to our fellow man. Perhaps the most popular story told in this ersatz Esperanto is that of the Christmas Day 1914 ceasefire between British and German troops. Ordinary soldiers from both sides laid down their rifles, it is said, and staged an impromptu football match in no man's land. They shook hands, showed family photographs and exchanged items of food and tobacco. For a brief moment, thanks to the panacea of sport, a ray of light shone down on mankind in its darkest hour.

And on Boxing Day they were all trying to kill one another again.

(* See also: If All The Nations Of The World Played Sport, There Would Be No More Wars.)

VI

🎐 Sport Is The New Religion

Tricky. A cliché the writer Giles Smith calls 'the hallmark of the baffled observer'. And yet, speaking as a baffled observer myself, sport today does seem like a religion, in a sort of corrupt, medieval way: all that mindless zealotry and worshipping of false idols, the conviction that salvation can be secured on earth by the payment of indulgences, e.g., season tickets, multi-channel subscriptions, more shoes.

The stadium as cathedral, the match as mass: these are certainly clichés. But they are clichés people want to believe. In fact, the *idea* that sport is a religion is the foundation stone of the whole sports industry, because the *idea* is easily converted into money and clout.

There can be no better expression of your passion for life than being part of a crowd that believes there is no better expression of your passion for life than sport. Now buy our shoes. Just do it.

Believing in a church of sport also legitimizes the kind of loony devotional behaviour that causes *Star Trek* fans to be laughed at in the street and gets actual religious extremists locked up. Fat, forty, and dressed as a Klingon? You must be a dysfunctional saddo. But fat, forty and wearing a shirt with **B E C K H A M** pressed on to the back, which you paid for by the letter? England salutes you, sir!

If sport is the new religion, it's a church whose doctrine is immutable. Fit in. Buy stuff. Be passionate, within recommended guidelines. Look like everyone else. Know your place. Three Lions good, Starfleet bad.

The idea or the thing itself: either way, we need less heraldry and more heresy.

VII

🎯 'Some people think football is a matter of life and death . . . I can assure them it is much more serious than that.' Bill Shankly

The worst of the lot, expressed in sport's preferred vernacular – weighty yet wry. Contains elements of all of the above. Bill Shankly was, by reputation, a kind and honourable man, but the exploitation of his words is at the root of the problem with sport.

I can't express this more eloquently than the Liverpudlian whose testimony concludes *Cheer Up Kevin Keegan*, Richard Alwyn's film about the rivalry between England and Scotland in the run-up to Euro 2000: 'It's been hyped as a battle of Britain. I think calling any football match a battle does not do the sport any good at all. Bill Shankly once said, "Football is not a matter of life and death – it's far more important than that." And we all went with that, until Hillsborough. And that gives you some perspective about the game. When you lose young people that were just out for a day out, when ninety-six people die needlessly to go to a football match, when you have to hold an assembly in school the next day and talk about people that have died, that puts football into perspective.

'Now, I love the game, I really do. I passionately love the game but it's still only that: it's still only a game. It gets hyped up now to the extent where you really can't believe . . . And I mean, it's two teams playing football for a place in Euro 2000. It is not life and death.'

*

These are the windmills I have devoted my life to storming, not doubting for a moment that they are giants. Through the years I have revised and rehearsed my attacks on them with military precision, seeking out their weak points, trying to expose their fatal flaws. It has been a holy war.

However, around the time of my thirtieth birthday, I began to have doubts. I realized I was turning into a lunatic.

'Whoever writes about his childhood,' said George Orwell, 'must beware of exaggeration and self-pity', which is good advice I have ignored my entire adult life. In my crusade against sport, exaggeration and self-pity have been my close companions since the day I was dismissed from the hockey pitch, along with indignation, sarcasm and dubious totalitarian fantasies about Red Teams and Blue Teams.

My crusade was becoming a reflex, a knee-jerk. I thought I still believed it, but I couldn't be sure. I knew I was displaying the kind of unthinking nutty fanaticism I was so quick to condemn when it occurred in sport. Strong opinions that had seemed audacious and iconoclastic when I was a teenager now just sounded cranky and weird.

In Michael Bracewell's novel *Perfect Tense*, the anonymous narrator, a middle-aged office worker, reflects on how much of his personality was formed by the experience of being one of 'the big girls' blouses on whom the football teacher had let loose his ridicule':

This dandyism of our youth – which mocked the sombre teacher and the tough delinquent alike – seemed only to hatch a disaffection through which we subscribed to a premature sense of futility; and from there we turned Puritan, bitter and parched, concluding that we hated the world because we'd found no place within it.

I didn't yet hate the world, not quite, but one day soon I would, and for what? A half-remembered disappointment from half a lifetime ago.

And so, at the end of the sportiest decade of all time, I set out on a new quest: to meet the world half-way. I would try to understand the New Religion. I would speak the Universal Language to the best of my abilities. I would set aside my prejudices and I would tell the truth.

But I could not relinquish the past so easily.

'Look over there, friend Sancho Panza, where more than thirty monstrous giants appear. I intend to do battle with them and take all their lives. With their spoils we will begin to get rich, for this is a fair war, and it is a great service to God to wipe such a wicked brood from the face of the earth.'

'What giants?' asked Sancho Panza.

The Adventures of Don Quixote,
MIGUEL DE CERVANTES SAAVEDRA

2

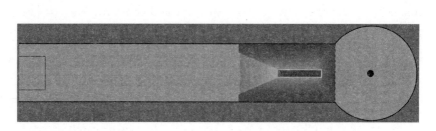

Rohrhügel – tunnel

Friday

'*Scheiße!*' screamed the man in the black baseball cap, '*SCHEIßE!*', and threw his putter into the bushes by the ninth hole. His second shot had missed the cup by millimetres.

The man stood for a moment, hands on hips, cursing himself under his breath. Then he picked up his club from where it lay beneath a conifer tree and grimly knocked the little orange ball into the cup. '*Scheiße,*' he muttered, one more time, as he stalked away to the tenth. This was André Kuhn, one of Europe's top minigolfers. He was not having a good day.

Nor, it must be said, was I.

At the eighth hole my ball had come to rest exactly beneath the obstacle, a diminutive Stonehenge-like monument. With two fives already on my scorecard for the round, not to mention a pathetic four at the first (all three of my playing partners had done it in two), I could ill afford to overshoot the eighth. But I had over-compensated and pulled the shot. As a result my ball was now barely playable. It had trickled down and settled just out of my reach. I couldn't get to it with a conventional putt, so my options were either to move the ball and take a penalty stroke, or get down on my hands and knees and play it like a snooker shot (possibly illegal). There wasn't much dignity in either. I felt the colour in my cheeks and a familiar sense of rising frustration and anger.

I took a deep breath and decided against the snooker option. Instead, I took the penalty shot and moved the ball. Now it lay just eighteen inches from the cup. With luck, I could still get a three at this hole.

But I missed.

'Oh, *FUCK!*' I shouted. '*Fuck, fuck, fuck!*'

But nobody seemed to mind. They had seen it all before. They understood. They knew an essential fact, the truth of which was only now beginning to dawn on me.

Miniature golf, like football, is not a matter of life and death.

It's *much* more important than that.

I had met André Kuhn the previous afternoon at the White Rock Gardens Adventure Golf Course in Hastings. The British Mini-golf Open is an annual one-day event organized by the British Minigolf Association (or BMGA), the UK's national governing body of minigolf sports. The tournament usually takes place on the first Saturday in September and is the highlight of the British minigolfing year, attracting competitors from around Europe. I had joined the BMGA some months previously. Perhaps minia-ture golf, in its small, sad way, was going to be just my sort of thing. I mean, how difficult could it be? And this was crazy golf, for heaven's sake, windmills, castles, all that stuff. I love crazy golf.

Anyway, the Open was my introduction to the world of competitive crazy golf. How did the rituals of this 'sport' com-pare with those of real golf (or, for that matter, with football, cricket and tennis)? What kind of people played crazy golf for kicks? I was hopeful, bitter experience notwithstanding, that these particular sportsmen would accept me as one of their own. I mean, they couldn't take themselves too seriously. Could they?

According to the letter I'd received from the BMGA's chairman, whose name was Peter, 'Entrants will be able to practise at the course free of charge on Thursday and Friday before the competition.' So I'd come down to Hastings on the Friday to have a look around and a laugh with – not at – my fellow BMGA members.

While in golf it's perfectly acceptable to study the terrain of a course prior to a major competition, I felt certain that because this was crazy golf we were dealing with (or minigolf, whatever) nobody would be treating it that solemnly and we could all have a joke and a beer and no one would be fussed about practising too much. But this proved not to be the case. André Kuhn, it turned out, had been there since Monday.

When I arrived, the dour German was sitting at a table near the course attendant's hut. He was with a group of three others: the hearty (i.e., fat and bearded) Thomas Zeininger (Austria), a perpetually smiling man called Christian Freilach (Austria) and a girl with short bleach-blonde hair and a stud in her nose, Corinna Plegnieres (Germany). I later discovered that she and Freilach were lovers. They were, perhaps unsurprisingly, all speaking German. There didn't seem to be anyone else around.

I loitered uneasily for a moment. This wasn't quite what I'd been expecting. What was going on? Where were all the British minigolfers?

'Er, hi!' I ventured, after a minute or so.

They all stopped talking and looked at me.

'Hello,' said the bearded Thomas Zeininger. The others nodded at me but said nothing.

There was an awkward pause. I noticed that their table was covered in minigolfing paraphernalia – different clubs, isotonic drinks, bags full of many coloured balls. All I had was one standard golf ball, white, and a putter that I'd borrowed from my mother. She had won it in a raffle. It was state-of-the-art, which meant it had a huge heavy head with directional lines on it. My mother found it very difficult to use.

'What is that?' said Thomas Zeininger, gesturing at the club.

'It's my putter,' I replied.

'Wow!' he said, weighing the head in his right hand. He turned to his friends. 'It's a driver!' And they all laughed.

'Ha ha!' I said mirthlessly. It had begun to rain. 'Um, is Peter here anywhere?'

Thomas Zeininger pointed over my shoulder. 'There he is,' he said, before turning back to his friends and adding something in German. They all guffawed.

'Thank you,' I said, through gritted teeth, and turned to look for Peter.

Out on the course a skinny young man, with round wire-frame glasses and an expression of great intensity, was playing the same hole again and again. Even from where I was standing I could see that he was using the same kind of balls the Germans had in their special holdalls. He was surprisingly young, in his mid-twenties, perhaps. Other than that he looked exactly like you'd expect the chairman of the British Minigolf Association to look, which is funny, because in his real life he's a fireman. ⚐

(⚐ Not really. I made that up. Actually he's a civil servant.)

Peter founded the British Minigolf Association ('for all those who enjoy playing miniature golf, crazy golf and adventure golf') in 1997. Its aims, as stated on the Association's website, are as follows:

- Increase the profile of minigolf in Great Britain
- Bring together those who enjoy playing minigolf
- Encourage the playing of minigolf as a competitive sport
- Organize minigolf tournaments, including a British Open
- Encourage the development of new minigolf courses in Britain which conform to the World Minigolf Sport Federation's approved designs

In all but the last of these Peter has been relatively successful. That summer, the BMGA had been officially recognized by the World Minigolf Sport Federation in Holland. The BMGA boasted over a hundred members. Forty people were competing in the Open – a BMGA record (not difficult admittedly: there had been only one previous British Open and only fourteen people played in that). Peter was clearly a man on a mission.

'Hello,' I said, extending my hand, 'I'm Andy Miller. I'm here to practise. Do I need to show you some ID or something?'

'Oh, hello. Let me just finish this . . .' said Peter. He effortlessly sank an eight-foot putt. As he looked up, I noticed his glasses had misted over.

'No need for your card,' he said, smiling. 'I believe you. The course is getting a bit waterlogged, though, I'm afraid.' Right on cue, a drop of rain fell from the end of his nose.

I was unsure of the etiquette of playing in these conditions. Little lakes were forming in the dips on the course. 'Won't all this rain be a problem for tomorrow?' I asked.

'Oh, no,' said Peter optimistically. 'This course is very absorbent.'

Right.

While I chatted to Peter, I couldn't help noticing that there weren't any windmills here. In fact, there were hardly any obstacles at all – no rockets, no water-wheels, none of the things you would traditionally associate with crazy golf. How odd.

'Where are all the windmills and obstacles?' I asked Peter. 'Do they keep them in the hut until the weather picks up?'

Peter laughed politely and said nothing. But I hadn't been joking. Where *were* the windmills? It began to dawn on me that I had made a mistake, that perhaps mini- and crazy golf were not the same thing after all. Suddenly I felt a stab of deep anxiety.

Peter took off his glasses and wiped them on the front of his sweatshirt. 'Would you like a game?' he said. 'Lionel's round here somewhere.' I noticed he seemed reluctant to involve the guffawing Europeans.

Lionel was the English – as opposed to the British – Minigolf Open Champion. I'd read about the impressive thirty-nine he'd shot at Eastbourne two months previously to clinch victory. He was the sort of person I'd come here to meet. Excellent, I told myself. I've only been here five minutes and already I'm making up a threesome with the best players in Britain! Peter put his glasses back on and peered around. 'Oh, yes, there he is,' he said, and waved.

Away in a far corner of the course, beneath some pines, was a short, balding man in a custard yellow golf jersey and what can only be described as slacks. He, too, was putting and re-putting one particular hole, and seemed to be making notes in a small book. He grinned at us ruefully and waved back. To his great credit he looked like he might be feeling just a little self-conscious. I warmed to him immediately. He might be an Open Champion but he seemed friendly. We walked over to the hole he was playing.

'Andy, this is Lionel,' said Peter. 'Lionel, this is Andy Miller.' We shook hands. I tried to smile at Lionel in a way that suggested I, too, felt this was a slightly absurd thing for grown men to be doing. He smiled back, ruefully again, it seemed to me. What nice people!

'I was just saying to Andy, shall we have a quick game?' suggested Peter.

Lionel's air of easy conviviality vanished. 'No, thanks,' he said, his face pinched. 'I'd rather practise on my own. No offence.'

'Right you are,' said Peter. Nothing more was said. Lionel returned pointedly to his ball.

The friendly atmosphere had disappeared in an instant. Did I detect a little tension between the BMGA's chairman and the English Open Champion? Was Lionel angry that Peter had invited an outsider to join them? It seemed that Lionel was a highly competitive man, albeit one who had learnt the knack of a rueful grin. Perhaps he practised it repeatedly, like his putting.

So we left Lionel to his solo pre-match preparation and set out to play a round at the White Rock Gardens Adventure Golf Course on our own, just me and Peter. The first hole was situated right next to where Andre Kuhn and pals were sitting. We played it under their mocking gaze. Peter took two putts to land the ball in the cup. So did I. We both felt a great sense of relief. Well, I did, and I assume Peter did. Now he was on the course Peter was giving nothing away. He was utterly impassive.

Peter was a very good minigolfer. While the course lacked novelty obstacles, it was much harder than it looked. For every solid three I managed, he effortlessly spun a two. For every hazard I negotiated by the skin of my teeth, he shot through and to the edge of the cup – twice actually into it. And for every curse I let out at my own incompetence, he displayed not a flicker of emotion at his own clear superiority.

After a few holes Peter's relentlessness became extremely dispiriting. I realized that in fact it was possible to take minigolf very seriously indeed. And not just that. Thanks to my appalling performance, I discovered that minigolf was also a game it was possible to be crap at after all. Of course! Why had I thought crazy, or mini-, golf would be any different from football, cricket, tennis . . . ?

It was the same old story. Here I was again, trying my best yet doing my worst, trampled by my playing partner. I began to interpret Peter's impassiveness as impatience at my lack of basic minigolfing know-how, rather than simple concentration on his part. My ability to make putts deteriorated accordingly. I took an unnecessary seven, the maximum number of strokes permitted, at the ninth hole and felt the familiar pangs of hopelessness. Why was I even bothering?

By the time we reached the fifteenth, Peter was comprehensively thrashing me but with all the excitement of someone filling out a tax return. This was no fun at all. I thought about calling it quits.

But then a miracle happened. Peter got the yips.

The fifteenth at White Rock Gardens is the most difficult hole on the course. Hidden beneath some trees, it has two separate greens, one lower than the other. The player starts the hole by putting his ball uphill. At the top of the hill the ball must cross a miniature bridge not much wider than the ball itself, under which flows a stream. If the ball lands in the stream it is carried downstream to the first green. The player must then putt the ball down a tunnel and on to the second and final green, where lies the cup. If the ball successfully crosses the bridge, however, it will scoot straight down to the final green, missing out the first green completely. A player who can do this is looking at a two or maybe even an ace. But there is a third, disastrous option. If you miss the bridge *and* the stream, the ball will rebound and land back at your feet. You are one shot down and you have to start again. For the serious minigolfer, this is ruin.

That was what Peter did with his first shot. And his second. And, unbelievably, his third. For the first time he was looking almost, but not quite, peeved. It was raining so hard by now that the little stream looked like it might break its banks. But with his fourth shot he was over the bridge and down the tunnel, coming to rest on the bottom green just six inches from the cup. 'Oh, well done,' I said. He sank the putt for a five and permitted himself a smile.

Now it was my turn. For the first time, I felt a strange surge of competitiveness. Here was my chance to claw back, what, three strokes? Not enough to draw level with Peter admittedly, but enough to restore a bit of self-respect. I wanted to let him know I could do it. I wanted to prove it to myself.

I took a practice swing or two and brushed back my wet hair from my eyes. Come on, now, concentrate! I drew back my putter and prayed. The club connected with the ball. The shot felt good.

Sure enough the ball ran straight up the slope to the tiny bridge. I thought it might shade left and rebound but, no, it was dead on target and as I watched it made its way up and over the bump, on course for the cup and the green and maybe an ace. *Yes*!

But it was not to be. Just as my ball cleared the bridge, there was an enormous clap of thunder, and lightning flashed across the sky. 'Oh dear,' said Peter, 'I'm not staying out under this tree. We'd better go in.' He turned and headed towards the shelter of the hut.

'But what about . . . ?' I cried, as my ball rolled into the top cup.

'Play it again when it's eased off a bit,' he called back. 'We'll finish up later.' And with that, he was gone.

Unwatched, my ball emerged on to the bottom green and glided effortlessly into the cup. It was a hole-in-one.

There was another sky-cracking rumble of thunder. I hoped for a moment that lightning would strike the hut and reduce it to smouldering matchwood. Then I remembered it was more likely to be me who'd be vapourized if I stayed under the tree. Regretfully, I retrieved my unacknowledged ace-in-the-hole and ran for cover.

Inside the hut, the atmosphere seemed tense. Lionel had taken shelter here too. It was quite cramped and damp and very quiet. The only noise was the drumming of rain on the roof. Once again Peter was wiping his glasses on his sweatshirt. Lionel was cleaning his clubs. Neither man spoke. Outside, the Germans and Austrians zipped up their hooded cagoules, presumably designed to European minigolf specifications, and carried on talking.

I thought about saying, 'Lionel, you know the fifteenth out there? The hole with the bridge? I just aced that. Peter took a five. A five! You wouldn't expect it from one of Britain's leading minigolfers, would you?' But I didn't. Annoyed as I was with Peter, I didn't want to fall out with him. He hadn't meant to be rude, he was just very focused on his game. Or something. Anyway, *I* knew I had aced the hole. That was what mattered.

The BMGA's Annual General Meeting was due to take place tomorrow after the tournament had finished. Golf-club committees are usually riddled with corruption, brinkmanship and backstabbing, and a bit of me hoped the BMGA wouldn't be any different. Did the members consider Peter a good secretary? Had he really done enough to encourage the development of new minigolf courses that conform to the World Minigolf Sport Federation's approved designs? Or not? Perhaps Lionel was planning to oust Peter as secretary. Was that, in fact, the reason for the tension between them?

'So,' I said, 'what's on the agenda for the AGM? Any points of order I should brush up on? Any money-laundering you don't want me to know about, ha ha?'

There was a long silence, punctuated only by the sound of

water dripping off my coat. Plip, plop, plip. Peter and Lionel were both looking at me like I was insane. It suddenly occurred to me that they probably thought I was as mad as I thought they were. Who is this nutter who's appeared from nowhere, and why is he so interested in our AGM? Money-laundering? What's he talking about?

'No,' said Peter, politely. 'Just the usual things.'

'Right,' I said. 'Just checking.'

There was another long pause. Drip. Drip. Drip.

I tried to change the subject. 'Lionel, do you play golf at all – you know, actual golf?'

'Oh, no,' said Lionel, the English Minigolf Open Champion, as if I'd asked whether he flew to Mars at weekends. 'No, no.'

Drip. Plop. Drip.

This was awful. The camaraderie I'd glimpsed earlier had disappeared completely. I'd had visions of me and Peter and Lionel laughing and congratulating one another as we played a hard-fought but fair round of minigolf as equals and, yes, friends. Instead I was stuck in a leaky hut with two strangers who clearly weren't in the mood for my light-hearted banter or, indeed, any kind of talk. Lionel didn't want to play with us. Peter had deprived me of my moment of glory, maybe deliberately. Both of them were suspicious of me. The only thing uniting the three of us was our mutual mistrust. To cap it all, I didn't even really know what game I'd been playing – crazy golf, minigolf or what. I decided it was time to leave.

'Well, see you tomorrow,' I lied.

'See you tomorrow,' said Lionel, flashing me the grin.

'Yes, we tee off at eleven,' said Peter.

'Absolutely,' I said, and fled.

All things considered, it had been a great disappointment. Minigolf, or crazy golf or whatever was just another club, it seemed, that wouldn't have me as a member; either you were in or you were out, and I was most definitely out. Well, it had been worth a go.

But as I made my way down the steps to the seafront, I heard a voice behind me. I turned round to see Thomas Zeininger smiling and waving at me. 'See you tomorrow!' he said.

'Oh, yes, see you!' I replied, smiling back. This was a pleasant surprise. Perhaps I had been wrong about the Europeans. Perhaps he and André Kuhn and the others were all right after all. Maybe I would come back tomorrow.

Thomas Zeininger pointed at my putter. 'Don't forget your driver!' he said, and laughed so hard I thought he might combust.

A windmill's sails turn in a sea breeze. A rocket points to the stars. A castle stands abandoned, save for the occasional golf ball that shoots across its drawbridge or smashes into its ramparts. This is crazy golf and it is beautiful.

Well, I think so. As a child, I loved crazy golf. Our holidays were mostly seaside ones, and I spent hours on mini links in Woolacombe, Cromer, Paignton . . . Crazy-golf courses are as much a part of the ailing British beach holiday as donkey rides and a bucket and spade. Pay your green fee at the shed to a bored teenager, who equips you with a putter and ball, and a scorecard and pencil (you MUST return the pencil). You then hack round a green felt putting course that has been enlivened by a number of miniature buildings – a castle here, a windmill there, a tricky ramp or some such at the eighteenth. You pretend it's a laugh, but secretly you want to annihilate your dad/younger brother/ older sister/friends. You want to win.

As the game goes on, you find yourself applauding displays of skill. You say things like '*Get in!*' or '*Shot!*' At the end, you might Win A Free Go by ringing the bell at the final hole. If you succeed, you do not claim the Free Go, but keep the token as a souvenir of your own amazing skill. It's OK: these are the universal rituals of crazy golf and they are observed, or used to be, in every seaside town from Brighton to Blackpool and beyond. It's the people's golf – open to all and playable by anyone. I loved it because it was about play, not sport.

And it was quite like golf, which is the only sport I do have some time for. There are several reasons for this. First and foremost, golf is not a team game (occasional aberrations like the Ryder Cup aside). It's you, the ball and the hole in the ground. If you mess up, you've only yourself to blame. If you fail, you're not letting anyone down but yourself.

Second, in golf there isn't much running about and little is required in the way of athletic prowess. A professional golfer can be fat (Craig Stadler), mad (Jesper Parnevik), a chain smoker (Fuzzy Zoeller) or, in the case of John Daly, all of the above and an alcoholic to boot, and still be at the top of his game.

Golf is also a badge of difference. Many people hate it. They've got no time for the game's politics, the perceived sexism or the plus-fours. Many middle-class football fans, like my friend Paul, hate golf because they think it's distastefully bourgeois, despite the fact that many actual footballers spend much of their free time on the golf course.

And the success of Tiger Woods and the enthusiastic endorsement of Bob Dylan, Iggy Pop and the Beastie Boys notwithstanding, golf is not, never has been and never will be, cool.

There's one more reason why I like golf. My father played the game and loved it. He wasn't a fit man, my father. Diabetic from his early twenties and not one of nature's athletes, he was no sportsman. But every Saturday afternoon, he would play a round of golf with two friends, and he would enjoy it. He wasn't a great player, a handicap of around twenty-two, I think, but that wasn't the point. For one afternoon every week, with his playing partners Don and John, he was like everybody else on the course, a golfer, let down only by his mistakes, not his health.

When I was a small boy, I was his caddy. I don't mean I gave him advice or support or any of the other things real caddies do. Having me around saved Dad carrying the clubs – I was child labour. I'd pull the trolley or, if the ground was wet, lug the bag round on my tiny shoulder, and I did it with spectacular ill-grace. The only good bit was at the end of the day when I was allowed to climb on to the trolley and ride back to the car. But generally it wasn't a happy arrangement. Unlike many men, for whom sport (especially football) provides common ground with absent fathers, I appreciate and understand only in retrospect what those Saturday afternoons meant to my dad. At the time, for me, they were a boring chore.

He died in 1985. I haven't followed him on to the course. Sadly my cack-handedness at every other sport also applies to golf. But I've begun to think that if my father could find it in him to understand and enjoy a sport, just the one, why shouldn't I?

My mother is nearly seventy now and a happily awful golfer. She lives near Hastings. When I got home after the first day's practice, we rummaged around in the box room and found my dad's golf clubs, the clubs I had so resented as a child, untouched since he died. 'Here,' she said, 'they're yours now, if you want them.'

Out of the bag, I drew the putter. This would be my broad-sword on the morrow.

'Don't you want to use mine?' said my mother, a note of disappointment in her voice. 'It's a really good one.'

'The thing is, it's a bit big for miniature golf, Mum,' I said expertly. 'A bit of a, you know . . . a bit of a *driver*.'

Saturday

As Peter had said, the tournament started at eleven. When we arrived at the course it was still raining. An oilskin-wearing official was sweeping water off the playing surfaces with a broom. My grandparents used to live in Hastings and in my memory the town is always grey and overcast and wet. When I was younger Hastings had a reputation as the drugs capital of the south coast. We always said it was because people were forced to spend so much time indoors.

There used to be a model village on the site of the White Rock Gardens Adventure Golf course – I remember visiting it with my grandmother – but about ten years ago the tiny residents were evicted and their churches, factories and cottages bulldozed to make way for these eighteen holes of adventure golf. In addition to this, just along the seafront lie a crazy-golf course, a miniature-golf course (no obstacles) and a good old-fashioned putting green. Four courses in one town! Hastings Town Council obviously thought they could wean troubled youngsters off mind-altering substances and on to putting. It didn't work. Troubled youngsters preferred to combine the two.

I remember as a teenager seeing two boys off their heads on the seafront crazy-golf course. One was lying on the ground, screaming with laughter and waving his putter around, while the other repeatedly ran at the flag on one of the greens, shouting 'Try again! I can do it! I can fit in there!' or something. At the time I couldn't see what was so funny.

There were a lot more BMGA members around than there had been the day before, maybe nearly sixty. Despite the Association's best efforts, minigolf in the UK seemed more like a hobby than a sport, and to judge from the people milling about by the first tee, its followers were firmly in the tradition of other great British hobbying groups: twitchers, trainspotters, Klingon imperson-ators. Nearly all of them were men.

Looking around, I saw the Germans and Austrians still huddled round their table. They had been joined by an excitable ginger-haired Frenchman, whose name was Edouard. He was dressed in a very athletic jogging top and green Lycra cycling shorts, and his bag of specialist minigolf balls was bigger than my holdall.

'So,' I said to him, assuming that a serious player like this had jetted in specially, 'how does this course compare with your courses at home?'

'There are no courses where I am from,' said Edouard.

'Oh,' I said, surprised. 'Aren't there courses in France?'

'No, I am living in Preston at the moment!' He laughed. 'Preston!' he said again, as though the full horror of it had just begun to dawn on him.

'I see,' I said. I looked again at Edouard's zippy sportsgear and his bag of balls and felt a bit sorry for him. It must be very lonely in Preston when you're far from home, French and you like miniature golf.

'But that is why today is so great!' Edouard exclaimed, rousing himself. 'It's great! Minigolf!'

You couldn't argue with that.

At the entrance Peter was greeting his people and directing them to check-in.

'Hi, Peter,' I said.

'Oh, hi, Andy,' he replied. 'Tee-off at eleven. Sign in – the weather's going to pick up later.'

'Right,' I said. Peter had clearly answered the when? where? and weather? questions several hundred times already today and was therefore presenting a sort of one-size-fits-all answer to whoever approached him. I left him to it.

As we waited to sign in at the Official Open Registration Centre (i.e., the hut) I chatted to a few of the people in the queue. These included Phil, a journalist who'd had a career crisis and was writing a novel about a journalist who has a career crisis and becomes obsessed with crazy golf, and the Vallory family: Steve, Martin, Gary, a cheerful teenager called Joe and his dad Robert. Steve was touting for business installing ornamental miniature golf courses in people's gardens ('No!' said my wife).

Interestingly, like Lionel, many of these pioneering British minigolfers had never played actual golf in their lives.

I had been joined for the day by my wife Tina, my friend Nick, his girlfriend Rachel and their small daughter Kit. Nick, actually a very good golfer, had decided to enter the Open largely to keep me company. Nick and I had a contingency plan if it looked like the day was getting boring. Rule thirty-three, subsection two of the Rules of Minigolf states: 'Before and during a tournament, it is forbidden to consume or be in possession of alcohol or drugs.'[1] If nothing noteworthy had happened by mid-afternoon, we would get as loaded as the two lads from the crazy-golf course years

---

1. *The Rules of Miniature Golf* is a thing of wonder and deserves to be published in its own right. Rule 26 is my favourite: 'The ball may only be taken out of the target hole by hand. The physically handicapped and members of the senior classes can use suckers.'

before and try to get ourselves forcibly ejected from the tournament.

The tournament itself consisted of three rounds of eighteen holes. The first round would be played in groups of four, drawn at random. At the end of the first round, these groups would be reorganized according to each player's score and these new groups would play the second round. At the end of the second round, only the top eight players would make the cut and go forward to the third and final round and possibly glory.

From what I could gather, the European players were unhappy with the condition of several of the greens and very unhappy with the fifteenth in particular. The bridge and the stream were too irregular for a major competition, they said.

This aside, the atmosphere around the course was very comfortable. At about ten to eleven, a list of the playing groups was posted in the window of the hut. I had been drawn in the first round with a bloke called Jet, a girl called Teresa (one of only three female contenders) and the perpetually smiling Austrian, Christian Freilach.

After the familiar traumas of yesterday, I was determined to enjoy myself. I had come back but I was, I told myself, unconcerned as to whether I won or lost. Teresa, Christian and Jet – this was going to be fun.

However, when I came to take my first shot, I confess I was feeling a little nervous. Unlike actual golf, where you play the hole together, in miniature golf there simply isn't room. Each minigolfer must play the hole alone, one after the other. And because we were one of the first groups out, we had a gallery of nearly sixty people watching us. My fellow players. Peter. The Europeans. And everybody else. As I approached the first tee my heart was thumping.

I shot a two. Thank God! So did Jet. So did Christian. Teresa took a three. We congratulated each other, signed our cards and moved on to the second hole.

And so it went. Christian Freilach was plainly a much better player than the three of us. Jet and I were evenly matched and

Teresa wasn't much good but didn't care. Christian wasn't even very involved in our game – he kept darting over to see how his fellow Europeans and his girlfriend were doing – but he was friendly and he even gave me a few tips. After a few holes, I realized I was enjoying myself. My fellow players were good company and I was playing well. It was fun. I took two at the difficult fifteenth. I even aced the sixteenth and found myself punching the air in triumph. By the end of the round I had shot a not-bad forty-eight (Christian Freilach shot forty).

'Forty-eight!' I said to Tina excitedly. 'Did you see me at the sixteenth? Did you see my hole-in-one? Forty-eight! I wonder if I'm anywhere near the cut?'

Tina looked at me oddly but said nothing.

The only problem I'd had in the first round was with my ball. In minigolf, if the ball drops into the cup but then bounces out again, it still counts as a stroke. The ball must be putted again to finish the hole. Because I was using a standard and quite light white golf ball and the playing surfaces were running so fast, this happened to me twice. It occurred to me that without these two extra shots I could have gone round in forty-six. I decided to use a proper heavy minigolf ball (just like the Germans and Peter) in the second round.

While we were waiting for the other groups to finish, we went to watch the Europeans in action. They were as thorough as their reputation suggested. Balls were bounced. Practice strokes were taken. André Kuhn lay down in a puddle at the sixth the better to judge the lie of the ball. When he missed a shot he would shout, '*Scheiße!*' or some elaborate variant. My German isn't very good, but I could make out, 'This is *Scheiße!*' or '*Scheiße* me!' If, on the other hand, he made a particularly difficult putt, the others would clap him on the shoulder or even applaud. For while the Europeans were very intense they were also very, very good. I watched Corinna Plegnieres ace four holes in a row. For the first time I began to feel respect for them. This was a real skill.

My friend Nick had been drawn in the same group as the

Preston Frenchman Edouard. Edouard was also a very good minigolfer, but his stance and swing were extraordinary. He stood over the ball, legs spread wide, green Lycra cycling shorts straining at the seams, while swinging his putter high above his head like a cricket bat. It looked ridiculous but it got results. When Nick's girlfriend Rachel asked for an explanation of how he had come to this method, Edouard launched into a long and in-depth discussion of the equipment he was using and all the different balls in his special bag. After about five minutes, it occurred to Rachel that perhaps she was being chatted up. Was this how it had started between Christian and Corinna? A careless word or two about ball density, and then . . .

Nick, meanwhile, caused a kerfuffle of his own at the eighth hole when his ball got stuck beneath the hazard (the stone obelisk I was to encounter later) and he used his club as a snooker cue to dislodge it. Nobody was sure if this was legal or not, but there was nothing in the rules to say it wasn't, so the shot was allowed and he finished the hole in three.

The remaining groups of four were finishing off. Because play was so slow, the competition was clearly going to take far longer than I'd originally envisaged. Both Kit (three and a half) and Tina (twenty-nine) were getting restless, but I wanted to be sure the AGM was still happening once the tournament was over.

'Oh, yes,' said Peter. 'We're still on for that. How did you do?'

At about one o'clock the first-round scores were posted in the clubhouse. In the lead were Corinna Plegnieres and André Kuhn, both of whom had shot thirty-five. Peter had shot a forty-two but the highest placed Brit was Don McPhee with a forty. Joe Vallory, the teenager, had shot an impressive forty-three. The snooker-playing Nick, I noted testily, had scored forty-six, two strokes ahead of me. But my forty-eight had placed me at joint twenty-first on the rankings and – oh, yes! – two shots ahead of the grinmeister himself, Lionel! Ha-ha! If I could just grind out that score again or lower . . . I thought about the two shots I'd lost bouncing out of the cup and went to trade my golf ball for a heavy red minigolf ball. And that's where my troubles began.

I don't know if it was the change of ball or the pressure I felt to keep my score down – to compete – but basically, in the second round, I choked. I couldn't make a putt to save my life.

My new group of four approached the first tee laughing, all 'cor, it's a bit tense' and 'what balls are you using, ha-ha', and I opted to tee off first. But my new red ball was heavier than I was expecting. I didn't hit it hard enough. It ran half-way up the slope then right back down again. Shit. Yesterday, under the mocking gaze of André Kuhn and pals I had putted this first hole in two. This morning, with more than sixty people looking on, I'd done it again. But this afternoon, with really only myself watching, I fucked it up. I shot a four. Ominously, my three playing partners all sank their putts in two. Oh, God . . .

Soon, my scorecard told its own sorry story. After a lucky two at the second, it went four, four, five, four . . . I couldn't get used to the new ball. Either I hit it too hard or I didn't hit it hard enough. I became impatient at my own uselessness and began to play petulantly, taking putts too quickly and paying the price. Five, three, four . . . After nine holes and the débâcle at the eighth I had shot a pathetic twenty-nine. If I kept this up I might even manage sixty by the end of the round. I felt a bit sick.

My playing partners included Joe Vallory's dad Robert, and a local man called Danny, who had a tremendous mullet. While they were sympathetic at first ('Come on, you cunt,' said Danny kindly, after that first disastrous five) I began to feel embarrassed on their behalf. We were supposed to be equals – we'd played as equals in the first round – but they were shooting twos and ones and here I was screwing around with my fours and fives. I was letting the side down.

And then everything changed. I aced the tenth. It was a fluke, a rebound, but it was still a hole-in-one. I couldn't believe it. And then Robert and Danny laughed and applauded me, like the Europeans applauded one another at these moments, and I felt great.

I followed this with a two at the eleventh. But this wasn't a fluke. I read the hole; I made that two happen. I could still make a go of this.

At the fifteenth, with its bridge, its stream and its two greens, Danny got stuck on the rebound and took a six. 'Well, that's me fucked,' he said philosophically. 'Come on, show us how it's done.'

Yesterday, I'd aced this hole. Earlier today, I'd done it in two. I had a good record here. But I'd had a good record at the first until this afternoon and I'd still made a mess of that. Never mind, I thought, what's the worst that can happen? If you don't get it first time, you'll get it next time. Just play it. I hit the ball and it somersaulted over the stream and the bridge and down into the tunnel and on to the bottom green. It didn't fall right into the cup, but it did with the second shot and suddenly *I got it*. I understood how this stupid little game could open up a whole new world to me.

I ground round the remaining holes, actually played them, a three, a two and a one. And when I aced the last hole, I knew from the moment the ball left the club that it was going into the cup. I shot twenty-one on the back nine, bringing me to a total of fifty for the round. I finished last in our group, but the leader, Bob, was only three shots ahead of me. More to the point, I felt like I'd proved something to myself: that I could take control, however briefly, and I could really compete.

It felt weird, but it felt good.

It was half past three before the third round commenced. The deputy mayor of Hastings had arrived to present the winners with a trophy and a cheque for three hundred pounds. A reporter and a photographer from the *Hastings and St Leonards Observer* were hanging around to capture the big moment.

The tension of this last round affected everyone on the course, with the exception of the teenage Joe Vallory, who won his group with a tournament record for a British player – an amazing thirty-seven. He came fifth overall, winning a cup for best British player, a cheque for two hundred pounds, a bear-hug from his dad and a firm handshake from Peter. 'Well done, Joseph,' he said. I wondered how Peter really felt about being flattened by a fourteen-year-old.

Meanwhile, the leaders' group, the Germans and Austrians who'd been the first people I'd encountered here in Hastings, were battling among themselves for the title of British Minigolf Open Champion. Every shot was vital. Every shot was slow. It was incredibly skilful. But it was also rather boring. By about the fifth hole, most of the spectators had drifted off to watch the other group and Joe the child prodigy, leaving only me, Nick and a very bored-looking course official, a girl wearing a yellow staff sweatshirt with her hair in bunches, watching this clash of the Titans.

André Kuhn's game collapsed. Like Peter before him, he got the yips at the fifteenth. After his second rebound, his arms dropped to his side, he looked despairingly up at heaven and, like Job on the ash-heap or Charlie Brown on the pitcher's mound, slowly and sadly uttered his most expressive curse of the day: 'Jesus Christ, why must I put up with this *Scheiße*?' He never recovered, finishing with a forty-three and a total of 114 for the day.

Corinna and Christian kept the spark in their relationship by doggedly battling one another round the whole course, only settling it on the last hole. She shot thirty-eight, he thirty-seven. But it wasn't enough. On aggregate he had a total of 111 shots for the day. Corinna had a mighty 108. She was clearly on course for the title.

But then Thomas Zeininger, the bearded, laughing Austrian who had found my putter so comical, did something extraordinary. He shot thirty-three, a course record, and by doing so, came from fourth to joint first. There was going to be a play-off. Thomas and Corinna would play until one of them won a hole, and that person would be the champion.

It was now five o'clock and it was starting to get dark. People were getting restless. The deputy mayor's smile was fading a little. Even I was weary of all the European throat-clearing and ball-bouncing that was going on. But the bearded Austrian and nose-studded *Fräulein* were impervious to it all. They were lost in thought, weighing up balls, laying their clubs along the playing surface of the first hole and psyching themselves up. They tossed a coin. Corinna would play first.

Inadvertently, Peter chose that precise moment to break her concentration. 'Excuse me, Corinna,' he said, tapping her on the shoulder. 'Could you hurry up? The mayor's got to go.'

'*Wass?*' said Corinna Plegnieres.

'The mayor's got to go.' Peter pointed at the smiling lady holding the trophy. 'Mayor. *Muss. Gehen,*' he said.

Corinna Plegnieres gave him a look that said: 'You stupid, bloody English amateur. What do you know of true miniature golf? I'm about to make a crucial putt here. I don't care if the mayor's having a fucking heart-attack, you don't call an ambulance until I've finished. Got it?'

But it was no good. The spell was broken. Like me earlier, she pulled her first shot and the ball failed to climb to the top of the slope. She was done for and she knew it. She shot a four.

Now it was Thomas Zeininger's turn. His first shot stopped two inches from the hole. He tapped the ball and down it went. Thomas Zeininger raised his putter and both arms above his head. All hail the victor! Those spectators who were left gave him a desultory round of applause and then about half of them departed immediately. The deputy mayor swiftly handed out the prizes, smiled for the photographer and then she, too, was gone. The Europeans all looked delighted with each other. I took some photos of Edouard's bag of balls for posterity then went to find Peter.

He was standing by the hut talking to a man with hedgehog hair and glasses and saying goodbye to people.

'Great day, Peter,' I said. 'Thanks for organizing everything.'

'No problem,' said Peter. 'Have you met Scott? He's our treasurer.'

'Ah, yes,' I said. 'Peter, where's the AGM happening?'

'Oh,' replied Peter, 'we were going to have it on the train home but nobody seems that bothered.'

'But I can run through the books for you, if you like,' said Scott hopefully.

'No,' I said. 'That's fine.'

So much for a leadership coup. I felt slightly ashamed at looking for intrigue where there was none. I'd misjudged Peter, Lionel and the rest of the British minigolf contingent. After the day's events, I could see the game from their perspective. Minigolf was their hobby; but it was also their sport. And maybe it could be mine too.

'Well,' said Peter, 'good to meet you, Andy. See you at Southend in May?'

'You will, Peter,' I replied. 'You will.'

Tina, Rachel and Kit were waiting for us back at the car.

'Where have you been?' said Tina. 'You've been ages.'

'Yeah, sorry,' I said. 'It dragged on a bit.'

'Well, hurry up, we want something to eat. God!'

As I walked round the car and opened the passenger door I noticed for the first time we had parked right next to the seafront crazy-golf course. It was a real old-fashioned windmills-and-water-wheels number. It was floodlit and still open. I shut the door and leaned in at the window. 'You go on without me,' I said. 'I just want to play this course quickly. We don't know when we'll be down here again.'

'Andy, it's pissing with rain!' said my exasperated wife.

'No, really, I'll catch you up, I just want to have a quick turn round here.'

There was a long pause. 'All right,' said Tina resignedly. 'We'll see you later.' She wound up the window and they drove away.

The first hole was a fairly straightforward run, no obstacles, but slightly zigzagged. I aimed my first putt so that it rebounded off the left wall but I pulled it slightly and it came to rest about four feet short of the cup.

As I stood there alone in the rain on Hastings seafront, I thought about the day, and everything that had happened at the British Minigolf Open. I'd loved it. I respected the skills of the other players. I thought about that first frustrated hole-in-one at the fifteenth and about that twenty-one on the back nine and then Thomas Zeininger raising his putter above his head in victory and about my own putt, which was currently lying four feet from the cup, and I knew what I had to do.

I had to do better next time.

3

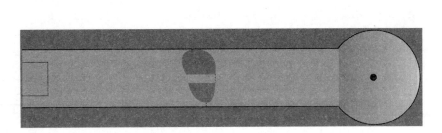

Schräger Kreis mit Niere – sloping circle with kidney

Football is all very well as a game for rough girls,
but it is hardly suitable for delicate boys.

OSCAR WILDE

It was cold where we were, and the wind was making it colder.
In the upper reaches of the Ellerslie Road stand at Loftus Road
Stadium, the home of QPR, five old men were singing themselves
hoarse.

> *'AND IT'S QUEENS PARK RANGERS!*
> *QUEENS PARK RANGERS FC!*
> *WE'RE THE FIIIINEST FOOTBALL TEAM THE WORLD*
> *HAS EVER SEEN!'*

I didn't join in. This chant was ridiculous. Not only were QPR
not the finest football team the world had ever seen, they weren't
even the finest football team on the pitch.

But football was not a game, I knew, where it did to applaud
skilful play from the visiting team. However magical the pass,
however spectacular the goal, if it wasn't scored by one of your
lot, best to keep quiet. And as my lot found scoring beyond them

most of the time, there wasn't much to shout about. Not that it bothered the old men. Nothing would silence their noisy loyalty, the idiots.

Fifty-seven minutes played. Queens Park Rangers o; Grimsby Town o. I pulled my coat round me and hunkered down to sit out another thirty-three long minutes.

They say, with the sort of sentimental wisdom that characterizes football, that a man doesn't choose his football team – it chooses him. Whatever the truth of that, in our first season together neither Queens Park Rangers FC nor I had shown very good taste. They were rubbish and so was I.

On the pitch, there was a flurry of activity. Grimsby had been awarded, in my view, a perfectly reasonable free kick. The old men disagreed. They responded by booing the referee and calling him a wanker. '*COME ON YOU Rs! COME ON YOU Rs!*' they bellowed.

Yes, come on, you Rs, I thought, and wondered if it was too late to start supporting Grimsby instead.

Being a real football fan is like joining the Army. It requires a blind and unquestioning devotion to your side, however questionable their actions might be. You also need a high tolerance to wind and rain and the company of antisocial men who can't wait to see combat. And, God, it's boring. I had developed a skill for not looking at the clock that hung above the School End at Loftus Road. Doing so usually added another couple of weeks to the game. But after another half-hour of hoofing, shoving and falling over, I caught a glimpse.

Fifty-nine minutes: QPR o; Grimsby o.

Shifting about on my tiny bucket seat – a snip at seventeen pounds – and trying to find a position that was merely very uncomfortable, I reflected on my progress over the last few months.

I had decided to support Queens Park Rangers as an experiment. This was more challenging than it sounds. I'd never followed a football team and I'd only ever been to one football match. I didn't really know how to go about it. But after the triumph of Hastings, I felt liberated. I determined to face down my own personal sporting demon – football.

(✱ Actually, I did have a brief history with a team. When I was eleven, for one season only, I had fallen in a big way for Liverpool. The Beatles came from Liverpool. At the time, Liverpool FC was the biggest team in the country. I had a replica shirt with Hitachi written on it, Liverpool being the first English club to carry a sponsor's name on their chests. The club won the old First Division that year. It was all the glory an eleven-year-old boy could want.

But it wasn't enough. When the new season started after the summer holidays, my passion for Liverpool departed as swiftly and mysteriously as it had arrived. Some of my favourite players had gone, retired or been sold to other clubs. It wasn't the same team, so what was the point? My brand loyalty wavered and died.)

So my reasons for supporting QPR were ruthlessly unsentimental. I had no family allegiances to consider – no one in our family followed football at all. QPR were my local team. I could walk to the ground. They weren't in the Premiership. I was told by people who knew about such things that there would never be any problem getting into a game. Also, the Superhoops (so-called, I read, because of their blue and white hooped shirts) had some quite good celebrity fans: the comedian Bill Bailey, Mick Jones of The Clash, and the composer Michael Nyman – come and have a go if you're avant-garde enough.

And I had several friends whose teams, Nottingham Forest and Ipswich, were, like QPR, currently playing in the Nationwide League Division One. So there would be a chance to compare notes and express my shamefully ignorant opinions to people who would not, hopefully, take offence and punch me in the face.

It was, I admit, a motley assortment of reasons for supporting a football team. But I was starting from scratch. It's not the sort of decision most people have to make consciously. Real fans don't look for reasons, they just do it.

Because I didn't know what I was doing, my initial attempts at 'support' were therefore based almost entirely on hearsay. Every Saturday I would look at QPR's results on Teletext simply because that's what you were supposed to do. But they were only numbers. On Sundays I made a point of reading match reports but because I didn't know who anyone was, all the reports seemed the same. The rest of the week . . . well, I didn't do much, really.

The stats were these. Over the course of half a dozen matches, Rangers won twice, lost once and drew the rest. They seemed to be settling in the middle of the table. Was this good? I didn't know.

After a month or so, I realized I wasn't going to get far by just *saying* I was a supporter (although this seemed to suit a lot of people): the only way really to get to grips with QPR was to go and see them play. I checked the fixture list. My team's next home game was the following weekend against Sheffield United. In my naïvety, I called the box-office to check ticket availability. There were, they assured me, still plenty of seats.

I put down the phone. So there it was. I was going to a football match. Immediately a pit of anxiety formed in my stomach. Was I really going to go through with something that every fibre of my being was telling me not to do?

But I got lucky. On the Thursday before the game it was announced that one QPR player, George Kulcsar, had been diagnosed with meningitis, and two more players, Matthew Rose and Karl Ready, were showing similar symptoms. The ground had been quarantined; the game was off. I breathed a sigh of relief then felt slightly ashamed. But only slightly.

It transpired George Kulcsar was suffering with viral, rather than bacterial, meningitis and therefore was in no immediate danger. The other players and ground staff were in the clear too. But the fact remained that the game, my first game as a supporter, had been cancelled in a dramatic fashion. Clearly, I reasoned, someone didn't want me to be doing this. Me, a football fan? It was against nature.

And so, content that God had spoken directly to me, I didn't get to Loftus Road until the New Year. I can't offer any excuse for my shameful lack of commitment to Rangers at this stage, beyond reiterating that I just wasn't very committed. Fundamentally, I didn't care because I had permitted myself so little to care about. As long as I didn't invest any real time or interest in the club, I was safe.

At the end of January, my Forest-supporting friend Paul was in town for the QPR game. Paul is a teacher. He was so outraged that I hadn't managed to drag myself down the road in five months that he went ahead and bought tickets in the Ellerslie Road stand, QPR territory, to guarantee my attendance.

Wearing the blue and white bobble hat I had carefully selected four months previously, I joined the crowds heading down to Loftus Road with Paul at my side. It was like the first day at a new and very remedial school. I made eye-contact with no one. We walked along Uxbridge Road, past the Coningham Arms and the Queen Adelaide, full of hard cases in QPR shirts. Down Bloemfontein Road, past houses with 'Official Rangers Supporter' stuck on the front window, and into Ellerslie Road. I assume we went this way. At the time, I was too busy looking at the ground.

'Stop bumping into me,' said Paul. 'We're there.'

On the corner of Ellerslie Road a man was selling fanzines. The magazine was called *A Kick Up The R's*, subtitled *The Alternative View of Queens Park Rangers Football Club*. I bought a copy. It was completely impenetrable, a thick fug of obscure club politics and in-jokes. Further along, I bought the official programme, *Hoops Magazine*, which was much the same but without the humour.

'Ready?' said Paul. 'Got enough to read?'

I smiled wanly.

'Pretend you're going to the theatre or something.' He pushed me through the turnstiles and into a brave new world.

My first impression was that Loftus Road Stadium, whether deliberately or not, had made an architectural feature of exposed concrete. It was either a bold design statement, reckless in its modernism, or it was ugly. The place had all the atmosphere of a multi-storey car park.

Directly in front of us was a small bar, which had been sub-divided into two much smaller bars. On one side was the Rodney Marsh Bar; three feet to the right lay the Jeff Probyn Bar. Next to that was a Ladbrokes booth where you could place bets on the day's match, a counter selling burgers and chips and another bar, this one anonymous, with a sign pinned on the back wall: 'We do not except £50 notes.'

Around us, stuck on the concrete walls, were more adverts for Carlsberg beer and Rollover hotdogs, and more signs. They were big on signs at Loftus Road. 'The New Blue and White Club – Members and Season Ticket Holders Only,' said one, with an arrow pointing to the end of the alley. The St John's Ambulance Brigade was operating an even more exclusive door policy: 'Casualties Only,' said theirs.

Climbing the, yes, concrete steps to my seat, I passed something called the 'QPR Behaviour Policy'. It listed the sorts of conduct that would not be tolerated at Loftus Road:

1. The Pitch – under no circumstances are spectators allowed to go on to the pitch
2. Racial and Abusive Chants
3. Throwing of Objects
4. Drinking in View of the Pitch
5. Prohibited Items (knives, guns, etc.)
6. Persistent Standing
7. Blocking of Exits
8. Flash Photography

'Just like the theatre,' I said sarcastically to Paul. 'And, look, under the Football (Offences) Act 1991 you can be arrested for points two and three! Brilliant! And I'm so glad I left my knife at home.'

We found our seats. The pre-match entertainment consisted of a series of announcements, team selection, and a few records: 'London Calling' by The Clash, the new Robbie Williams and Blur singles, and for some reason, Pigbag's 1981 funk workout 'Papa's Got A Brand New Pigbag'.

At about twenty to three, a man dressed as a giant cat ran on to the pitch. The cat was wearing a QPR shirt. 'Look,' I said to Paul, 'a cat.'

'That's your mascot,' Paul replied. 'We've got a bear.'

Apparently, it was the cat's job to work the crowd, waving at fans, giving them the thumbs-up, patting small children on the head and so on. According to *Hoops Magazine* the cat's name was Jude. Unfortunately Jude was a bit scabby and in need of repair. When he ran across to wave at The Loft, he had to keep one hand on his head to stop it falling off.

So this was the football entertainment revolution, I though – a new-wave disco and a bloke dressed as a cat. Fantastic.

A few of the Forest fans agreed. '*YOU'RE SUPPOSED*,' they sang, pointing at Jude and laughing, '*YOU'RE SUPPOSED, YOU'RE SUPPOSED TO BE ... A CAT! YOU'RE SUP-POSED TO BE A CAT!*'

I laughed, for which I received a hard stare from a bloke in front of me. Lesson one: he may be a scabby cat, but he's *our* scabby cat. You're in the blue and white army now.

The stand was filling up. We were joined by a man and his young son, and a couple of pensioners. The man lit a cigar-illo, which stank. As we were at such close quarters, all of us – me, Paul, the pensioners and the little boy – smoked it with him.

At about five to three, the DJ switched from the sounds of the eighties and cued up 'Ride Of The Valkyries'. Jude the Cat executed a few devil-may-care swoops and dive-bombs but man-aged to hang on to his head. The announcer ran through the teams again and this time people cheered each Rangers name and booed a few of the Forest ones. Forest were new arrivals in the First Division, having been relegated from the Premiership at the end of the previous season.

'*WE! ARE! QPR! SAID WE ARE QPR! WE! ARE! QPR! SAID WE ARE QPR!*'

At just before three, the PA system crackled into life. 'Ladies and gentlemen, *this* is Loftus Road, *we* are QPR, please welcome Nottingham Forest and Queens Park Rangers!' And out came the players.

People stood and cheered. There was a last-minute influx of bodies from the bars outside. Cigarillo Dad stubbed out his cigarillo, shouted, '*We! Are! QPR! Said We Are QPR!*' a couple of times, then lit up again. His son jumped up and down and held his nose.

Kick-off.

At half-time I went to get a hotdog but the scrum at the food bar was so huge that by the time I got to the counter there were only sausage rolls left. I bought two. I had one bite and threw the rest into the bin. Indescribable. The bin, I noticed, had quite a lot of sausage roll in it already.

On returning to my seat, I started counting the signs dotted around the pitch, and carried on doing so once the second half was under way: T. J. Dairies, Shamrock Building Supplies Ltd, British European Airlines, Le Coq Sportif, Konica copiers, Konica fax, Thrifty Car Rental, Truly Scrumptious Catering, McAlpine Building, Wall of Sound Records, Carlsberg, Nationwide, Sport England . . .

Two in particular caught my eye – Ericsson, and Dew Valley, the Cooked Bacon. The telecommunications conglomerate had been the club's sponsor since 1996 and it was Ericsson's logo that adorned the players' shirts. I didn't know how long Dew Valley, the Cooked Bacon had been associated with QPR but, ominously, their sign hung above the management dugout. I hoped they hadn't supplied the sausage rolls.

When the whistle blew the score was QPR 1, Nottingham Forest 1. It had been a long ninety minutes. A lot of people started filing out before the end, 'To beat the rush,' said Paul. 'Enjoy it?' he asked, as we shuffled past the mounted police and chip vans.

There was no easy answer to that. I could still taste the sausage roll and my hat stank of cigarillo smoke. As entertainment, the game had been a washout. It was so boring. Forest had got an early goal, significant for those in the know in that it was scored by an ex-QPR player called Quashie but meaningless to me (wasn't Quashie an ex-Tellytubby too?). QPR equalized in the second half with a scrubby effort by the number eleven (Chris Kiwomya, I checked). The DJ put on 'Papa's Got A Brand New Pigbag' again. '*Duh duh duh duh!*' the crowd sang. '*HOOPS!*'

And that was it, for the most part. There was a lot of kicking the ball way upfield and hoping someone would win it in the air, but there was little in the way of passing or sustained play. This was called 'the long game'. And it was surprisingly physical. Players really threw themselves around and into each other. This was called 'commitment'. Nevertheless, unless you cared about one of the teams, there wasn't much to watch.

But the crowd had been great. The crowd made the game. They were participants rather than just spectators. They took their cue from the players, but without them, the game would have been nothing. The action on the pitch was dull and laboured, but the crowd turned it into an event. They transformed a kick-about into a football match.

What a brilliant way to make money, I thought. Charge people seventeen pounds a time just to entertain themselves. Genius.

Further moneymaking nous could be found in the club shop, which was doing brisk business after the game. It was an Aladdin's cave of crap, albeit blue and white hooped crap – replica shirts, of course, but also pennants, pendants, mugs, lunch boxes, mouse mats, a set of six drinks coasters, a 'Best Dribbler at QPR' baby's bib . . .

I bought a pencil sharpener for a pound and a CD called *QPR The Greatest: The Songs of Queens Park Rangers FC*. The album was rubbish, of course (unless you liked QPR, in which case it was *Astral Weeks*.)[1] The compilers had struggled to pad it out to

1. Inexplicably, the album received a rave review in the *NME* the following week ('Sod Richard Ashcroft's boast with The Verve: *This* is music.'), inexplicable that is until I realized the reviewer was also a regular contributor to *A Kick Up The R's*.

forty minutes. Aside from the 1972 and '74 team records, there were no fewer than three numbers by a 'band' called the Bush Broadcasters, one of which was titled, optimistically, 'We Won't Get Beaten Anymore'. It even had the theme from *Steptoe and Son* on it.

The one exception was 'Supporters Support Us' by the QPR Supporters, the B-side of a 1967 single released to celebrate QPR's victory in the League Cup that year – the only major cup or title, it should be noted, that QPR have ever won. The track is a weird freaked-out jam laden with echoes and effects, three stoned minutes of the Summer of Love. It is beyond psychedelic.

'Supporters Support Us' starts with a crowd chanting, '*RANGERS!*' and some rather limp clapping. The mysterious group then picks up the motif. They thud it out on one note, over and over again. '*Rangersrangersqueensparkrangerzzz,*' slurs an unnamed lead singer. The beat is relentless. The chant changes, shifts. Others join him, like Alex's droogs. '*Rodney, rodney, we want rodney . . .*' they demand, as though rodney is Shepherds Bush nadsat for hard hallucinogenic drugs. The rhythm is hypnotic, omnipotent. 'RODNEY, RODNEY,' they howl, 'WE WANT RODNEY . . .' Pause. '*MAAAAARRRSSSHHH!*'

Two minutes in and the track is at meltdown. Doused in reverb the ecstatic singer is nearing the end of his journey. 'THEY'RE THE GREATEST,' he wails, 'THEY'RE THE GREATEST . . . *TEEEAAAMMMM!*' All that remains for him are sounds beyond language, wildly unhinged shrieks, moans and guttural sobs (clearly the rodney had kicked in by this point). Fade to black.

Wow. What a record. What a team. *My* team.

'You'll have to go back now,' said Paul.

So I did.

Over the next few games, I picked up some vital bits of knowledge, such as which QPR player was which. The captain Gavin Peacock, who was the kids' favourite; young Stuart Wardley, who had come to the club on a £15,000 transfer from a non-league side and who, miraculously, was that season's top goal scorer; Karl Ready, a bleach-blond hardcase defender, who had been with the club for nearly ten years and whom almost nobody liked; Richard Langley, a fast young midfielder of whom great things were expected; the slightly erratic Lee Harper in goal; Mikkel Beck, a Danish international on loan from Derby County, who seemed even less popular than Karl Ready; and finally the player who had snatched the goal against Forest, Chris Kiwomya. Kiwomya had come to QPR on a free transfer from Arsenal. He arrived at Christmas 1998 and had scored fourteen goals before the season was out. He had his own chant, sung to the tune of 'Volare':

> *KIWOMYA, OH OH OH OH!*
> *KIWOMYA, OH OH OH OH!*
> *HE CAME FROM ARSENAL!*
> *HE COST THE Rs FUCK ALL!*

By the time of the Grimsby game, however, my initial flush of enthusiasm was vanishing.

Sixty-one minutes: QPR 0; Grimsby 0.

'Rodney, rodney, we want rodney . . .' I recited to myself. It wasn't working. QPR had drawn six of their last seven games – 1–1 (Forest), 1–1 (Port Vale), 1–1 (Stockport), 1–1 (Barnsley), 0–0 (Fulham), and 1–1 (Sheffield United) – and looked on course for another draw today. And Grimsby were pretty grim. Their only celebrity supporter was somebody called Dean Reynolds, whom I'd never heard of. To a hardcore fan it would be dull; to me it was absolute torture. When were QPR going to win something? Or lose? On Wednesday, they had beaten promotion hopefuls Manchester City 3–1, but that had been in Manchester and I hadn't seen it. I knew nothing of the euphoria of victory or the anguish of defeat; I was, however, rapidly becoming an expert on the tedium of deadlock. Come *on*, you Rs.

In fact, by their standards QPR were having a good season. The club had declined from the glory days of the 1970s, when the team boasted five England internationals, among them Gerry

Francis and Stan Bowles. As recently as 1993, they had been the top London club in the Premiership, finishing fifth. But they had been relegated in 1996 and were now barely surviving in the First Division. The Superhoops had only just avoided relegation to the Second Division by beating Crystal Palace 6–0 in the final game of the previous season. In a lucrative bit of *Schadenfreude*, you could buy a video of the Palace game in the club shop.

Gerry Francis was now QPR's manager. It was his second stint in the job. He had returned to the club in October 1998, after a less than glittering spell at Spurs. At that point, Rangers had gathered only nine points from fifteen games. Francis said he would continue to the end of the season in a bid to save the ailing Hoops. Many, including chairman Chris Wright, said Francis had made the decision with his heart rather than his head. But he did it, just.

Now it was Gerry's task to ensure that QPR stayed in the First Division. Some fans didn't like him. His squads were always injury-stricken, they said, because he trained them too hard. He believed that Loftus Road should be sold and the club enter into a ground-sharing arrangement with someone like Brentford. And he was perhaps overly realistic. 'Even if we were promoted, you have to ask yourself whether there would be any chance of staying up, and the answer is a resounding no.' It was about as inspirational as his dubious haircut, a never-changing badgery mullet.

But there were also those who loved Gerry. They believed him to be doing the best he could, given that the club had very little money, another of his favourite topics. 'When I decided to take this job I knew that many difficult financial decisions would need to be made . . . a lot of people have worked very hard to improve matters at this club and at Loftus Road plc but there is still a lot more to be done.' And that was in today's match day programme.

Out on the field, Wardley had his header cleared off the line by the Grimsby defence. Gerry scuttled out from beneath the Dew Valley sign to bark something at the players, before retreating to the dugout to chew his nails.

Seventy-two minutes. Ho-hum. If I left now I could *really* beat the rush.

In the box in front of the QPR goal, the ball was passed on by the Grimsby number eight to one of his teammates, but ricocheted off the hand of Rangers defender Chris Plummer. Up went the Grimsby players' arms. 'Oh, come on, that's not a fucking handball!' shouted one of the old men behind me helpfully. But the referee pointed towards the penalty spot.

I sat up. Around me people were ululating at the unfairness of it. And it *was* unfair. There was no way Plummer had meant to touch the ball (I've just viewed the incident again on the *Season Review* video and can confirm this). Rangers players were clustered round the referee but he was immovable. Penalty.

This was almost exciting. Like many exciting football moments it was a simple story: it had a hint of injustice about it – a wrong that would be righted if Harper kept the ball *out*.

The Grimsby number five, Richard Smith, approached the penalty spot with irritating confidence. Harper swayed. He looked apprehensive. The whistle blew. After a slow run-up, the Grimsby player sent it low and left, slotting it away into the corner of the net easily and efficiently.

Seventy-two mins: QPR 0; Grimsby 1.

Only he didn't and it wasn't. Harper saved it. Diving to the left, he blocked the ball with his body, knocking it away with his elbow. And I was on my feet with eleven thousand other people, shouting out the keeper's name.

'*LEE HARPER! LEE HARPER!*'

Karl Ready ran over to high five his teammate but the ball was still in play and Harper ignored him. What a fighter.

'*LEE HARPER! LEE HARPER!*'

It was a corner. Come on, Lee! Lee plucked it out of the air easily and QPR were now on the attack once more.

'*COME ON YOU Rs!*'

Wherever and whoever he was, Dean Reynolds must have been gutted.

Five minutes later Chris Kiwomya was brought down in the

box and this time the penalty was unambiguous. Mikkel Beck sent the Grimsby keeper the wrong way and it was seventy-seven mins: QPR 1; Grimsby 0.

'*Duh duh duh duh – HOOPS!*'

In the next issue of *Hoops Magazine* Lee Harper said, 'I have now realized how important it is for me to believe in my own ability and focus on what I am capable of achieving. In the past I have allowed my confidence to be affected by the opinions of others, opinions I didn't necessarily need.'

So it was a turning-point for both of us. Lee Harper saved not only the ball but also his self-esteem and my interest in the club.

My friend Mike, the Ipswich supporter, is as fanatical about Ipswich as only somebody can be who doesn't live there. He had subjected me to a long advertising campaign on the subject of Ipswich Town FC. They were definitely going to be promoted this season. I had to come to Portman Road to see some real football. It was a family club with a really enjoyable atmosphere. Their mascot was hilarious. And so on.

Gallingly, it turned out he was right. A trip to see Ipswich play Blackburn Rovers had come very close to fun, even though it had been another goalless draw ('Jinx,' said Mike). From the good humour of the crowd to the fluid entertaining football practised by the team, to the easy availability of hotdogs, the whole experience contrasted sharply with the drudgery of watching and following QPR. Bluey definitely had the edge on Jude. Even the chanting was of a uniformly higher standard.

Of course, a real fan wouldn't be swayed by such trifling matters as better facilities, value for money and, heavens above, football. You can change your name, your wife, your kidneys, but you can't change your football team. Got it?

But I wasn't a real fan. I was an impostor. So why not Ipswich? QPR had had a few hundred pounds of my money for which I had received very little, so they could hardly complain. Why not write off the loss and relocate, football-ly speaking, to Suffolk?

After the Grimsby game, I was pleased I hadn't. In April, Ipswich Town came to Loftus Road. Improbably, QPR had beaten them 4–1 at Portman Road in October. It was a fluke, said Mike. Lightning wouldn't strike twice. Now, six months later, they were in contention for automatic promotion to the Premiership. The game really mattered.

We beat them 3–1. 'I'm really sorry,' I said to Mike, after the match. But I wasn't.

I started going to away fixtures. At Charlton I was accompanied by an American friend, a sports fanatic, who was taken aback by the crappy football and even more taken aback by the language. The two offenders were a couple of pre-pubescent boys in the row behind us. *'Cunts!'* they shouted at the Charlton players and fans in high, unbroken voices. *'Red cunts!'*

'RED ARMY! RED ARMY!' chanted the Charlton fans.

'Red *cunts*!' shouted our two brave boys.

'"Red army". What a stupid chant,' said one boy to the other.

'Yeah,' said his friend. 'Cunts.'

'Gerry Francis' blue and white army!' they screeched a minute later.

One of the boys was still clinging to the innocence of childhood. 'This is it,' he would say hopefully, whenever a Rangers player won the ball. 'This is our goal!' But then, inevitably, the ball would be gifted to a Charlton player, and a little bit more of the child's youth would drain away.

'Cunts!' shouted the older boy.

'Yeah, cunts,' agreed the younger, dejectedly.

Cunts or not, Rangers were going to finish the season in the top half of the First Division but nobody seemed very excited about it. Around the time of the Manchester City game, fans talked about making the play-offs, but as the draws piled up, hopes of promotion dwindled. As Gerry said, 'We'll probably be relegated before Christmas.'

The last home game of the season should have been a party – the club was, after all, about to conclude its most successful campaign for five years – and yet the atmosphere was muted, almost tired. Jude ran around clutching his head, *this* was Loftus Road, *we* were QPR, but still things didn't really spark. The game was against West Bromwich Albion and it was crap. But it was all a preamble to the real business of the day.

If we stayed in our seats after the match, the announcer promised, one of us would win a season ticket. Gerry and the players wouldn't take a lap of honour if we didn't stay put, he said.

But his efforts at crowd control were a waste of time. As soon as the final whistle blew, the players sprinted for the tunnel and fans spilled out on to the turf, waving at their mates, darting to avoid capture by the stewards. The police formed a well-drilled line of horses and forced the fans back into their seats. The club probably had to pay extra if horses were deployed, I realized, hence the attempts to bribe or bully the crowd. But even this bit of civil unrest felt forced, a rather weary ritual before the grass was rolled up and put into storage for the summer (or whatever they did with it).

Five minutes later, Gerry and the players trotted heavily round the pitch. Gerry smiled and waved, job done. Gavin Peacock applauded the supporters. Lee Harper grinned and appeared relaxed for the first time in six months. Karl Ready skulked around at the back, not looking at the crowd. The unpopular Dane, Mikkel Beck, was long gone, back to a club in his home country but, bizarrely, still on loan from Derby.

All that remained was an away fixture at Portsmouth. Even the Rangers website described it as pointless. But I felt I should finish what I hadn't properly started. And so, on the first Sunday in May, we got into the car and headed for the coast.

Of course, I also wanted to combine this away trip with a bit of field research. The Portsmouth area, it turns out, is quite light on crazy-golf courses. Eventually we found one at Clarence Pier in Southsea, an old-fashioned pleasure beach. Treasure Island Adventure Golf was situated next to an arcade, opposite a roller-coaster and, just over the road, a car-boot sale. It was strewn with pirate paraphernalia – treasure chests, cannon balls, upturned barrels and numerous skulls and crossbones. The terrain was split into two nine-hole courses, called, with a neat eye for local detail, the Victory Trail and the Warrior Trail. Of course, this meant that to play all eighteen holes you had to pay twice. But given the lack of other courses in the area, it was a seller's market. So we did.

It was a beautiful day and as the breeze came in off the sea, and the smell of ozone mixed with chips and diesel, I was pleased to be there, on my little holiday. And I was, so help me, looking forward to the football.

By the time we found Fratton Park, the sun was blazing away and, without the sea air to cool things down, burningly hot. The away fans' end at Portsmouth isn't covered. We were going to be Sunday roast. Around me, QPR supporters were fanning themselves with *Pompey Chimes – the Official Matchday Magazine*. Jesus, it was hot.

The game kicked off at one thirty. And it was good – really good. In fact, it was the best game we saw all season. Passes were long and creative; tackles were committed but not foolhardy. There was a rhythm to the action in front of us. Pointless the game might have been, but for the first time in six months, Queens Park Rangers FC's football could be enjoyed for its own sake. It wasn't football as a vehicle for form or firms or histories or whatever. For once, it was almost football about football.

And then, after exactly half an hour, Richard Langley scored the best goal of the season. Out of nowhere he drilled the ball into the top left corner of the net from thirty yards out, brilliantly. It was a World Cup goal, the sort of thing you couldn't believe had just happened in front of you. You wanted to see it again and for a moment you forgot that you couldn't, because this wasn't TV, this was the real thing. There was something, I had to concede, beautiful about it.

The Rangers fans, stunned by the goal, roused themselves to cheer but not long and hard, it was too hot for that, which just added to the unreality of the situation.

'ONE–NIL AND YOU STILL CAN'T SING!' chanted the Portsmouth fans, but that was easy for them to say. They were in the stands. We were dying out there.

We won the game 3–1. Portsmouth suffered the indignity of an own goal. We left early to avoid another pitch invasion and staggered into a pub to cool off. It was over.

Looking back, I'm glad I made the effort to go to Portsmouth. It was QPR's last golden day for a long time. Things would be very different a few months from now, for both of us.

On the way home Mike called us. He had just seen Ipswich beat Walsall 2–0. They were in the play-offs. And when, three weeks later, they battled their way through the play-off final against Barnsley, and into the Premiership, he called us again, from Wembley Way this time. He was so happy. 'Yahayyyy!' he kept saying, 'Yahaaayyyyyyy!!' which, if you knew what he meant – and for the first time in my life, I think I did – was all he really needed to say.

This all sounds very lovely. And, by and large, it was. I let a little empathy into my life. I felt better for it. By the end of the season, I felt qualified to walk down Ellerslie Road and actually look where I was going. But I still couldn't embrace football whole-heartedly. Nagging doubts remained.

In the 1990s football did, indeed, come home, but home to the middle classes whose game it was in the first place. They'd let Alf and his cloth-capped mates from the factory have a kickabout for most of the century and now they wanted their ball back. But if QPR was anything to go by, reports of the middle-classing of football have been greatly exaggerated, outside the top Premiership sides.

Football in the UK is still overwhelmingly white, male and working class. According to figures from the Sir Norman Chester Centre for Football Research, only 14 per cent of season-ticket holders are female. This figure has risen in the last ten years, but that's still 86 per cent men (as opposed to the 51 per cent of British people who are, on a daily basis, women). The biggest concentration of black faces at Loftus Road was to be found behind the counters serving the filthy sausage rolls or on the pitch. Not in the stands.

In February, I went to a midweek derby with local rivals

Fulham FC. There was going to be a 'good atmosphere'. Their last meeting, back in the autumn at Craven Cottage, had seen extensive crowd trouble and a number of arrests. There were conspicuously more police in evidence and the chanting was loud and strong already, both inside and outside the ground.

Sitting next to me was a middle-aged man in a grey fleece jacket and blue and white scarf, on his own. Ten minutes in, when a fight broke out in the row behind us, he didn't even turn round. He just carried on watching the game.

Richard Langley flew up the wing past us. 'Go on, you little jigaboo,' said my neighbour, almost fondly, as he passed. Then he said it again, louder. 'Jigaboo!' I couldn't believe it. It wasn't just the racism, it was the choice of word. It was almost quaint. And it was directed at one of our players. '*Come on you Rs!*' he offered next. I did nothing. I felt ashamed of myself. I was aware of more and cruder abuse around me.

Most of the behaviour outlawed by the QPR Behaviour Policy was in evidence at that Fulham game, tolerated and tolerated to the point of encouragement. There was drinking in full view of the pitch and the policemen who did nothing about it; objects were thrown (pound coins – you could tell it was West London); chants were both abusive and racial. It was pretty foul; violent, pissed up, ugly. I left at half-time.

Walking back home, I felt angry for the first time since I'd started this experiment. The racism was just one part of an evening whose only point appeared to be a rancorous hate-in (with optional football). Because it was Fulham, and we had a history with Fulham, there would be a 'good atmosphere'. It would be a bit 'lively'. Why? Because it was Fulham. And we hate Fulham. Why? Because we do.

What this meant, I now knew, was that the football would be as bad as ever, but that the lack of entertainment would matter even less than usual, because there was a received and pointless rivalry to fill the vacuum. That made it an exciting game. It mattered more. And why did it matter more? Because it did. Because it was Fulham. And we hate Fulham.

Over Christmas a friend of mine went to see a couple of matches, First Division West Bromwich Albion at home, and then Manchester United at Old Trafford. He had enjoyed the West Brom game much more. 'The thing is, Andy,' he told me, after the Man U game, 'the football was so skilful in comparison with West Brom, it was like watching a different sport.' But had he enjoyed it? 'At first it was great – the old cliché, like watching chess on grass, that clever and creative. But after a bit it was just boring. There wasn't any singing. When United scored, people just clapped.'

In other words, Manchester United play a beautiful game but West Brom was a better match. Football, beautiful football, is boring unless you can find something to make it matter.

Tribalism makes football what it is. It is tribalism that turns a lifeless game into an event. I had seen that at my very first QPR match against Forest. Without the cheering, the laughter, the in-jokes and the chanting, the game is almost nothing. It's a vacuum, a Beckham-like blank space. It's mostly benign, most of the time.

But now I could see the downside. There is a void at the centre of the game, which tribalism can fill – local, national – and turn in an instant into something less amiable and more dangerous. And yet, without that edge, without that sense that things could slide, maybe, into proper disorder, as one writer has said, 'You might just as well be watching snooker.'

'And . . . ?' you might be thinking. 'A bit of chanting, the odd ruck, it goes with the territory. What do you expect? That's football.'

That's football. I hear this apparently innocuous phrase all the time. The games are boring, the seats uncomfortable, the sausage rolls inedible – that's football (accompanied by wry shrug). The middle classes are taking over, the grass roots are disappearing – that's football too. And so is the use of mounted police and punch-ups at local derbies and deportations and 'No Surrender to the IRA' – it's all football. But – and this got worse in the nineties – football accommodates this as part of the sport's rich pageant, embraces it, because it reinforces the myth that football is like life, full of life's primal energies and emotions, good and bad. But it isn't. It's just a game.

'In Britain, football itself is almost incidental to fan culture,' says Simon Kuper, in his excellent book *Football Against the Enemy*. He is writing about the rivalry between Celtic and Rangers, whose scope encompasses just about every expression of hate you can think of, including murder. 'British fans enjoy fan culture, and most of all they enjoy hating their rivals. Celtic and Rangers fans need each other.'

Football writers love to talk about Celtic and Rangers. The subject gives them full scope to explore the passions that football can inspire and demonstrate how the rivalry is entrenched and entangled with history, nationality, politics and so on. Lesser accounts than Kuper's inevitably focus on tragedies around the clubs, stabbings, wasted lives, killed for wearing the wrong shirt. That's football, they seem to be saying – rich, isn't it?

Fulham versus QPR was not on the same scale as Celtic versus Rangers, thank God, but the attitude I saw displayed there and, moreover, the acceptance of it, is at the heart of football culture. It runs in a direct line to sectarianism, racism . . . It has a good side, of course – the sense of community that still clusters around football is precious and probably unique – but people think they need football so badly that there's a widespread denial that it could be anything other than wholly positive. And it's what people use to convince themselves that football is more meaningful than snooker or dog-fighting or miniature golf.

I didn't want to go back but I did go back, so the Grimsby game was both a breakthrough for me, and a defeat. Because, at whatever level, by jumping to my feet and shouting, 'LEE HARPER! LEE HARPER!' I was choosing to ignore the protestations of common sense – the expense, the boredom, the prejudice, the stupidity – and, like a real fan, to accept all those things as part and parcel of the game. I wanted to belong. Was this a good thing? Thinking about it, no. But I wasn't thinking about it any more: I was just doing it. But I felt uneasy, like I had betrayed the younger me.

I started saying 'we' when talking about the club, not 'they'. *We* were robbed on Saturday. *We* need to sort *our* midfield. And friends and colleagues would look at me strangely and say, 'It's we now, is it?' And I'd laugh and say, yes, it's we now. Because it was.

4

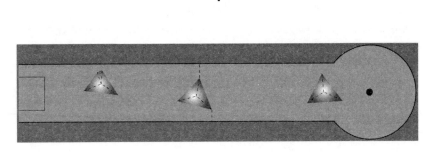

Pyramiden – pyramids

In August 1999, not far from where Neville Chamberlain once waved a piece of paper and promised Peace In Our Time, an event took place that might, eventually, have a similar seismic effect on the nation's sporting life. In Croydon, on an industrial estate just behind Ikea, the Lost World Adventure Golf Course opened for business.

Its unveiling featured little of the razzmatazz one associates with great sporting occasions or even, for that matter, the opening of a supermarket. No celebrities came to cut the ribbon. No famous minigolfers turned out to celebrate, because there are none. The mayor of Croydon played a few holes for the benefit of the cameras, but there weren't any names from the world of real golf – no Faldo, no Lee Westwood, not even Bruce Forsyth. Get real! This was minigolf! This was Croydon!

But the appearance of the Lost World in the last months of the old century seemed highly significant nevertheless. For the Lost World is Britain's first *indoor* miniature, or adventure, golf course. It's like Tomb Raider with putting. On Saturdays, terrifyingly, it is open until three in the morning.

I'd first heard about the Lost World in the British Minigolf Association's newsletter. 'Depressed by the prospect of a long winter ahead?' it said. 'Is the thought of not being able to play minigolf again until spring getting you down? It has come to our attention that indoor adventure golf courses are now open in Bristol and Croydon!'

Croydon was nearer than Bristol and, besides, I had a sentimental attachment to the place. To many people, Croydon is synonymous both with town planners' worst excesses – tower blocks, shopping centres and ring roads – and an ugly suburban small-mindedness. 'It was everything I wanted to get away from,' David Bowie said famously, in one interview. 'I think it's the most derogatory thing I can say about somebody or something: "God, it's so fucking Croydon!"'

But David Bowie can fuck off back to Bromley. I grew up near Croydon, and it was on Croydon's municipal playing-fields and recreation grounds that I failed at whatever sport I turned my hand or foot to – football, rugby, cricket, all of them. To me, Croydon's tower blocks and shopping centres were an escape from all that. It was the grassy bit that was a nightmare.

The BMGA newsletter also contained details of a big-money minigolf tournament that was taking place in Denmark in the summer, with a first prize of several thousand pounds. 'That sounds like fun,' I said to Tina. 'I've never been to Denmark. We could go together. I might even win some money.'

'I'd love to come with you,' said Tina, 'only I don't want to.'

Hmm. I decided to think about it. In the meantime, I rang the Croydon Tourist Board (yes, it does exist). Could they tell me if there were any indoor minigolf courses in the Croydon area?

'Yes, dear, there's one down at Valley Park,' said the woman from the Tourist Board, apparently unfazed by the question – but, then, if it's your job to talk up Croydon as a great holiday destination, you probably don't faze easily.

'Do you know where Ikea is?' she continued. 'It's behind there.' I did. The first shelves of my adult life had come from that very branch. 'I'll send you a brochure. There's a map on that.'

'Great!' I said, hoping to strike a sort of grateful, enthusiastic but not insane note. 'That's great!'

The brochure, when it arrived, made the Lost World sound very exciting indeed. 'The UK's 1st Indoor Adventure Golf Course,' it announced proudly, above the course's logo – a golf ball set in an Inca crown. Inside were photographs of a pretty young couple experiencing the full range of emotions that the course could provide – surprise, horror, joy, but not, it must be said, much golf. In the first photo, they were putting with glassy smiles, their eyes fixed firmly on each other rather than on the ball. They were clearly In Love and not much competition for even the most average minigolfer.

But all too soon, disaster struck! Suddenly, they were on a rope bridge, gaping open-mouthed in terror at some unseen assailant; and in the next photo the girl was alone, so startled by a wax tribesman in a ceremonial headdress she had dropped her putter. Of her cowardly partner there was no sign. Had he abandoned her? Or had a more sinister fate befallen him? 'Why not bring your friends,' ran the blurb underneath, 'invite the office, bring the family, get the girls together or make a boys' night out?' It was like an offer from Butlins to go hunting for the Blair Witch. It looked fantastic.

And so the following week, I made a nostalgic return to Croydon, taking four different buses to get there. The Lost World was situated at the back of a futuristic bowling alley called the Superbowl, which, like the rest of Valley Park, wasn't designed to be accessible by public transport.

The Lost World's unique mixture of the sinister and the naff, so convincingly dramatized in their brochure, was in evidence at the entrance to the course. A smiling teenage boy and teenage girl were behind the desk. They were both wearing blue sports tops emblazoned with the Inca golf-crown logo.

'Hi there!' beamed the boy.

'Hello,' I said. 'One, please.'

'Sure thing,' he said. 'That'll be three pounds twenty-five, please.'

I handed him a fiver. He grinned at me. This was all a bit strange. It struck me as odd that I hadn't struck him or his colleague as odd. No 'Are you here on your own?' or 'Are your kids on the way?' It was half-term. I might be a pervert. At best I was clearly eccentric. Or did they get single thirtysomething men here all the time?

'Do you get single thirtysomething men here all the time?' I enquired.

Not a flicker. 'Oh, yes,' he said. 'We get all sorts of people here.' He turned to the girl. 'Don't we?'

'Oh, yes.' She smiled, and handed over my ball and scorecard.

The Superbowl had obviously done their recruiting in Midwich. I persisted. 'And, er, is it popular? Lots of, you know, young people?' I asked, dodgily.

'What do you mean?' said the boy, looking puzzled.

Oh, come on. 'You know . . . kids?'

'Oh, yes,' he said. 'We get loads of kids. But we get loads of other people too.'

I gave up. 'Really?' I said, choosing a putter from the rack.

'Yes,' said the girl. 'But if we get any weirdos, Security get rid of them.'

'Right,' I said. Was my bluff being called? 'Well, I'll just . . .'

'You should come back on a Saturday night,' the girl continued. 'We get loads of people then, even at three in the morning. Don't we, Liam?'

'Oh, yeah,' said Liam. And they both laughed.

I stepped gratefully into another world. The 'stone' walls were illuminated with an unearthly orange sodium glow. Wild animals howled in the distance, on tape. The first hole was a long twelve-foot run tapering upwards, with a rocky outcrop jutting in from the right of the cup. This'll be a two-par, I said to myself, consulting my scorecard, or 'Expedition Log', as the theme has it. It was a three. They're making this too easy, I thought.

Before starting, I ran through the other details on my 'Explorer's Passport'. The rules were fairly standard, maximum six strokes per hole, tee off from the tees provided, that sort of thing, but with the occasional 'Adventure' twist – 'Do not swing putter carelessly above your waist: leave swinging to the monkeys,' for instance, or 'Do not attempt to retrieve balls from water hazards, all lakes contain piranah [sic.]!' You had to give them full marks for consistency, if not for spelling.

I placed the ball on the tee and took a few practice swings to loosen up. The trick would be to get the ball as near to the hole as possible without it rebounding off the back wall of the cave and coming back down the slope. Elementary stuff, really. Addressing the ball, I gently pushed it uphill and watched it glide towards the cup. However, I was so concerned not to overdo it, I pulled the shot. The ball limped to the lip of the slope, hesitated, then rushed back to greet me at the tee. It came to rest between my feet, a few centimetres back from where it had started.

I see.

Clearly a different tactic was in order. I whacked it. The ball rocketed up the slope, ran up the back wall, somersaulted over the cup, bounced back off the rocky outcrop on the other side and came to rest six inches from the hole. It was a terrible shot, but it did the job.

I approached the ball and carefully knocked it into the hole to preserve my par three. Not a great start.

As I bent down to retrieve my ball from the cup, I heard a great explosion of noise behind me. Children were here. Lots of them.

A group of about ten kids were waiting impatiently at the tee for me to get out of the way. They were all about ten or eleven and nutty with half-term fever. My self-consciousness cranked itself up another couple of notches, in the process coming very close, I realized, to shame. Trying to muster a little insouciance, I headed back down the slope to meet them.

As I walked, I thought quickly. Although they were clearly contravening Rule Number One of the Explorer's Passport ('No more than 4 explorers per group'), I was a single man in an Eskimo parka and therefore in no position to argue with anyone about anything. So I would set them a good example and behave in a gentlemanly and sporting manner ('Rule 6. Courtesy: Please

Allow Smaller or Faster Expeditions to Play Through'). By doing so, I would therefore avoid taking every shot under the noisy gaze of ten pairs of mocking eyes. Also, once they had gone through, I could slyly play the first hole again, and by doing so enter a two-shot birdie on my scorecard. I congratulated myself on my cunning.

'There you go,' I said to a little boy in a blue anorak. 'I'm going to let you through.'

He didn't need telling twice. Turning to his friends, he said, 'I told you! He's gettin' out the way!' They pushed past me, their whoops and yells blending with the jungle sound effects of the course. I tried to look anywhere except directly at them.

The boy in the blue anorak was first off the tee. Swinging his putter carelessly above his waist (NOT permitted) his ball ricocheted off the back wall and flew straight into the cup. 'Hole in one!' he shouted. 'Hole. In. Wuuuurrrrrnnnnne!!'

Well, I thought, a sickly smile fixed on my face, at least they'll be quick.

They weren't. Anorak's great skill did not extend to the other Explorers in his group. It took them a good ten minutes to clear the first hole, what with all the screaming, stamping and hacking that goes with the younger game. I waited patiently for them to move on.

Once the last little urchin had left the green, I placed my ball once again on the first tee. I had a good sense now of how to play this hole and knew better than to pull the shot a second time.

Sure enough, the ball slid effortlessly up the slope and over the top, coming to rest just inches from the cup. What a great shot! What a golfer! It was a shoo-in for a birdie at the first. Conveniently forgetting the tragic fact that I had already played this hole and was therefore effectively *cheating against myself*, I marched up to claim my two.

But it was not be. A small child darted out from the entrance to the second hole, where he had been waiting to take his turn. Spying my perfectly placed ball and assuming it to be a spare, or one left behind by one of his group, he kicked it into the cup.

Before I could stop him, he grabbed the ball and proceeded to start playing football with it, dribbling it and bouncing it off the cave wall.

Wordlessly I approached him and held out my hand. He picked up the ball, gave it to me, and bolted back to his mates. 'Hey!' he shouted in delight. 'It was that bloke's ball!' This must have been who the couple in the brochure had been screaming at. Rather than replace my ball or go through the whole thing again, I awarded myself a gimme as compensation. Two shots at the first. Very good. I waited for the yelling in the next cave to subside then made my way through to the second hole.

The fiasco at the first more or less set the pattern for the round. I would play a hole, badly, then have to wait while the Lost Boys ahead of me finished putting, driving, hitting one another over the head, etc., and moved on to the next cave. To fill in the time, I would play the hole again and again until I got a sufficiently low score to enter in my Expedition Log, all the while feeling somewhat embarrassed by such ludicrous self-deception, and desperate not to attract any further ridicule from the party ahead. It was wretched.

Thus I slowly battled on, down Witch Doctor's Run (hole four), through a revolving, disorientating tunnel and across a pool of fire (hole six), playing badly, feeling ridiculous and cheating like a bastard.

Things came to a head at the seventh, a difficult par three called the Snake Pit. The hole was a dog-leg, doubling back on itself. You putted uphill, round a bend, and back down to where the path then split into two. If the ball headed down the right fork of the path, it plopped down on to the green, which the player accessed by crossing an illuminated pit of hissing fibreglass snakes; if, on the other hand, your ball ran down the left-hand fork it was deposited back at your feet, from where you would have to restart the hole, a stroke down.

I played a great shot first time. The ball ran up the cave wall on my right, hugged it all the way round the bend, then ran smoothly down the right-hand path to the green where it came to rest beside the cup. I negotiated the Snake Pit (which was about as scary as Noddy) and sank the putt for a birdie two. Easy.

For once I didn't have to play the hole again to get my score down: I could do it for 'fun' while I waited for the kids ahead to move on.

But try as I might, I could not duplicate that perfect initial shot. Every time I hit the ball, instead of hugging the wall down the tunnel to the green, it would repeatedly rebound off it and shoot down the left-hand fork, ending up back at my feet.

Putt, bounce, fuck.

Putt, bounce, fuck.

How had I done it? After a few goes, I couldn't remember. I tried everything – nudging it, pushing it, smashing it off the near left wall, all to no avail. Every time it was the same; up, down, return. Putt, bounce, *fuuuuuuuuck*!

Eventually, I fluked the ball back on to the green where, in a fit of righteous indignation, I missed a one foot shot, double-putting for a risible eleven. Eleven! On a par three! For a minute I was tempted to scribble that eleven on my scorecard for the world to see, so contemptuous was I of my own failure. But I didn't. I entered the two and trudged on.

Is there a sadder sight in the world than a grown man in a parka playing a miniature-golf course on his own and taking notes? Well, yes, actually: a grown man playing miniature golf on his own who takes eleven shots to sink the ball then pretends it was a two. Thus I forged ahead.

By the time I arrived at the ninth and final hole (par four), I'd had enough. I was fed up with those kids, and I wanted to make a run for it. Away behind the final green was a staircase that led back up to ground level and the exit, the fluorescent lighting of the Superbowl shining down invitingly into the subterranean caverns of the Lost World. But between me and the exit lay a sheer 'rock face', with three equidistant holes at the base. A sign above read, 'The gods are pleased! You have done well to reach the Aztec Temple. Now choose your path wisely to the last hole.' Oh, piss off, I thought.

After checking which of the three holes led directly to the final green (the one on the left), I scooped my ball into the tunnel, illegally but accurately before, *yes*, two-putting again for a birdie three. It should have been an eagle.

I didn't care. Without taking my ball out of the cup and without looking back, I left the underworld and headed towards the light.

'See you again!' grinned Liam and his colleague at the front desk, as I handed back the putter.

'Probably not,' I replied, and left. Security, I couldn't help but notice, followed me discreetly all the way to the door.

The Lost World at Valley Park in Croydon is an adventure-golf course rather than a crazy or minigolf course. The distinction is more than academic. Adventure-golf courses are emphatically *not* the same thing as crazy golf. Unlike crazy golf, the courses are high-tech, exciting, dramatic. There are no windmills in adventure golf – or if there are, they are enormous and called something like the Windmill of Terror. In other words, the emphasis is very much on the adventure rather than the golf. If you presented Thomas Zeininger or any of the top Europeans with the putt, bounce, fuck of the Lost World's seventh hole, they'd probably refuse to play it – it's just too silly.

Mike Newman is a designer of adventure golf courses, and would definitely refute any accusations of silliness. For him places like the Lost World are about 'taking the player into a story.'

'It's all about not growing up,' Mike told me, when I met him at the Leisure Industries Fair in Birmingham. 'For a designer, adventure-golf courses are incredibly fulfilling because your imagination hasn't got a boundary.'

The Lost World had certainly been designed by an unfettered imagination – unfettered to the point of mental illness. The World that was Lost and then uncovered many centuries later in – let's not forget – Croydon was a hitherto unimagined fusing of Aztec, Inca and Egyptian mythology and architecture, with a nine-hole putting course thrown in.

What an archaeological puzzle this place was. Human sacrifice loomed large in the culture of both the Aztecs and the Incas. Presumably, then, the lost tribes of Valley Park spent their days holding thrilling miniature-golf tournaments, the losers of which were slaughtered at the foot of one of the course's fibreglass pyramids – a real sudden-death play-off.

Mike Newman's speciality was pirates and smugglers. He had designed and supervised courses all over Britain, from Little-hampton to Whitby. He had even built the new course at Center-Parcs. All these courses had a pirate theme. Mike had long hair, a gold earring and a goatee beard. Perhaps he had fallen into adventure-golf design because the pirate navy was full.

'There are certain themes which are timeless,' Mike told me excitedly. 'The *Treasure Island* story, Robert Louis Stevenson, has been going since eighteen-something, so it's a timeless story. For children, you're supplying adventure. I mean, a ship is such a wonderful shape to explore. And for adults, when you're dealing with pirate flags, shipwrecks, smuggling, there's something romantic about it, something that captures people's imaginations whether they're old or young.'

Pirates aside, Mike's work, he felt, was influenced by the council playground he had frequented as a child in Port Talbot, South Wales. 'Concrete floors covered in broken glass, the most dangerous play equipment you could possibly imagine. My brother broke his arm in there. I cracked a tooth. But, as a kid, you don't care. You just have fun.' For Mike, a buccaneer of the baize, the adventure-golf experience was all about fear. 'The core of the design is to instil fear into the child – because if it's boring and safe, why go there?'

Well, I certainly had the fear and, after my first trip to the Lost World, I had the loathing too. It had been a disaster. I had played terribly and I'd left feeling stupid and embarrassed and, yes, punished.

However, within hours I wanted to go round again. The experience was addictive and I was hooked. And, like all great addictions, I wanted to turn others on to my trip. I began to plan my own tournament, a Saturday-night showdown. I had already begun to forget my first pathetic expedition to the Lost World and to rationalize the advantage it would undoubtedly – *undoubtedly* – give me.

Nick had enjoyed his performance in the British Open, so it was comparatively easy to persuade him to give up a Saturday night in the interests of 'research'. And, I reasoned to Paul, I would need him as the third corner of the triangle.

'What triangle?' said Paul.

'Adventure golf,' I replied, 'has, I believe, mysterious healing properties. As a result of the great sports plague of the 1990s, we live in troubled and divided times. But the Lost World is a place where we can all meet as equals: a lifelong sports hater like me, a consummate nineties man like yourself and an actual sportsman like Nick [golfer, fourteen handicap]. It's like A Level Playing Field, Paul. Do you see?'

'You need a patsy,' said Paul. 'That's OK. I've beaten you before. I'll be happy to do it again.'

Paul was right. He had beaten me before, the only time we had ever played crazy golf together. It was, coincidentally, the first time he had ever picked up a putter. It still smarted.

If there is such a thing as a Bad Loser – and I think we know that there is – then Paul is a textbook example of a Bad Winner. So reasonable and temperate in most other areas of his life, victory at games brings out the worst in him, transforming him from a decent, personable guy into a strutting, toilet-mouthed delinquent. And that's just at Monopoly. Football has a far more deleterious effect, as it does on many men. And as for our sole foray into crazy golf . . . After his fifth hole-in-one Paul startled passers-by by jumping up and down on the eighteenth green, waving his club in the air and shouting, '*Yeeeessssss!*' like the secret yobbo he is. What a git.

To beat Paul in Croydon, therefore, would be sweet indeed, the kind of deeply satisfying victory that only comes with the abject humiliation of a close friend. And, like a fool, he agreed to accompany Nick and me to the Lost World.

So, a few weeks later, I stood in the car park of the Superbowl, waiting for Paul and Nick to show. Nick's car had broken down and they were late. It was after midnight and bitingly cold. Behind me were the twin towers of Ikea, once the Croydon B power station. Running off to my left was a Burger King, Frankie and Benny's restaurant (Italian American) and the impressive Warner Brothers multiplex cinema, whose fake art-deco frontage recalled the long-demolished Croydon aerodrome. In spite of the lateness of the hour, the cinemas and restaurants of Valley Park were full of people. Most were teenagers and many were drunk. Kids rang their mates in other areas of the park. Groups of lads in football shirts whistled at girls and jeered at each other. I saw two scrappy fights break out. Courting couples snogged against trees. Some did considerably more.

I couldn't work out if this was a happy ending for Valley Park or not. On the one hand, where once there had been a power station, now you can buy shelves. Where once the crowds had come to mob Charles Lindbergh and Amy Johnson, now they come to enjoy Frankie and Benny's hospitality and have sex behind their Italian American restaurant. Where once Valley Park had rung with the sound of industry and endeavour – oh, happy Valley! – now it rings with the sound of text-messaging and people enjoying themselves.

On the other hand, I thought, please hurry up, boys. Let's just remember where we are. In a retail park in Croydon. On a Saturday night. The Superbowl's alleys and bars are still open and thronged with lager-drinking Croydonites. And we have to play two rounds of adventure golf. Pirate Mike would appreciate the fear-instilling potential of the situation.

At just after one a.m., Paul and Nick arrived.

'Do you like my shoes?' said Nick.

For tonight's challenge he was wearing an actual pair of Arnold Palmer's golf shoes, which he had won in a bet with Palmer's legendary caddy Tip Anderson.

'Very nice,' I said.

'They don't really fit,' said Nick, 'but they're lucky.'

This being a serious sporting occasion Nick had brought his

own putter, as had I. As we pushed open the big glass entrance doors, two of the Superbowl's security team headed straight for us. 'Where the fuck do you think you're going with those?' said one, a shaven-headed bruiser with an earpiece and a walkie-talkie, nodding at the putters.

'Er . . . We've come to play the golf,' I said wetly. 'That's all.'

'It's all right, Brian,' said the other, even more mountainous security guard. 'I remember this bloke from a few weeks ago. He's harmless. On you go, gentlemen.'

'Have you been here before?' spluttered Paul, as we made our way to the course. 'Did you really come here on your own?'

I ignore him. Now I have to win. And to prove that his last victory wasn't a fluke, especially now he knows of my rigorous preparation, Paul wants to make me suffer again. Meanwhile, for understandable reasons, Nick the Real Golfer wants to beat both of us. After six holes our scores are as follows: Paul and I are tied at seventeen while Nick lags two shots behind at nineteen, after a careless five at Witch Doctor's Run. The absurdity of our surroundings notwithstanding, the atmosphere is anxious.

Fortunately, after a comprehensive bout of putting, bouncing and *fuck*ing on the seventh, at the end of the first round, I am just about in the lead. This is thanks to some skilful play on my part and, vitally, Paul taking seven shots, the maximum permitted, on the difficult final hole. I know the left-hand tunnel is the one but Paul doesn't. We murmur our condolences. In an eerie echo of what's yet to come Nick jokes about 'using a sand wedge' to bypass the complex layout of greens and interconnecting tunnels. Little does he realize how his words will return to haunt him. We shake hands, sign each other's Expedition Logs and head for a half-time drink at the bar.

'Well done, Andy!' says Nick, unconvincingly.

We sit under the blue and pink neon of the Superbowl's main bar. It's packed. There's ten-pin bowling, snooker, fruit machines and cutting edge kill-'em-all video games; every hi-tech plaything that twenty-first-century man could possibly desire. Why would such a successful and hip amusement arcade (which, under the neon, is essentially what the Superbowl is) even consider adding an attraction so, well, *unattractive* as putting?

After a couple of pints, we head back to the course, pausing only to join a small crowd who are watching a Japanese boy play a video game called Dancing Stage, a super-athletic variation on the old Simon bleep 'n' follow game of the late seventies. You can find it in most British arcades, but in Japan it's a sensation. The Japanese boy executes a rapid series of dance steps in time with the music and at the prompting of the machine. He's very good at it, spinning and skipping impossibly fast, and when he finishes, he gets a round of applause from the semi-circle of boggling spectators. Impressively, he ignores us, disdainfully snatching up his coat and heading off into the night. What would we know, anyway? A member of staff tells me later that the boy comes here every Saturday, on his own, and dances on the machine for hours at a time, the leading authority in a field of one.

Of course, the Lost World fits in snugly with attractions like Dancing Stage, the driving simulations and slot machines. The Lights! Props! Sound effects! – set to 'stun' on a Saturday night – are the reason why the course is here. This is a fairground ride, whose cost was in excess of a quarter of a million pounds; the putting is almost incidental. It could just as easily be Adventure Snooker or Adventure Ping-Pong.

Our second round is quieter, more determined and more intense than the first. Sport finds a way. '*Shit me!*' says Nick, as he misses an easy putt at the fifth, his head dropping in momentary despair.

At the seventh I take another three – putt, bounce, fork, hurrah! – Paul a four and Nick a five. Nick has played consistently badly all night and is beginning to look a bit punch-drunk and slightly woozy. The scores are me forty-six, Paul fifty and Nick fifty-three. Fatally, I allow myself the beginnings of smugness at my impending victory.

At the eighth hole things start to unravel accordingly. Paul takes a two. So does Nick. I, however, take four shots to traverse the comparatively simple terrain of the hole, with only the lava pit to negotiate. As a result, Paul now trails me by only a couple of strokes. Another slip-up like this and the novice will once again be turning cartwheels on the final green. I cannot allow this to happen.

Because our play, tense and precise, has now slowed to a crawl, there's a big backlog of families and late-night golfers queuing behind us. Given that it's now nearly two o'clock and the bars are still open, we decide it might be prudent to let them play through. The first lot are a party of five, two mums, two daughters and a boyfriend, whose it was hard to say. In marked contrast to our painstaking, not to say painful, approach to the game their whole group plays off in one go, wildly. The mums in particular smash their balls off the cave walls with such alarming ferocity that I worry someone might lose an eye.

Once all the other groups have passed safely through we approach the ninth and final hole, the Aztec Temple. It's a clear-cut situation. I have fifty, Paul fifty-two and Nick fifty-five. Nick trails me by five shots and is effectively out of the game. The gods are pleased and so am I. Paul is the one I have to beat. 'Now, choose your path wisely to the last hole.'

The tunnel on the left is the wise choice. But getting the ball up the narrow slope to the entrance of the tunnel proves nearly impossible. And, indeed, I can't do it. The ball just won't run up the slope the way I want it to. After three shots I give up and try one of the other tunnels. By the time I make it to the bottom green, I'm already at the permitted stroke limit. I take a seven.

So Paul now has a five-shot advantage. If he can play this hole in four or under, he'll win.

With his first shot, Paul tries to box clever. He lays up, putting his ball just to the edge of the slope – safe but sound. Now he just needs to nudge it into the left-hand tunnel and he could be looking at a three and victory. He takes a minute just to check his bearings. Slowly, carefully, he takes his putt. The ball rolls slowly up the slope . . . and then rolls down again, running half-way back to the tee.

'Fuck,' says Paul, matter-of-factly.

'Bad luck,' I fib generously in return. He knows, and I know, that that was it – the deciding shot of the night. He chooses to play through the other tunnels, ending up with a six, better than my attempt, but it leaves the scores at fifty-seven and fifty-eight. I've beaten him, admittedly by just one stroke, but I've still done it. I've won!! To coin a phrase, *Yeeeessss!* All that there remains to do is wait politely for Nick to sink his ball and then we can go home.

But then something extraordinary happens, something bad. Without meaning to, Nick wins the match.

Instead of doing the decent thing and meekly seeing out his terrible round, instead of laying the ball up or playing it safe or skilfully shooting it up the slope and into the tunnel as neither Paul nor I could manage, Nick the Proper Golfer decides to show some last-minute flair. He doesn't putt or push or nudge – he chips. The ball arcs high above the suddenly irrelevant slopes and tunnels and bounces heavily on to the lowest green. Is such a shot legal? I don't know. I don't think so, but . . . As Paul and I look on dumbfounded, Nick's ball, his facetious chip, bumps hard against the back wall and pops, just like that, into the cup.

It's a hole-in-one.

It's fifty-six.

It's all over.

Nick can barely believe it. And neither can we. It's unbelievable. He smiles the smile of the redeemed, the born-again, the transformed man. I feel empty, yes, *gutted*. Paul and I offer our hands and our congratulations but Nick doesn't hear us. He is caught up in his own fairytale ending. He was lost but now, gentle Jesus, he is found.

As I say, I hate sport.

Outside, we try to hail a cab, not easy in Valley Park at two thirty in the morning. I have plenty of opportunity to reflect on the night's events. Was tonight fun? Absolutely. Was it fair? Not really, no. Maybe adventure golf isn't such A Level Playing Field after all – or, at least, it's as level as any other sport. Because, it seems to me, whether you like, love, or loathe sport, winner or loser, the one thing tonight proves conclusively is this: in sport as in life, a smartarse will always spoil it for everyone else.

A couple of weeks after the match, I received this e-mail from Peter, whom I'd asked for adjudication on Nick's chip at the ninth.

'I played the course in Croydon over the Christmas break – although only once. Managed a twenty-seven. How does that compare to your scores? As regards your specific question, there are, if I recall correctly, three possible paths to the cup on the last hole. In a tournament you would need to 'correctly negotiate the obstacle' by any of these three paths. So Nick would have had to replay his tee shot – counting the original stroke in his score. Incidentally, the use of pitching wedges or indeed any golf club other than a putter is also forbidden in minigolf.'

So Nick had lost after all! Ha ha! All right, he'd shown wit, imagination and actual skill – and he'd worn lucky shoes – but so what? He was a rotten cheat and I, after all, had won! I was the winner! At last! And if I could do it in Croydon, maybe I could do it in Denmark . . .

Adventure golf had not united us, as I'd hoped it would, but who cared about that? I won!

A hollow victory is still a victory.

5

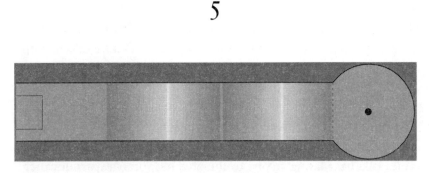

Bodenwellen – waves

This is the humiliating story of how I fell in love with the Boat Race.

One Saturday in late February, after another goal-free afternoon at Loftus Road, Tina and I were waiting for a bus to take us into town. As one pulled up, Tina suddenly grabbed my arm. 'Look,' she said urgently, pointing upwards. I followed her gaze and laughed. In the gap below the upper deck, a space where normally you'd find a reclining Spice Girl, there flowed a curling and very blue Thames. It was an advertisement for the University Boat Race. '*The Boat Race,*' said the big unlikely letters, '*a great day from start to finish. Sponsored by Aberdeen Asset Management.*'

So even the creaky old Boat Race gets the full treatment these days. '*Hundreds of viewing points along the course,*' promised the ad. '*Giant TV screens at Putney Bridge and Furnival Gardens, Hammersmith . . . and it's free!*' Oh, come on, I thought, of course it's free – it's the Boat Race. If it weren't free, no one would go, not even the oarsmen.

Antipathy to the Boat Race can be summed up in two words: bloody toffs. The pre-race weigh-in takes place every year at the Hurlingham Club in Putney. This is where, thirty years ago, Monty Python filmed the 'Upper-class Twit of the Year'. But wouldn't you rather watch 'Kicking the Beggar' or 'Taking the Bra Off the Débutante' ('Well, there'll certainly be some car-door slamming in the streets of Kensington tonight') than 'Yomping the Blue Boats Up the Thames'? I know I would.

Where does it come from, this intolerance? Unlike fox hunting, the Boat Race is harmless enough. Nobody dies. No saboteurs try to disrupt it and no one, to my knowledge, is attempting to ban it. Yet the inverted snobbery directed at it can be ferocious. 'Britain's biggest sporting anachronism,' blasted one London listings magazine, in a preview the week before the race. 'Varsity japes on the Thames in an event of a monumental irrelevance,' they snarled, before going on to list the start time and the best pubs along the route.

Of course, those who consider themselves well informed about such matters have a more cosmopolitan prejudice against the Boat Race than just class: the boats are crewed not by Lord Snooty and his pals but by bloody foreigners, and probably Yanks at that, brought in as ringers and reading Applied Mechanical Breathing or some equally suspect degree of convenience.

I subscribed to a mish-mash of these two points of view – the boats were either full of toffs, damn their eyes, or Americans who obscurely made you yearn for the days when the boats were still full of toffs. More to the point, who cared?

Even the rowing community didn't seem convinced. In 1997, Steve Redgrave infamously referred to the race as 'a Mickey Mouse event', and when asked what it had done for international rowing, replied, 'Absolutely nothing.' He went on to say, rather wittily in my view, that the Boat Race does for international rowing what go-karting does for Formula One. Redgrave sub-sequently apologized, and talked about the wonderful traditions of the Boat Race and what a great day out it was, but many serious oarsmen agreed with his original comments. The Boat Race, for all its publicity value, does little to enhance the sport.

Of course, at this early stage in the year, it didn't matter to me what Steve Redgrave thought of the Boat Race because I didn't know who Steve Redgrave was. I'd never knowingly heard of him. If you'd asked me I think I would have guessed that he was an actor, a little-known cousin of Vanessa, maybe.

As for the race itself, all I knew about it was that on a fine day in spring Oxford rowed against Cambridge and it was all jolly dramatic and then it was over for another year. Sometimes Cambridge won. Sometimes they didn't. So what? It was almost post-modern in its meaninglessness – the blue team versus the other blue team.

And so, although I'd started the year with the best of intentions, it was primarily in a wholly sarco-sceptical frame of mind that I approached this clash of the varsities. They could emblazon every bus in London, a whole fleet of Routemasters By Appointment – it wouldn't make any difference to me.

In the pub after work a couple of weeks before the big day, I was gaily setting about the Boat Race to some long-suffering colleagues. At the next table, a tall man in glasses smiled politely throughout my monologue. 'Sorry to bother you,' he said, when I'd finished. 'Hope you don't mind. I'm one of those "dreadful in-bred cretins" you were just talking about. I'm a rower.'

I was mortified, but luckily the tall man was indeed pretty posh and therefore impervious to real embarrassment.

We discussed the race – well, he did. I just listened.

'The Boat Race is the entire *raison d'être* of both OUBC and CUBC,' he said. 'They train all year for the one race. It takes place at the arse end of winter, when the tide and the wind can mean it's really not ideal for delicate rowing shells. There's no prize, other than the blue, and you get that if you lose anyway, but to lose is a waste of a year. I've rowed it downstream a few times, from Mortlake to Putney, and that nearly killed me – those idiots do it upstream! And it's not friendly rivalry at all. They really do loathe one another.'

As he talked it occurred to me that I had never really made a connection between the Boat Race and rowing. They seemed like two completely separate concerns.

'The feeling of rowing in an eight,' said the man, whose name was Alex and who was slightly drunk, 'when you're all pulling together and the boat is balanced and the blades aren't bashing on the water either side, you're going into the water together, coming out of the water together – it's unbelievable. It's like you're *singing* along, you can hear the boat hissing through the water, and there's a thump-thud, thump-thud as you go along, and it's an incredible feeling.'

I bought him another pint.

'I've never known a sport that's as demanding in every way,' enthused Alex. 'It's the best workout you can have. To be in a rowing crew you have to be cardiovascularly very strong, you have to be anaerobically fit, aerobically fit, you have to have good strength all over your body, your stomach is important, stomach muscles, back muscles, legs, arms, shoulders, the whole works. At the end of a race, you're puking, you don't know where you're going to get the oxygen from. And rowing is a sport that, if you're going to be any good, you have to do seven days a week – you can't have a social life, you can't go near the beers or anything like that. And the Boat Race is extreme – it's like the distillation of all that.'

'God, it sounds awful,' I said.

Alex shrugged and took another sip of his beer. 'You asked me,' he said.

I told him I was thinking of going to watch the race.

'Well, you'll get the best view if you look from the front. By Barnes, one team will be in the lead. They don't tend to be close races. Get on a bridge, if you can, Barnes Bridge, say. But if you want to feel the emotion, obviously be at the end of the race at Mortlake. You can usually work your way into the Boat House. And take a radio, otherwise you won't know what's going on. If you can be bothered, read Dan Topolski's book about the American mutiny in 'eighty-seven. Topolski was the Oxford coach and he writes about rowing for one of the papers. But for God's sake don't watch the film.'

I thanked Alex for his time and went straight home and rented the movie. Like the book, it was called *True Blue*. It was a highly amusing *Chariots of Water* clash between stiff-upper-lipped Brits and tradition-spurning megalomaniac Yanks that could have been produced as anti-Boat Race agitprop:

Dan Warren, Olympic oarsman, enraged at draconian training schedule: 'What is this Victorian *bullshit*?'

Donald MacDonald, OUBC president (stoically): 'It's what we do to win the Boat Race. Then we go to the gym.'

But the book was much better. 'With the possible exception of an Olympic marathon, or a World Boxing Championship,' says Patrick Robinson in the foreword, 'the race between the Dark and Light Blues represents the most brutal, harsh and uncompromising struggle in all of sport.' It was a view shared by Dan Topolski. His sincere belief that the race is a unique and punishing event suffuses every page of *True Blue*. In addition to the physical challenge, Topolski maintains that the Boat Race is one of the last remaining sporting contests from an age when it really was about the taking part and not the winning – a Corinthian struggle.

Well, maybe. In fact, the inaugural Varsity Boat Race took place in 1829 and therefore predates by some forty years the rise of Amateurism and the foundation of bodies like the Football Association and the Amateur Athletic Association. At this time rowing was a highly popular spectator sport, and it shared a common purpose with cock-fighting, bear-baiting and bare-knuckle boxing: the winning, or losing, of money. As Richard Holt says in his book *Sport and the British*: 'These gentlemen displayed none of the scrupulous disdain for money which was later to mark off amateur oarsmen. They backed themselves in races and wagered on others just as patrons of pugilists or owners of horses would do.'

From the participants' point of view, the Boat Race may be the last bastion of true amateurism but wagering, patronage and ownership still surround the event, as they did at its inception. Sponsorship, advertising, PR, news and sport mingle and merge with one another. In its own quiet way, the race is a case study in how the symbiotic feeding pool of modern British sport works.

The race is watched in 180 countries by an estimated 400 million viewers worldwide, over six million of them in the UK alone. It's one of the top five live televised sporting events of the year, along with the Grand National, the FA Cup Final, the Wimbledon Men's Final and the British Grand Prix. Clearly somebody likes it.

In addition to Aberdeen Asset Management's sponsorship, which I had started noticing on more buses, the tube and in magazines, the BBC was making a big deal of the 146th University Boat Race. Rather than a great day out, they were packaging the old dependable as the ultimate gladiatorial grudge match. Trailers ran for what seemed like weeks beforehand, misty-lensed slowmo replays of the crews in action, their muscles pumping, grimacing either with pain or residual upper-class twittedness.

The BBC needed to plug the Boat Race as real sport and plug it hard. Following the ravages of the 1990s and the dominance of Sky, the Boat Race is one of the few major national sporting events the Corporation has left. Their logo was featured prominently everywhere and they had commissioned a mini-documentary to follow Oxford's preparations. In the words of Victor Lewis-Smith, 'This isn't really a sporting event at all – it's a meaningless annual television ritual, like the Queen's Christmas Speech or *The Last Night of the Proms*.' But it is still a ritual that pulls in the viewers.

In addition to its above-the-line spend, Aberdeen employed a PR agency to get stories on to the airwaves and into the newspapers, and preferably in sections other than the sport pages – for while there was undoubtedly a certain audience for tactical debates, there was a bigger one for personality-led material. All the broadsheets, not just the *Telegraph*, were full of pre-race performance reports and profiles of individual oarsmen – the former joiner who had left school at sixteen and only started rowing three years previously, the Oxford crewman who was a world-class juggler ("'Getting to see my girlfriend is another thing I have to juggle!" laughs Ayer'). Most attractive to the media was the Oxford number five Dan Snow who, as the son of BBC broadcaster and pundit Peter Snow, attracted coverage in the *Radio Times* ('It's not hard to pick out Dad's voice booming across the river'), the *Sun* ('HERE WE ROW, DAD! – Dan wants boat win for TV Peter') and even a fashion shoot in *OK!* ('Dan wears navy cricket sweater by Mulberry, £115; Nicole Farhi drawstring trousers from Barkers, House of Fraser, £130; slip-on mules by Buffalo, £49.')

Because Oxford hadn't won the race for seven years, it was they who dominated the media coverage. Oxford wanted to win, we were told, they needed to win. Several world-class oarsmen, such as Kieran West of Cambridge, had withdrawn from the race to concentrate on preparations for the Olympics, so there were more genuine undergrads in the boats. There was a better atmosphere in the Oxford camp as a result, said Dan Snow, 'and there are less egos around, so hopefully we'll go a bit faster.' Cambridge were judged to be more technically proficient but Oxford had the hunger. 'They are like little dogs, they try and bite and bite,' ventured Jürgen Grobler, the coach of the Olympic coxless four.

Wherever you looked in the papers, there were also a lot of Facts. They love Facts in the Boat Race – longest, tallest, shortest, thickest. A photo-opportunity was staged next to the Thames, the Oxford cox Kajsa McLaren (four foot ten, the race's eleventh female cox) dwarfed by the towering Cambridge number five Josh West who, at six foot nine and half, was, yes, the tallest oarsman in Boat Race history. Photographs of the two, appearing cordial but not overly friendly, were reproduced on-line and in print, replete with the appropriate statistics, bitter but dignified rivals with Aberdeen Asset Management logos on their chests and the necks of their racing shirts.

As 'Managers of Britain's Top ISA Fund', the event's sponsors, Aberdeen Asset Management, had more in common with the wagering origins of the Boat Race than any spirit of philanthropic amateurism. In addition to their advertising spend, they paid for the PR agency and an official website, maintained close links with the BBC, and had even commissioned a new Boat Race Trophy, to be presented by AAM chief executive Martin Gilbert at the end of the race. According to the *Financial Times*, the company had 185,000 direct clients when it had started sponsoring the event in March 1999. One year later, it had 400,000. 'The Boat Race has taken our name into places where it is never seen,' said Gilbert, 'such as *OK!* magazine, the *Radio Times* and one or two of the tabloids.' He should have thanked Dan Snow by name.

And so it went. The sponsors employed the PRs who rang up the newspapers who ran stories about the crews who you could watch on BBC Television where you could see and hear the name of the sponsors: a perfect circle. On the day of the race, Aberdeen extended their sponsorship to 2004. I wasn't so naïve as to think this kind of mutually rewarding relationship was unique to the Boat Race – no doubt the event is slim pickings in comparison to the Premiership or Formula One – but I was still taken aback to find it thriving at the heart of an event that many believed was the last outpost of good sportsmanship. The real tradition of the Boat Race had survived and prospered – people made money out of it in 1829 and people – many more of them – were still making money out of it now.

I wasn't unduly outraged by this, but it did make me feel a bit sorry for the oarsmen. The veneer of amateurism, along with a cloud of money and prejudice and Facts, obscured that what the crews were going to do on Saturday was both difficult and exceedingly painful. It was 'extreme rowing', as Alex had called it in the pub. Still, I told myself, that's up to them. Silly bastards. Let them half kill themselves and be dumb enough to be exploited for it too. But I could feel old certainties groaning a little.

By the morning of the race I had accumulated an impressive portfolio of Boat Race-related statistics. Oh, how seductive they were. How easily they lodged in the brain. This year's crews featured oarsmen from Great Britain, the USA, New Zealand, South Africa and Norway. The oarsmen were secured to the boat with their shoes, which are permanently fixed to the footplate (or 'stretcher'), adding an extra frisson of danger to the potential results of a sinking. Oxford were deploying a crew that was both heavier (ten pounds per man) and taller than Cambridge – the tallest Dark Blue crew of all time, in fact, with an average height of six foot four and five-eighths inches. Golly! Stats and stats and stats . . . Anyway, if the weather was poor, this weight imbalance might work in Oxford's favour. And, of course, they had a secret weapon.

For the first time a Boat Race crew were employing the services of a full-time sports psychologist. Oxford had recruited Dr Kirsten Barnes, herself a double Olympic gold medallist in rowing for Canada, to help them get the edge over Cambridge. Dr Barnes had had monthly sessions with the squad since October, helping them rehearse the day of the race by using creative visualization: imagining the feeling of victory, the roar of the crowd, and so on. The crew had been taught to envisage three race strategies, it was reported; leading from the start and finishing easily, winning by a narrow margin or coming from behind to overtake Cambridge and win. Whatever the method, the only result contemplated was victory. 'Constantly, we emphasize the right messages,' said Dr Barnes in one paper. 'If someone imagines himself catching a crab, then he goes back and starts again.'

He goes back and starts again. Wasn't the Boat Race painful enough without being mentally cruel too?

The last word went to OUBC president Nick Robinson: 'It's all or nothing,' he had said profoundly. 'You either win or you lose.'

Nick didn't need to worry. Having 'studied form' for a week, I *knew* Oxford were going to win. It was a dead cert. Was this because I was now an expert on the intricacies of the Boat Race? Possibly. Or had I fallen for the idea of Oxford as little biting underdogs? Probably. Whatever, I decided to join in the oldest of Boat Race traditions and put a tenner on Oxford to win. I got odds of eleven to four, not bad. But I also felt placing a bet was insurance against a non-event and a wasted afternoon. I was doing it for the oarsmen. I was doing it for tradition. I was bribing myself to care.

On the morning of the race I bought a copy of *The Times* ('your perfect Boat Race paper'). On the front page, above the headline 'Oxford Launch Dream Team', was a large picture of a glamorous, smiling woman standing on the towpath by the Thames. This, it turned out, was Kirsten Barnes, the Oxford sports psychologist. 'At their last session on Monday, Dr Barnes handed each member of the crew eight long white slips of stiff paper, on which they wrote what quality every other member contributes to make the boat go faster,' reported *The Times*. 'These were collated and sealed in white envelopes, which the crew then opened, read and have kept with them during the past five days.' My money suddenly felt very vulnerable.

I had been determined to crack the Boat Race and had invested time, money and effort in doing so. I was, I felt, at least a little closer to understanding it than I had been. But as the day wore on, it became clear that I had over-prepared. On the day, what was needed was not a strong grasp of the race's history or the fine points of rowing technique, but a strong stomach. Of the quarter of a million people lining the banks of the Thames, 99 per cent cared nothing for catching crabs or comparative stroke rates. They hadn't come to watch the rowing: they had come to get pissed.

This is the great secret of the Boat Race that television never picks up: nearly everyone is drunk. Not for nothing does Aberdeen produce a map with all the hostelries along the route highlighted, rather coyly, with a wine glass. There should have been pint mugs marking the pubs and a chain of lager cans for the towpath. At Putney, the bars were overflowing with pissed-up Sloanes and rugby-shirted hoorays; at Hammersmith, a surprising number of Australians and South Africans were staggering about; at Chiswick, families and associations held barbecues in front gardens and guzzled good wine. The people who actually liked rowing – and, of course, heavy drinking – hung out at Mortlake.

We arrived in Putney at about half past eleven. The riverside was already busy. You could buy blue rosettes (dark and light) from trays. Young men in blazers wandered around shouting at each other. The presence of Aberdeen Asset Management announced itself with blue balloons (light and dark) on lamp-posts, and with banners and bunting on the pubs and bridges.

Even the official souvenir programme contained a pull-out Aberdeen Unit Trust ISA Lump Sum Application Form. The crowd was overwhelmingly white.

'If the weather turns nastier,' I informed Tina, 'Oxford's weight advantage will come into play. However, if the weather turns against the tide, that might be sinking conditions and we might see a repeat of the race of 1912 when both boats were swamped and the race abandoned.'

'Right,' said Tina. 'Shall we get a drink?'

In the Star and Garter, two rugby-shirted men were sharing their experience of the Boat Race with their girlfriends.

'Yeah, well, the race itself is pretty boring!' yelled one of the shirts.

'Yeah, it's like watching snails racing!' the other yelled back. 'Har har har!'

'Har har har! Snails!' brayed the first, practically spewing into his pint.

The two girlfriends honked into their Bacardi Breezers and I asked for our beers to be poured into plastic cups.

We wandered back outside. Across the river at Bishops Park a big screen was showing highlights of previous years and flashing up questions, many of which, annoyingly, I now knew the answers to.

As we made our way along the embankment we saw a familiar-looking man in a blue blazer with gold buttons and smart tan trousers. Where had I seen him before?

'Look,' said Tina, 'why has that man painted his head orange?'

She thought the orange-headed man was a local Boat Race Day eccentric. In fact, it was BBC anchorman Steve Rider, who had just emerged from Makeup.

We walked on down past the boathouses, past the outside broadcast trucks with their tall masts, past the cameramen in cherry-pickers high above the river and past the young man who had just vomited on to his shoes. Cyclists whizzed past us, joggers trotted and ramblers rambled. We left Putney behind and entered Al Fayed country. On the other side of the river was Craven

Cottage, the home of Al Fayed's club Fulham (we hate Fulham), standing empty today. They were playing away at Ipswich. In some flats just past the Harrods depot, two middle-aged women were pouring themselves large glasses of wine. They had draped a Union Jack over the edge of their balcony. We waved to them and they raised their glasses to us. It wasn't even lunchtime.

Hammersmith – half past twelve.

First South African: 'Which are you, mate, Oxford or Cambridge?'

Second South African: 'I don't give a shit as long as the beer's cold.'

We stopped at the first pub past Hammersmith Bridge for another pint. With three and a half hours still to go before the race, everyone was riotously drunk. A man with a banjo had stripped to the waist and was standing on a table, belting out 'Brown Sugar' and 'Can't Get Enough Of Your Lovin'' to roars of approval from the crowd. As he climbed down, I asked him which boat he was supporting. 'University of Hard Knocks, mate, ha ha ha,' he said, looking at me uncertainly. 'Nice parka.'

We carried our beers outside and bought hotdogs from a stall in front of the pub, eating and drinking and laughing as we manoeuvred our way carefully through the gathering throng. This was almost fun.

A little further on, on the green next to the Dove, there was a funfair. 'If you're a boy, win a cuddly toy,' shouted one stall-holder. 'If you're a yuppie, win a puppy,' but the yuppies were mostly back in Putney. Here, there were young families and tourists, eating candyfloss and playing skittles, children running around with their faces painted like tigers. One stall had an ergometer, the machine that oarsmen trained on. You could pay a pound and 'Take the Ergo Challenge'. Emboldened by the beer, I did so. Fuck! I paid the man another pound to get off it before I ruptured something.

Onwards, past the Dove towards Chiswick. The houses started to get bigger. Through net curtains we could see tables stacked with open bottles of red wine, apple juice, French bread, Brie and mineral water. Outside one house, a group of young men lifted their cans in a toast to a woman with her hair in a bun. She tried to ignore them, but eventually relented and graced them with a regal wave. They cheered.

Outside the Old Ship Inn, roughly the half-way point, there was a bottleneck, a mass of people trying to get in or out or past the pub, virtually at a standstill. Right in the middle a woman was attempting to carry a bike and two small crying children through the crush. 'I didn't realize,' she kept saying, 'I didn't realize . . .'

Further on, in a playground strewn with empty lager cans, a woman was breastfeeding her baby while her partner emptied a bottle of beer and watched their toddler fall off the swings. Two hours till race time.

At Chiswick, the houses sprouted high gates and fences. There was a marked increase in blue plaques. We stopped for another pint in the Black Lion. I was knackered. Four and a quarter miles might be a feat of endurance on the river but it was no easy stroll for me on land. My feet were aching.

As we arrived at Barnes, the police were closing the bridge to pedestrians, so we were forced to take a twenty-minute detour. Thanks! The route took us past allotments and a health club. But normal race-day service was soon resumed. As we regained the towpath, the same policemen who had shut the bridge were frisking four young boys for lager.

The wind was getting up and we felt the first spots of rain. On the river we started to pass houseboats and barges painted in blue and gold: the *City Slicker* and the *Elizabethan*.

I stopped to use the Portaloo opposite the Duke's Meadow golf club. Inside, a very posh man had locked himself into the cubicle and was throwing up, loudly and extravagantly. He was clearly as well brought up as his breakfast, for his manners were impeccable. 'Sorry!' he said plummily, to no one in particular, before releasing the hounds once more.

Between Barnes Bridge and Chiswick Bridge, the finish line, the crowd began to take on something of the character of the county set. We saw more three-wheeler pushchairs, open hatchbacks, mobile barbecues and huge dogs – St Bernards, perhaps on hand to administer emergency Pimm's. We saw our first deerstalker and a fat man in a checkerboard suit, broad-brimmed trilby and spats, like an extra from a seventies revival of *Guys and Dolls*. I bought an RNLI badge from an old man in a tam-o'-shanter, whose long ginger beard had bits of food in it. His wizened face was ruddy with sea air and grog. He looked like I felt.

It was now raining. As we trudged heavily along the long final stretch of towpath towards Mortlake we heard cheering from across the river, and as we turned to look, two boats passed us, oarsmen pulling together in unison. Oh, bollocks, I thought, don't say we've missed it. But it was only five to four. I scrabbled to get the radio out. Had we got it wrong? No, this was the race between the reserve crews, called for some reason Isis (Oxford) and Goldie (Cambridge), which traditionally preceded the Boat Race. One boat was in front of the other by quite some margin. But who was in it? I couldn't see which boat was which. We tuned in the radio to hear that the leader was Isis, the Oxford boat. 'Go on, Isis,' I said, casually.

When we got to Mortlake, I bought a couple of cans of warm lager and two fairy cakes to celebrate the Isis victory, or whatever. We tried to find a spot on Chiswick Bridge as Alex had suggested, Barnes Bridge being shut, but it was already full so we opted instead for the slipway next to the bridge, just by the finish line. Although it was raining and the slipway was wet, I sat down. The cumulative effect of the alcohol, the walking and, frankly, the prolonged exposure to fresh air were beginning to take their toll.

We switched on our radio. The race was due to start at any moment. A middle-aged man in a Barbour jacket approached us. 'Would you mind terribly,' he said, 'if we listened in? It's just that we've forgotten ours.'

I stood up. 'Not at all,' I said magnanimously. He beckoned his wife over. They looked like old hands at the Boat Race. 'This is a good spot, isn't it?' I said. 'I bet you get the real enthusiasts down here, don't you?'

'Yes. There's lots of different types here,' said the man, looking around at his fellow Barbourees, 'but they're all *of* a type.'

We huddled silently in the rain for a minute. Were they Oxford or Cambridge? They weren't wearing any visible colours. I tried to flush them out.

'This is sinking weather, you know,' I said.

'Is it?' said the man.

'Oh dear,' said the woman.

'Yes,' I said, 'but Oxford have the heavier crew. That gives them an advantage in bad weather, I'm happy to say.'

'Really?' said the man.

'Yes,' I said weakly. 'It does.' They weren't biting. 'Actually,' I continued, 'this is the tallest Dark Blue crew of all time.'

'Crikey,' said the man, looking impressed. 'You're a bit of an expert. Oxford, are you?'

'Er,' I said, flustered. Was I? 'Er . . . yes,' I said. 'I am. I'm Oxford.'

'We don't have a side,' said the woman. 'We've never been before. But we'll be Oxford too.'

'Be rude not to, under the circumstances,' shouted the man, 'listening to an Oxford radio!'

Five Live were utilizing three or four different commentators, including Tim Foster, tipped for a GB Olympic boat, and Richard Treharne Jones, one of the official timekeepers and source of many of the useless facts now littering my brain. Cambridge had apparently won the toss and chosen the Surrey bend, giving themselves a slight advantage. After an initial period of jostling to hold their chosen line, Oxford were marginally ahead at the one-mile mark (Fulham FC), the umpire still warning both boats to keep apart. Going into the Surrey bend Oxford were ahead by no more than a couple of men.

'Come on, Oxford!' said the woman, and nudged me.

Oxford's style was more ragged but also more aggressive and, it seemed, effective, to judge from the commentary – it wasn't pretty but it was moving the boat through the water. Clearly it was already a cracking race. 'Come on . . .' I muttered.

The two boats were neck and neck at Hammersmith Bridge, side by side down Chiswick Reach. The crews were probably in real pain now. Also, and significantly, it was raining, really raining. The water was choppier than it had been for Isis and Goldie half an hour earlier. If Oxford could stay in contact with Cambridge round the final bend, which in theory favoured the Light Blues, the weight advantage meant they might be able to edge ahead. Come on, Oxford, come *on* . . . As they passed beneath Barnes Bridge, the Dark Blue boat had a length on Cambridge and a lead of three seconds.

They were going to do it. For the first time in eight years, they were actually going to do it!

Cambridge made a bold effort to 'get on terms' but the wisdom was that by Barnes Bridge the race was usually over and so it proved. As the boats finally pulled into view, Oxford were easily in the lead.

'Come on, Oxford!' I shouted. They crossed the line. I had miraculously backed the winning team. The boat disappeared beneath Chiswick Bridge and we lost sight of them, but we could hear their yodels of elation echoing off the underside of the bridge. And, full of fairy cake and booze and Facts, tired and very emotional, I found myself yodelling with them.

'Well done,' said the man in the Barbour, clapping me on the shoulder.

We ran under the bridge, across a rugby pitch to the Boat House where the crews would moor the boats and the Aberdeen Asset Management Trophy would be presented. On the river's edge there were crowds of people: the reserve crews, journalists, family, cameramen, PR girls. We could see Nick Robinson clambering down the boat congratulating his crew and Kajsa McLaren excitedly splashing the Thames with her hands. As the boat approached the shore, the crew leapt out, hugged their friends, jumped and screamed in triumph; Alex Reid, the stroke, somersaulted out of the boat.

Behind them drifted the Cambridge boat, heads down, even at this distance utterly beaten. They came ashore in silence, filing past us, not merely crying but sobbing with pain and exhaustion, their enormous shoulders shaking with emotion. It was humbling – still pointless, but humbling none the less.

'I just can't think of anything to say,' said Nick Robinson tautologically to Steve Rider, as he held the new Aberdeen Asset Management Trophy aloft. 'It's just the moment I've been waiting for four years now and it's happened and, I dunno, it's just incredible.' Two members of the Goldie crew stood just behind us, silent tears running down their faces. 'We just stayed in the fight. We kept at them like . . .' He thought for a moment. 'Like . . . a small dog yapping at their heels!'

If you look closely at the TV footage as Nick Robinson makes his way from the podium, you can see a bedraggled, bleary man in an Eskimo parka slap him on the back. Rather more embarrassingly, he then tries to do the same to Steve Rider.

But it had been, I had to admit, a great day from start to finish. And there was a new statistic to add to the record books: at eighteen, the Oxford number two, Matthew Smith, had become the youngest winning oarsman of all time, another bit of factual flotsam drifting off down the river of Boat Race history.

When we got home, I sat down to watch the highlights of the race on TV and promptly fell asleep on the sofa. I woke up at about ten o'clock feeling slightly foolish, with a thick head. First QPR and now the Boat Race: for someone who despised sport, I was turning out to be a real pushover.

But I had enjoyed it, really enjoyed it. I was also beginning to grasp how important drink was in the appreciation of these things. Just like at QPR, the outcome of the game was almost incidental to the spirit of the event. Take your pick. The Boat Race was a Corinthian pageant, a corporate circle jerk, a giant piss-up, or all of the above. The contest was nothing without the context.

They talk a lot about pain in the Boat Race – the pain of defeat, the physical pain of the race itself – but, ironically, the popularity and enmity it inspires rest on the appearance of the race as 'varsity japes', rather than what it actually is: a marathon on water. Its charm, if you find it charming, relies on your *not* knowing quite how much torture those oarsmen are putting themselves through, nor how close it is in reality to the cash-and-carry of modern sport.

The thing that makes the Boat Race so popular with a general audience is that it looks easy, and its rules and customs are easy to comprehend. Who cares how mentally and physically demanding it is? For one day you can be the blue team, or the other blue team, with no effort and no consequences. It's instant, harmless fanaticism – just add water. Which is precisely why, when combined with hang-ups about class and nationality, a sizeable chunk of the 'real' sporting audience dislikes it so much. It isn't about passion™ or commitment™ or anything else used to sell trainers; it's a sports fixture for people who don't care about sport. And if they knew how demanding the race really is, it wouldn't make a scrap of difference. It's varsity japes if you like it and varsity japes if you don't.

The Boat Race also shows up the snobbery that exists between sports. I think I'd always assumed that if you liked one you liked them all. But no. Alex told me he loved cricket and rugby, and rowing obviously, but couldn't stand football. Similarly, many people would happily take darts or snail-racing more seriously than the Boat Race. But they're all the same, really, aren't they, darts or rowing or football or minigolf? So why be a snob about it?

The following morning I rang Paul, who had been up to see Forest play at home. 'How was it?' I said.

'Yeah, good,' replied Paul. 'How were Rangers?'

'Oh, I didn't go,' I said. 'We went to watch the Boat Race instead.' I felt a bit embarrassed even as I said it.

'Oh, right,' said Paul. 'I don't like the Boat Race.'

'Yeah,' I said, 'yeah, it was a bit . . .' No, what was I doing? I was going to tell the truth.

'Actually,' I said, 'it was really good. Everyone drinks. If you got into it it was really exciting. And these seven-foot oarsmen were really sobbing. It was quite moving, actually.'

'Mm,' said Paul, 'but I don't like the Boat Race.'

'Hold on', I said, 'hold on. This is an event with two teams in the peak of physical condition, who rely on skill, endurance and teamwork to pull them through. These teams feature international athletes, and the event draws spectators from all round the world, male and female, and a huge television audience, united in sport. Does this sound familiar? It should do – it's the line you always spin me about football.'

'Fair enough,' said Paul. 'But I don't like the Boat Race.'

Postscript: following the Olympics and the beatification of Steve Redgrave and Matthew Pinsent, the 2001 Boat Race was a much happier affair for the media. 'Blue is the colour,' trumpeted the London listings magazine. 'Prejudice aside, the Boat Race is an occasion to celebrate rowing's growing popularity and record of success,' they noted, before going on to list the start time and the best pubs along the route. On race day Redgrave and Pinsent could be found with the BBC commentary team, in a launch, bobbing along in the wake of the blue boats and their own life-changing success.

'I love the event,' said Sir Steve. 'I love the tradition of it. It was a classic race last year.'

The blue team won by the way.

6

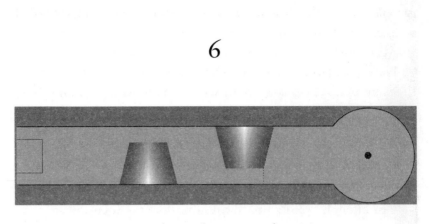

Stumpfe Kegel – truncated cones

And so the tour began.

I had a lot of work to do. The Danish Invitational Open was only three months away and I had practised hardly at all – because there was almost nowhere to practise. Most crazy-golf courses live at the seaside and, like the seaside, shut for the winter. Gates are chained up; windmill sails are stashed in scorers' huts, and huts are padlocked. Aside from the trips to Croydon, I hadn't picked up a putter in five months.

But now April sprang, and so did I. All over Britain, bed-and-breakfast landladies stowed their good furniture and unpacked the crates of small china dogs and horrible antimacassars that had wintered in the shed; ice-cream men stockpiled imitation Flakes and reset the chimes of their vans from 'Kashmir' to 'Greensleeves'; and amusement-arcade owners stuffed their lucky-dip machines with bootleg orange Pikachus. And I slung my dad's putter in the back of the car and hit the road, motivated more by the prospect of a few days out at the seaside than any genuine conviction that practice would make perfect.

Was I concerned by this lack of decent preparation time? Not in the slightest. Three months seemed like a lifetime. In the coming weeks I would play in two British tournaments: the BMGA Players' Tournament in London and then, a month or so later, the big one – the British Masters in Southend. And I would supplement these with a comprehensive recce of the south coast's various courses. Two tournaments and a tour. That would be a whole lot of minigolf in three months – more than anyone I knew, more than sounded reasonable. Three months! I had come twenty-sixth in Hastings just by turning up. I was confident that three months would be enough to reach tournament standard.

The first stop on the winding road to Denmark was Clacton. I had never been to Clacton before. I had no idea if Clacton had courses. There were none listed in the *BMGA Yearbook*, but it seemed likely that somewhere with this town's cheap and cheerful reputation would have at least a couple. How could somewhere like Clacton survive without crazy golf?

It was a blustery Saturday morning as I walked down from the town centre to Clacton Pier, a toothpick set in a stony sea, a bit of driftwood washed up from jollier times. The pier was advertising its own website, but its presence in cyberspace clearly wasn't doing much for business. The shops in town were full of people but the attractions on the seafront were not, the few that were open. The flags that flew above the pier – the Union Jack, the Stars and Stripes and, incongruously, that of the European Union – rippled and cracked noisily and conspicuously. There appeared to be no courses in the immediate vicinity.

At one side of the pier was the Cockney Pride Fun Pub. When I peered through the window, it looked even worse than it sounded. But it was open.

'Excuse me,' I said to the solitary barman, a blond Australian, 'any crazy golf round here?'

'You're keen, mate,' he said, nodding at my putter.

'Yeah. Well, there's a load of us,' I lied instantly and creatively. 'Stag, you know. Probably see us in here later!'

The barman nodded. 'There's one up at the top of the hill,' he said, 'and another about a mile up that way. But they might not be open for the season yet.'

I thanked him. 'We'll *all* see you later!' I said, a bit too emphatically.

The invisible roaring boys and I climbed back up to find the first course the barman had mentioned. It was hidden behind Anne the Clairvoyant's caravan ('skilled in psychometry and healing; a reiki master') and a go-kart track, which was shut but not empty. A group of teenage girls were sitting in the stationary go-karts, their bare legs goose-pimpling in the wind, throwing a mobile phone to one another.

'You call him!'

'Fuck off, Kimberly, you fucking call him!'

'Kelly,' drawled Kimberly, slowly and deliberately. 'Piss. The. Fuck. Off.'

Wow, I thought, as I edged gingerly round the girls, that's what I call swearing.

I approached the hut. The course was called Augusta Masters Adventure Golf. I paid the green fee to a dumpy man with a Zapata moustache and a squint, who handed over a scorecard, a ball and a club.

'I've got my own putter,' I said apprehensively. 'Hope that's OK.'

He didn't even blink. 'Do you need a pencil?' was all he said.

I stood at the first tee and surveyed the course. The Augusta Masters, Clacton, was not in the immaculate condition of its full-scale Georgia namesake. The greens were wrinkled and threadbare. In addition, each of the nine holes had been assigned a gripping name (e.g., Eagle Falls), and a small sign by the tee with a poem on it. However, the names bore little or no relation to the dilapidated holes, and the doggerel that accompanied them was not particularly illuminating:

> *The object here*
> *At Eagle Falls*
> *Is Just to Putt Your*
> *Own Golf Balls.*

You don't say.

Still, I managed to ignore this sage advice, and played Eagle

Falls in a lousy four strokes. It should have been three, but the ball jumped off a snag in the felt, and wobbled away from the cup.

I played on. The third hole, Traitor's Gate, featured a miniature lake, which was empty, its blue paint blistered and flaking away. The cup, however, was a deep, dank well, full of dirty water – rain and who knew what else? To recover the ball I had to plunge my hand into its muddy depths. On resurfacing it smelt . . . *tangy*.

After three holes, I had a three, a couple of fours and a hand I had to remember not to eat with. It was difficult to know if I was putting well or not, such was the unpredictability of the playing surface. The ball would catch or bounce or curl inexplicably. I suppose it all added to the Craziness!! of the golf but I found it merely irritating. Peter's phrase about courses being 'a true test of skill' came to mind.

Ahead of me a father and son were playing together, while Mum kept score. The boy was laughing, delighted just to be allowed to hit something, anything, with a big metal club. The dad was not.

'Bollocks,' he said, as his ball ran confidently two inches wide of the cup his son had just aced.

'Dean!' said the woman.

'Did you see that?' said Dean, ignoring her. He stood, hands on hips, exasperated.

'Look at you!' chided the woman. 'Don't take it so seriously!' But he can't help it, I thought. He's a bloke.

The seventh hole was called the Khyber Pass. The kid stopped at the tee to read the rhyme aloud, slowly and carefully.

'The – Mum, what's that word?'

'Khyber.'

'The Khyber Pass. "Hit the Ball, Aim Straight and Low, Up the Khyber, It Will Go." Dad, what's a Khyber Pass?'

But Dad didn't answer, preferring to concentrate on his shot. Either he had a poor knowledge of Cockney rhyming slang or he was protecting his son.

'Bollocks!' he said again, as his shot rimmed the Khyber.

'Ha ha ha!' laughed his son.

'Jackson Pollocks . . .' muttered Dean, as he bent to retrieve his ball. He knew.

I finished the course on level par, twenty-nine: five fours, two threes, a two and a fortunate ace at the last, a rebound off a twig. Par, I said to myself, as I returned the ball and pencil to Zapata. Not bad. Imagine if that had been a *real* course. It would have been a walkover.

By a neat coincidence, that very weekend at the other Augusta Masters in Georgia, Vijay Singh was on his way to receiving the famous Green Jacket. It was a great Masters victory, a feat of skill and self-possession under pressure. However, Vijay had it relatively easy. His fairways didn't have rips in them; no one talked Pollocks in his vicinity; and presumably he lacked a few lines of William McGonagall at every tee.

I strolled along the promenade. Clacton was agreeably desolate in April – the rough grey sea, a few flapping deckchairs. I'd expected fortune-tellers and chip shops and drunks at noon but Clacton seemed to be keeping most of these delights to itself, or they were clustered in the town centre or on the pier. Out here it was surprisingly residential. There were more retirement homes on the seafront than niteclubs.

As we approached the other end of the prom, I could see another flag, a green one this time, fluttering at the top of a proper flagpole. It featured a sort of crest, a putter and ball arranged within a circle, and the words 'Miniatur-Golf'. I quickened my pace. This must be the other course the barman had been talking about.

Miniatur-Golf, when I reached it, was situated in a fenced-off playing area, adjacent to a café. 'Nine Different and Attractively Designed Mini Golf Courses,' said a sign by the small hut, which was closed. Another notice directed you into the café if you wanted to play.

I went in and asked the woman behind the counter if I could have one for the, er, minigolf.

'One crazy golf, love. Just hold on.' She shouted out the back, 'Jim! Jim! Have you got the crazy-golf stuff?'

'I don't need a putter,' I said, 'just a ball and a card. And a pencil.'

'No club, right you are,' she said, as apparently unsurprised as her colleague at the other end of the prom.

'It's round the side,' came a voice from the back.

'Oh, yes. Just over here, love,' she said. Arranged on the wall in the corner behind me were a selection of new-looking putters and balls, in red, green, pink and blue, and perforated rolls of yellow scorecards.

'Now,' she said, 'it's two pounds for nine holes, or three if you go round twice.'

I opted for the bargain full eighteen.

I went back outside. There was no one else on the course. Like the Augusta Masters by the pier, this place accepted 'no responsibility for persons entering this golf course and incidents thereafter'. But there the similarity ended. In contrast to the Augusta Masters, there was no green felt on the Miniatur-Golf Course, tatty or otherwise, and no poetry. In fact, it didn't look much like any crazy-golf course I'd ever seen. There were nine holes, made of what looked like flecked grey fibreglass, all about eight feet in length, and all bordered with a metal rung. Each hole was a different shape, and most had different coloured obstacles – some red and blue pyramids on one, a metal sort of maze-like thing on another. And each hole had a name, most self-explanatory – in order of play, Pyramids, Somersault, 'Volcanoe', Middle Hole, Double Brook, Labyrinth, Zigzag, Helter-Skelter (which looked like a lavatory bowl) and the not-very-thrilling-but-named-with-pinpoint-accuracy Right-angle. Like the putters and the balls, the course looked very new.

A hedge bordered the playing area. Leaning against it, broken in half and forlorn, was an old sign. 'Crazy Golf!' it said, in bright, excited letters. Another sign on the small hut said the same, contradicting the flag. And indeed, looking carefully, it was clear that a crazy-golf course had been here until recently:

the outlines of its holes were discernible on the cracked pink concrete, like shadows. This utilitarian set-up had replaced it. Shame.

But those feelings of sadness for the passing of a course quickly turned to righteous anger. Once I started playing Miniatur-Golf, I soon discovered that while the nine holes didn't look much, they were ridiculously difficult. The grey surface, whatever it was, ran very fast, and balls shot off the sides or dribbled out of control or, if you were lucky, into the cup. I took seven shots at the metal maze, the Labyrinth, without even trying. The course was infuriating. The cup wasn't so very far from the tee but might as well have been in another country. It drove you crazy, without having any inherent craziness itself. Fun it was not.

While I swore and cursed my way round the first of my two rounds, the owner of the café came out to talk to me. This must be Jim. He was an open-faced man in his early forties. In his white coat and a red and white striped cap, he looked like a member of the Rubettes.

Jim was keen to know what I thought of the course. I was the first paying customer to play it. Did I like it?

I didn't have the heart to tell him, actually no, I didn't like his stupid little ding-dong course. 'It's quite, um . . . a challenge,' I said. 'Is it minigolf or crazy golf or what?'

'Miniature golf,' said Jim inaccurately, pointing at the flag. They had decided to replace the old crazy-golf course, he told me, apparently without regret, with something more hardwearing. The felt had got very scruffy, what with the rain and seawater, and, of course, vandalism was a real problem. After searching the Internet, he had turned up this system. The nine holes were made of prefabricated concrete panels and were bordered with galvanized steel. They had come from Germany at a cost of roughly a thousand pounds per hole and been installed by a British company.

'And they're adjustable,' said Jim, moving one of the plastic pyramids on the first hole so that it blocked the path to the cup, 'for difficulty.'

'That's great,' I said. 'And the flag?'

'That's their flag,' said Jim cheerfully. 'That was free. Course, after I got the flag, I realized I needed a flagpole. That was another grand.'

Jim went back in. It was the café's first day open and the griddle wasn't working. I carried on playing. Ten thousand pounds for this portable torture chamber. The flag had a telephone number and the name of the company that had supplied it. They were called, inquisitorially enough, Bishop. Cardinal would have been more appropriate.

But something about that name rang a distant bell. Bishop . . . Wasn't Bishop one of the BMGA sponsors? And there was something else . . . I couldn't remember.

I had lunch in Jim's Café, which looked out over the blasted Clacton shore. Once, there'd been a Butlins here and donkey rides on the beach and laughing, well-behaved nuclear families playing real crazy golf. That had all gone. I felt old.

Over seventeen holes I had scored forty-eight. I didn't even have the energy to award myself a probable hole-in-one on the unplayed eighteenth. My score was already so poor, so demoralizing, there was no point.

After one morning and just two courses into the crazy-golf tour, I had already spotted a flaw in my pre-Denmark training plan. It was going to be difficult to improve my putting skills if Clacton was a true picture of the general standard of playing areas. The Masters was in poor condition and the so-called Miniatur-Golf was just stupid. And neither course had a windmill. Furthermore, the seaside wasn't quite as congenial as I remembered it. Sitting alone in Jim's Café, I felt suddenly foolish – not for the last time. The gap between what I was trying to achieve and my means of doing it seemed vast, and its vastness incommunicable to anyone save the nutters in the BMGA.

Over the next few weeks, I played a lot of crazy golf. I was diligent. I had to be. I journeyed to Bognor and Great Yarmouth and Margate and round the cape to Broadstairs and all over. I covered the waterfront, and as I did so I became increasingly unsure of the usefulness of what I was doing.

Great Yarmouth, for instance, had two adventure-golf courses, one with a pirate theme, the other a jungle setting, and one more traditional crazy-golf course with a windmill, a rocket and a water-wheel. If fun was what you were after, the adventure courses were fun, particularly the pirate one. At the twelfth hole, you had to putt from inside Bluebeard's giant fibreglass head, through a gap in his teeth and down on to a sprawling green. The course also featured a narrative and educational angle. Between the scattered swords, cannons and human bones, small informative signs lined your route: 'The pirate known as Captain Kidd was born in 1645', or 'Pirate or Privateer – When is a pirate not a pirate? When he is a Privateer!'

Along the prom, Great Yarmouth's crazy-golf course was delightful. It was an exact duplicate of the seafront course in Hastings, a little haven of red, white and green. It was called the Arnold Palmer Putting Course, in honour of the great American golfer. So, under normal circumstances, Great Yarmouth would have represented a carnival of crazy golf – three rounds in the morning, with an ice-cream in between and fish and chips for lunch. Smashing.

But, in my new frame of mind, it wasn't fun I was after: it was rigour, self-improvement. Therefore only the Palmer and Pirate's Cove courses were of any use to me, because they were playable. It didn't matter if the obstacle was a stumpy lighthouse or a pair of giant fibreglass crossed cutlasses. All that mattered was putting the ball in the cup, which the jungle course in Yarmouth conspired against. It had been designed by some joker who, not content to litter the course with gurning Disneyfied giraffes and monkeys, had sought to add to the wackiness of the experience by planting hidden hillocks and ruts in the playing surface. And what good was that to me? What was the use of a good straight putt if a hillock interfered for no purpose other than its own amusement? *And what are you looking at, you big gorilla?*

The novelty of the adventure courses wore off fast. I was a

reluctant frontiersman in Eastbourne, an exasperated explorer in Margate, a pissed-off pirate in Portsmouth, Hayling Island and Littlehampton. Many of these places had orthodox crazy-golf courses too, often Arnold Palmer-style, but either they were in a state of bumpy disrepair (Bognor) or so full of people that a round of eighteen holes could take ninety minutes: fifteen minutes of putting and an hour and a quarter of standing around – the father making sure all three of his toddlers finished their turn, the lawless stag parties, the bastard, bastard urchins.

In municipal parks, on promenades and at a golf centre near Chichester, I also encountered more of the Clacton-style concrete torture courses. These I really hated. They were the very opposite of what I thought of as fun. Prefabricated, hygienic, trim, conservative, and really bloody difficult. I made myself play them. All putting was useful, even on these barren landscapes. 'Kerazee Golf!' their signs declaimed. 'Fun Golf! Wacky Golf!' I played them as though I were digging my own grave.

And through it all, one question remained: was I getting any better? In a more relaxed frame of mind, I would have enjoyed the variety of courses, the silliness of the setting, the happy, laughing children and early summer days with nothing to do but putt, putt, putt. But I wasn't relaxed. As the month wore on, the crowds, the jargon, the keraziness all became increasingly irritating and obstructive.

The problem was that I didn't yet believe in miniature golf, not really. I was trying to improve at something that I felt I wasn't any good at and, more to the point, something no one really thought you *could* be good at. Including me.

But I persevered. This was the Wall, I told myself. Keep going.

I learnt a few tricks. I got up earlier to avoid pensioners and children, often arriving before the course owner had appeared to open up for the day. I became increasingly appreciative of good courses, those that combined imaginative layouts with realistic playing terrains. I looked forward to finding the windmills and water-wheels of well-maintained Arnold Palmers, whatever they might be called. Good courses were to be played twice, and the

Arnold Palmers offered a chance to build up some consistency, largely because they were all the same. The holes might be in a different order, not every course might always have the full eighteen – the one in Broadstairs, for instance, had twelve and some well-tended geraniums – but in theory, by operating a steady-as-she-goes policy of playing for twos on these courses, you could easily score thirty-six or under, although in practice I had yet to break forty. They offered a real, quantifiable challenge. They offered sanity in a Crazy world.

And they were, I felt at some deep level, the real crazy-golf courses of my childhood, their windmills, rockets and warehouses and smart bordered playing areas harking back to a golden age – the atom age, in fact – a glorious industrial present laid out neatly in white, red and green. At Cliftonville, on a well-preserved Arnold Palmer course, now called Lillyputt Minigolf, I made a giant leap. I went round in the magic thirty-nine strokes for the first time.

'This is a really good course,' I said, exhilarated, to the blonde woman in the hut. Maybe I was getting better.

She looked at the wild-eyed man in front of her and laughed. 'Great,' she said chirpily. Her name was June.

There were, in fact, two courses on the Lillyputt site. They had opened as Arnold Palmer Putting Courses, June told me, in the late 1960s. A round cost three and six. Ronnie Corbett – who else? – had played the inaugural round in front of a crowd of dignitaries, holidaymakers and locals. It was a big do: the pictures had been in the local papers.

In those days, Cliftonville was the posh bit of Margate. Families stayed in the bed-and-breakfasts, frolicked at the lido or, if they wanted a ride of any kind (donkey, roller-coaster, other), walked down the hill into Margate proper. In a sense, it was still posh, but Margate, in common with many British coastal resorts, had been in a slump for twenty years and Cliftonville had slumped with it. Opposite the courses, a kitschy selection of mobster-themed businesses squatted in the crumbling Victorian buildings – Bugsy's American Pool, Frank's Nightclub, a rubbishy amusement arcade. Vegas it wasn't.

Still, a little bit of Cliftonville pride remained in the Lillyputt courses. Over the way in Margate, the Aztec Temple Adventure Golf Course was unfriendly ('Players only allowed on course. Sorry, NO spectators') and neglected. It was part of the town's famous Dreamland amusement complex, a mess of dodgems and concrete, a fairground in a car park. The Aztec Temple course lay in the shadow of a rickety waterchute ride called the Log Drop. The fairways were covered in bird shit and the felt had turned dark green in places, saturated with damp and slimy with mould. Rainwater collected in pools in the connecting tunnels, dripping from the stalactites that hung down off the fibreglass. Putting on this surface was a nightmare. I could connect nothing with nothing.[1]

But June and company looked after their courses. She had been a beach photographer back then, taking pictures of daytrippers on the Margate sands. Now she was part-owner of the Cliftonville Lillyputt courses, and another one along the coast in Broadstairs, the geranium garden. They sold sweets and drinks from the hut, kept the area free of litter, made sure the motors for the windmill sails were running smoothly, and relaid the felt every two or three years – it only took a season for the wear and tear to show, said June, particularly around the tees, what with the mis-hits, the footfall and the weather. Like Paul in Clacton, they suffered the unwanted attentions of vandals on a fairly regular basis. But June could make a decent living off her little empire. In high summer, they were always busy. They were still popular with holiday-makers, families, courting couples and Germans.

'They take it so seriously, it's funny,' said June, 'and it takes

---

1. Margate, despite its slump, is still one of Britain's most popular spots for artists and writers to come and indulge their horror of modern life, from T. S. Eliot to Lindsay Anderson in his 1953 short *O Dreamland* and right up to the present and Pawel Pawlikowski's 2000 feature film *Last Resort*. Twenty years ago, Paul Theroux began his grumpy trudge round Britain's coastline in Margate (*The Kingdom by the Sea*). Tracey Emin's work, however, bears all the scars of someone who has lived in the town.

them ages to finish a round. Ages! But they're very good, I must be fair.'

June told me how well organized the business had been back in the sixties. There had been courses all over the country. They were run as franchises from the office of Arnold Palmer Enterprises in London. Franchise-holders were supplied with a handbook and suggestions on everything from course maintenance to marketing opportunities. There were kids' clubs on a Saturday morning, tournaments from time to time, even soirées where prominent local businessmen, accompanied by their wives, could make the acquaintance of other prominent local businessmen – the funny handshake across the eighteenth green, and then Win A Free Go.

June's business partner in the courses was the man who had run the Arnold Palmer franchise in Britain for a while. 'Give him a call,' she said. 'He'll be able to give you more details. He'll have photos and all sorts.' She gave me his number. 'Tell him I said to ring.'

I went to play the other course, and effortlessly shot a horrendous forty-eight to put next to my earlier thirty-nine. Forty-eight! I wonder what that little sod Corbett went round in, I thought spitefully, as I walked back to the car. An hour ago, Arnold Palmer had seemed like the egalitarian father of the greens, a bringer of style *and* substance. I had had his courses pegged as traditional, British, skill-enhancing. But it seemed they were none of these things. And forty-eight . . . I made a mental note to call June's business partner and complain.

My suspicion that this practice method was improving my game hardly at all was confirmed at the BMGA Players' Adventure Golf Championship the following weekend. At Broomfield Park in North London, the rain came down and my score went up. And up. And up again.

Fifteen players turned out for the event. They included Peter and Scott, Lionel, his son Étienne, and a clutch of Vallorys. 'All right?' said Steve Vallory. 'Hello, Andrew,' said Robert. Joe raised an eyebrow in my direction. It was good to see them all again.

I played a quick practice round with Lionel.

'Do those help?' I asked, as he rooted around in his minigolf bag for the correct ball.

'Not really,' said Lionel. 'Not in these conditions.'

Rain was obviously a constant at BMGA events, but unlike the Hastings ground staff, the Saturday staff at the venue showed little or no interest in keeping the fairways free of water. Several holes were so waterlogged that putting them entailed pile-driving through ponds, slashing and splashing at the ball just to push it onwards by a few feet. The ninth in particular, its cup submerged under two inches of water was, as Peter said in his post-match report, 'more akin to a paddling pool than a minigolf hole'.

Peter, who by his reckoning had paid a 'premium price' to hold the event, had received little or no assistance from the park authorities in setting it up. The weather was appalling and, to complicate matters further, he had the media to deal with. A student radio reporter called Rudy was playing today, hoping to pitch a ten-minute feature to Five Live about the global minigolf phenomenon. With good weather and some *simpatico* assistance, this tournament could have been a great showcase for the cause. But it showed every sign of being a washout. I felt sorry for Peter.

However, once the competition was up and running, I soon felt rather more sorry for myself. In the first round, I shot a hard-to-comprehend sixty-three, a number as big in minigolf terms as the universe itself. And, under the circumstances, Peter seemed buoyant, racking up fifty-one and placing himself in joint third place behind Robert and Joe Vallory, and tied with a newcomer – Tim Davies from Hastings.

This was our first sight of Tim. He was shortly to become a significant figure on the British minigolf scene. He was a tall man in his late thirties, with glasses and greying hair, wearing a red Welsh international rugby shirt. He was accompanied by his girlfriend Vicky, whose eyes flashed with amusement and, as the event went on, fatigue. She was pregnant, and quickly got tired of standing around in the rain watching our prowess, or lack of it – although I don't believe even a perfect eighteen would have impressed her. She was normal that way.

I liked Tim. He was unashamedly focused on his game, yet endearingly aimless in life. I asked him what he did for a living.

'I do fuck all for a living,' he said cheerfully, puffing on a rollie. 'Actually fuck all.' Later he told me he had a degree in business studies and had taught English as a foreign language for a while. In theory he was now a computer contractor. But with the baby on the way, he planned soon to be on extended paternity leave. Which would give him ample scope to work on his putting.

Tim had lived in Hastings all his life, had played the Arnold Palmer on the seafront since he was eight, and the White Rock Gardens course since it opened. He remembered, as I did, the model village that had once stood on the site. They had discovered the BMGA via the Internet. 'Our mate Ted said, "Look up minigolf or crazy golf." To us, it's what we do at the weekends, you know, with a wager or two. We're in Hastings, after all. There's not a lot to do.'

They had missed the Open by a day. 'We were all a bit upset that we hadn't had the opportunity to play. They didn't tell us, although we were regulars. We're there all the time and no one mentioned it! We were a bit miffed.'

Tim and two of his mates had joined the BMGA. 'We're the core members of our little minigolf set. There are three others who didn't join.'

Why not?

'There are some very strange people in Hastings. One of them said they wouldn't be able to beat me, so what was the point?'

'I can understand that,' I said.

'Well, I can't,' said Tim brusquely, as affronted as he ever got. 'Even if I know someone's better than me, I still believe I can beat them, 'cause otherwise you're not *going* to win, are you?'

Tim, uniquely among the minigolfers I had encountered, was a real sportsman.

'I grew up with sport you see. It's been my life, basically. Every sport. I've enjoyed every one.'

Tim's real passion was cricket. He described Curtly Ambrose's last test appearance as tear-jerking. I didn't like to tell him I didn't know who Curtly Ambrose was. Tim himself had been a good player, village cricket mostly, but 'It got a bit serious so I opted out. There was all the internal politics to deal with. We had a pub quiz team where the same thing happened. It just wasn't fun any more. We loved the questions but there was this other team we had to beat, there'd be griping, so we stopped it.'

Fun, it seemed, was the key for Tim.

'I'm past playing most sports competitively but I do still play a lot of them. I still ski, I still play tennis. I don't play football much any more except for a knockabout. Rugby, certainly not. I've played golf since I was ten or eleven. Not very good at it. I can hit it a long way but I don't like the rules and regulations and the dress code. Cricket, I've got quite a few little trophies. I've also got quite a few in skiing, but that's within the British framework of skiing, mind you, which is that we're all crap. We race each other to find out who's the crappiest.'

'Ah, good old Eddie the Eagle,' I said.

'Well, respect to the guy,' said Tim unflinchingly. 'He still has to jump off that bloody thing!'

Plainly Tim saw no reason not to take minigolf as seriously as any of his other sporting passions. 'Would you consider minigolf a sport, then?' I asked him.

He didn't pause. 'Yes. It is,' he said, without a hint of doubt. 'I mean, any sport, and I've played a few, it's not about the medium – you know, such as rugby or cricket or whatever one you want to talk about – it's about your belief in it.'

'But don't you feel a bit . . . silly?'

'No. Never. 'Cause it's a game I want to play. And I do believe it's a good game. And I believe that everybody, and I do mean everybody in the whole population, can play the game – which is not true of other sports. I do have a problem when I go somewhere and tell somebody that they *should* be playing it. But when I'm playing it, certainly not. No.'

In the second round, the rain stopped and people's scores improved a little as the course dried out. I shot fifty-two, but my heart wasn't in it. After the reshuffle of groups I had been first out, lumped in with Martin Vallory and Scott, the C-stream, hacking round unattended and unloved by the leaders. It was a parody of my school sports career. Scott and Martin were fairly hopeless, but they were good losers and jovial company. I didn't want to be jovial any more, though: I wanted to be a contender.

Meanwhile, at the top of the table a tussle was developing between Peter, Tim and Robert and Joe Vallory, father and son. This is how Peter described it in his post-match report.

By the sixth tee, just two shots covered the final quartet of players. However, just when it looked as though Robert's challenge might be starting to falter, he steadied his ship with a well-taken two from off the raised green at the sixth.

Joe lost ground with a four at the same hole; and further dropped shots at the 9th and 11th effectively ended his chances. With Peter putting his ball out of bounds at the 10th, it was Hastings-based Tim Davies who was emerging as Robert's main challenger. A puddle still lay between the teeing-off area and the entrance to the castle at the 12th hole but, unlike Peter, Tim decided that the path was playable. He struck his shot through the obstacle and – thanks to a double rebound – saw his ball cannon straight into the hole. Suddenly he was in a share of the lead.

Up ahead, Lionel was completing a blistering round. While Lionel himself seemed resigned to the fact that a personal best total of 41 wasn't going to be enough to win him the shield – his opening round of 55 had left him with too much ground to make up – it certainly set a respectable target for the final quartet to chase.

Robert matched Tim's scores at the next two holes, but his first shot at the 15th hit the back wall at the wrong angle, and stayed on the plateau several feet from the hole. Unlike Peter, who had hit a fine recovery shot from a similar position to keep alive his own slim hopes, Robert just failed to make the putt. For the first time in the tournament Tim was on his own in the lead.

Both of the main protagonists hit twos on the 16th, and par threes at the 17th. That left Peter with just the slimmest chance of forcing his way into a play-off. But it was always asking a lot – and he eventually slumped to a five after failing to putt his tee-shot through the building on the final hole.

Next to play the 18th was Tim Davies. Sensibly he opted to play to the left of the obstacle, settling for the four that would almost certainly be good enough to at least book his place in a play-off.

It left Robert needing a three to take the competition to an extra hole. Having already seen Peter fail to make the daunting putt, he thought better of aiming his tee-shot through the obstacle. A good first stroke, taking into account the one-shot penalty, would have left him with a short putt to force his way into a play-off. But luck was not on his side. His putt bobbled off some debris and out of bounds. The resulting four meant that he would have to settle for a two round total of 94 – one shot behind the victor.

My fifty-two had been enough to give me a two-round total of 115, but because most other people's scores went down accordingly with the improvement in conditions, I still only managed thirteenth place. Great. Rudy the radio student, who had never played before, finished joint ninth. 'You know,' he said to me, 'that was great. I thought it would just be stupid but it was quite tense, wasn't it?'

Oh, piss the fuck off, I thought.

Tim won a bottle of Moët & Chandon, a shield and a cheque for a hundred pounds. He was obviously very pleased to have won; and Peter, too, looked happy, delighted to have discovered another enthusiast and, crucially, a real talent.

'Vicky was chuffed, really chuffed,' Tim told me later. 'She was coaching me.'

'What, from the car?'

'Ha ha. No, earlier. Vicky's a training consultant. I've been a bit resistant but it's worked. It's given me more focus, more thought to what I do.'

Tim's positive approach, I reflected, was something I could learn from. If you don't believe you can win, you're not going to win, are you?

It was now mid-afternoon. This tournament had taken up most of a Saturday, in the wind and rain. On my way home, I told Peter of my plan to go and play in Denmark.

'Oh,' said Peter, 'you're going to Denmark?' A mixture of emotions played across his face. He looked surprised, pleased and slightly alarmed; surprised that I should be so keen, pleased that British minigolf would have a representative in a European tournament, and slightly alarmed that the representative had just finished a full twenty-two shots behind the tournament leader.

'I'll need to send you the paperwork,' he said, recovering himself, 'and issue you with an international playing licence.'

'Right,' I said. I'd had no idea it was all so formal.

'And you'll need a proper minigolf putter like mine, and some balls,' continued Peter. 'If you turn up with that, you'll be laughed off the course.'

'Oh,' I said. 'Right. And where do I . . . ?'

'I can order those for you. It'll be a putter and balls like Lionel's got. We've got contacts with someone in Germany who can send them over. You'll need to give me the money to cover the bank charges as well. I can't remember if Denmark is played on eternit or beton, I'll have to check.'

'Wh–?'

'But you'll need specific balls. You should be able to buy them at the tournament or borrow them off other players, otherwise you won't be able to make the shots. I mean, the Pyramids hole on eternit, if you don't have a 3D 053, that's an impossible shot.'

'What's Bet On and, er, –'

'Eternit. Or beton. They're the courses that WMF – World Minigolf Federation – competitions are played on. They're concrete. The eternit courses are supplied over here by Bishop, the BMGA sponsor.'

Bishop . . . Bishop . . . Finally, bits of information gathered over the last few weeks coalesced in my brain. A lightbulb appeared above my head, but it quickly metamorphosed into the countenance of a member of the Rubettes, laughing. For the first time I realized just how steep was the mountain I had set out to climb, not just because of the skill I lacked or the equipment required, but because the mountain itself was pitiless and cruel. Pyramid, Labyrinth, 'Volcanoe' . . .

'Peter,' I said, 'have you ever been to Clacton?'

7

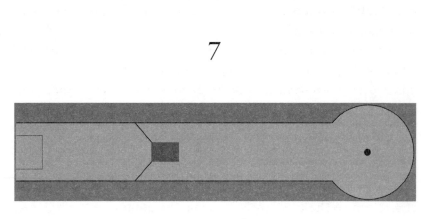

Wippe – rocker

The following weekend I headed south, to Camber Sands in Sussex. I was going to a rock festival and I was really looking forward to it. In contrast to my recent activities, you didn't get much more unsporty than the sickly ragbag of musicians and drug addicts who had been lined up to play over the three days and nights ahead.

The festival showcased some of the more leftfield, experimental acts on the scene, many of whom retained a touching faith in the power of guitars and the racket they could make. The two dominant musical forms of the nineties had been tainted by sport – Britpop, with its tracksuit tops and trainers and cheeky fraternizing with Parklife and football, and dance music, which involved dressing up like an athlete, and passing the night in strenuous physical exertion while necking copious amounts of Ecstasy, a performance-enhancing drug if ever there was one. But there would be little dancing this weekend. Here at Camber Sands, the emphasis was on the static, both in terms of how much you would be required to move and also what you could expect to hear coming out of the PA. It was an old-fashioned celebration of beer, cigarettes and terrible brain-fucking noise. It was going to be great.

Normally this would have occupied me wholly. However, this

year I was distracted. The festival, in homage to the old soul weekenders, took place at the Pontin's holiday camp near the beach. And that meant there would be crazy golf. This wasn't a hunch on my part. I knew there would be crazy golf because much of the pre-festival coverage used the camp's crazy-golf course as a motif through which to emphasize the sheer genre-busting uniqueness of the event – see the bands, drink in the bars till three a.m., EVEN PLAY ON THE CRAZY-GOLF COURSE! That kind of thing. And sure enough, on arrival, there was the course, just a few feet from Reception, a non-specific sort of buried-treasure affair with the hole numbers picked out in yellow and purple on a green Astroturf surface.

We checked in, found our chalet and played a quick round. I lost. No matter, we had all weekend. I went inside, watched a band then dragged one of my companions out to the course again, where I lost. Again. It was getting dark and the first of the weekend's big acts was due on the main stage. We watched them. They were great but I couldn't get into it. Those two losses were preying on my mind.

The following morning, after breakfast and another round, which I lost, we explored the area around Pontin's. By the beach there was an amusement arcade, shops selling inflatables and postcards, a couple of pubs and cafés, and – yes – another crazy-golf course. It was a homemade number, red-brick and green baize, situated in someone's back garden, where the greens were split-level and the connecting pipes were either old chimneys or plumbing parts.

We played it. I lost. But even as I lost, I felt a mounting sense of excitement. It didn't look much, but this was a good course. Someone had clearly taken a bit of care in its construction. The only thing that stopped a putt going where it should was the player's incompetence, not subsidence or kinks in the layout. And another thing. The Pontin's course was worn and silly and always full of festival-goers. But this one was mostly empty, probably a bit too 'boring' for the thrill-seekers back at camp. The prospect of a full weekend of meaningful practice presented itself.

And so I vowed that, when I was not watching the bands I would live at the crazy-golf course by the beach. I challenged anyone I could think of to rounds of crazy golf. I kept losing. But when I lost, I tried to do so with good grace and the inner conviction that this was all roughage in my miniature-golf diet. And surely, I felt, I can't keep losing: the law of averages is going to have to reward me sooner or later.

But the law of averages had been revoked. By Saturday afternoon, I had still to win a match. A parade of whey-faced indie kids had passed me on their way to the beach, and again hours later on the way back and still I couldn't get my game together. A small kind of mania had gripped me. I kept having to dash back to Pontin's, see twenty minutes of a band, then run back to the course again to pick up where I'd left off. By this stage, it should be noted, I was playing alone. I knew I looked odd, a troubled loner, but I couldn't stop. Just one more round . . .

Music for me, and the culture around music, has always existed as an alternative to sport, in direct opposition to sport, in fact.[1] I know this isn't consistent – tribalism, commercialism and snobbery are rife in music too – but I've always drawn righteous energy from the pop life, the better to help me fight the evil of

---

1. I've never bought the theory about the special relationship between football and pop music; it's only ever pointed out by people who like football. Football records are rotten, aesthetically and spiritually. Even 'World In Motion', the single New Order made with the England football team in 1990, is rotten. It was a collaboration in the Vichy France sense of the word. Here were former members of Joy Division cheerfully doing their bit for the war effort – love will tear us apart, but football and England will bring us together. And you'd be hard pressed to find a starker contrast with the polymorphous perversity of punk than the sight of Peter Hook pissing it up with Gazza. This became a regular gangshow over the next few years – footballers, fans, comedians and pop stars getting blitzed together in the national interest.

Of course, 'World In Motion' was quite a good record, but who cares about that? In retrospect, we can see that New Order invented the nineties. The fucking, fucking bastards.

sport. However, there wasn't much energy on display in the big Pontin's ballroom, righteous or otherwise. The audience sat on the floor in threes and fours, smoking and drinking lager. 'Thanks for coming in out of the sun,' the singer from Ligament told the supine crowd at one point.

'Fuck, yeah,' added their weary bassist, 'I wouldn't have come.'

Most of the bill played rather uninspired, mostly instrumental post-rock, fine in small doses but lethargy-inducing when strung out over a whole day, and particularly uninvolving, it turned out, if you kept having to puncture the epic soundscapes and transcendental interludes with trips to the crazy-golf course.

So I found the appearance at teatime on Saturday of a Texan band called . . . And You Will Know Us By The Trail Of Dead inspirational. They were loud. They were fast. Unlike many of the weekend's acts, they looked fantastic and had no discernible facial hair. They began their set with a sample of Pete Townshend on stage with The Who (*'This is a fucking rock'n'roll concert, not a fucking tea party!'*) and twenty minutes later ended it by smashing up their instruments. I loved them. So did the crowd. Some people even stood up.

. . . And You Will Know Us By The Trail Of Dead were ever so slightly ridiculous and ever so very derivative. If you believed the name, the trail of dead in question began with Keith Moon and worked down from there. And yet they were up on stage, they were doing it – extremely well – and in the context of that particular weekend, they were superstars. Perhaps, I thought to myself as I went to the bar, I could apply some element of their rock'n'roll attitude to my putting.

The following day, I walked with a new swagger past the accommodation blocks and perimeter gates, swinging my club like a low-slung axe, tossing it from hand to hand and dropping it only once. When I got to the course, I didn't thank the boy in the hut as he handed over the ball and scorecard. This wasn't a fucking tea party. I tried to putt dynamically, cockily. I scowled at the ball as I hit it, a sneer playing across my lips when it didn't do what I wanted. The ball can fuck itself, I thought. Fuck you, ball! Yeah!

But it didn't work. I played as appallingly as ever. I still looked like a troubled loner, only now I was a troubled loner with a Billy Idol complex. On his own. At the seaside.

A group of girls on their way to the beach stopped to watch. I lined up a putt on the sixth hole, aware they were looking. Concentrating, I tried to look mean and as though I meant business. 'Ooh, the tension!' giggled one of the girls, a poppet with a hair-slide, and her friends laughed. I fixed her with what I hoped was a hard stare and putted. Unbelievably, the ball rolled straight into the cup.

And in an instant, a new dilemma presented itself. It was a great putt, a spectacular shattered Stratocaster of a putt, but this was the wrong time, the wrong place. I was scared to celebrate it, for fear of looking like even more of a loser than I did already. These girls were as cool and cruel as only young girls can be. So I opted for a nonchalant ladies-I-do-*that*-every-time raise of the eyebrows. The girls gave me a slow, satirical round of applause, and headed off to the beach. 'Sad,' said one.

She was right. It was sad, and not just the business with the eyebrows. Over there, a rock festival was taking place. Self-awareness hit me like a bucket of lukewarm lager. What was I doing here, for Christ's sake? What was I thinking of? Enough! With a rebel yell I cried, no, no more, handed back my ball and went to get drunk.

Initially it worked. The noise was tremendous. These were my people. This was where I belonged. But later, as the day wore on, the itch began again. In front of me was all the fire and brimstone modern indie rock could muster; but at the edge of my increasingly blurred vision was a carpet of felt, a straight putt, a lucky last round before Monday.

'Excuse me,' I slurred to the lead guitarist of a once all-conquering New York art-rock quartet, 'would you like to play crazy golf with me?'

But he declined even quicker than his career.

And so the weekend ended with an incandescent set from the festival headliners, and a very drunk man – who had his own putter – knocking a rolled-up bit of paper round the Pontin's course, the ball dispensary having long since shut for the night. Did he win? He thinks so. He can't remember.

Two weeks later, my new putter arrived from Germany.

It was like a standard golf putter, but with two significant differences. The shaft joined the head at one end, rather than somewhere along the crown; and the head itself was fitted with a pink rubber cushion on the playing side. In the box with it was a selection of nine minigolf balls, a bag to keep them in and a protective blue polyvinyl sock for the head of the club, all branded with the logo of the manufacturer – the oxymoronic Fun-Sports. The cost, including postage, packing and bank charges, had been a little under a hundred pounds.

I unzipped the sock, spilled the balls on to the sitting-room carpet and took a few experimental putts across the room. The pink of the putter head clashed with the bright yellow, red and purple balls. They were slightly smaller than golf balls, and made of what felt like rubber or silicone. Each had a number from one to eight: 1 (dark green), 2 (pink, matt), another 2 (pink, gloss), 3 (black), 4 (red), 5 (dark green), 6 (purple), 7 (yellow), 8 (light blue). Confusingly, they were not classified, as far as I could tell, by bounce. The light blue 8 was the springiest, but then so was the red 4. The blue ball was softer, with more give to the touch but if you dropped both balls simultaneously from shoulder height, both jumped back up to the knee. Repeated bouncing revealed the harder 4 to have the slight edge. The dark green 1, as might be expected, was the heaviest and deadest of the selection, a pill-sized medicine ball; so dead, in fact, that when you dropped it, its sheer lack of rebound made you fear it might crack open the floor, small though it was. But the purple 6 was heavy too; the black 3 was just as dead but lighter than either, almost like wood; and the 7, the 5 and the two pink 2s were, after repeated trials, much of a muchness. In any case it was academic; on felt or carpet, their properties were almost indistinguishable. They were designed to be used on a hard surface, on concrete; only then would they come into their own. Or that was the idea.

All the ball bouncing had caused our downstairs neighbour to start playing the Dixie Chicks at high volume, so I collected up the balls and returned them to their bag. It was like a strapless bum-bag, blue, waterproof, and with a ribbed rubber underside; the sort of thing a door-to-door condom salesman might carry his samples in. The putter sock seemed to be made of the same stuff, with a white fake-fur lining. The whole set-up was unaccountably, yet unmistakably, European, like French crisps or an 'I Am Top Gun Rocking Boy' bomber jacket.

The Fun-Sports logo was a putter and ball on a grid of crossed lines, as though copied by an eight-year-old on to graph paper. And much as I tried to convince myself that I had just paid a hundred pounds for a really professional bit of minigolf gear, when I looked at the brightly coloured balls and club and bag, it was difficult not to conclude that this was a child's starter kit. But then I was a child, eight years old in minigolf years.[2]

In a symbolic, probably Freudian moment, I put my father's putter away in the wardrobe, and accepted a new putter into my life.

In the days after the North London competition, Peter confirmed for me that the Danish Invitational Open was to be played on beton. This was both good news and bad news. It was good news because I wouldn't have to play on the horrific eternit courses; but it was bad news because there was nowhere I could practise how to play the beton course. There were no beton courses in the UK.

I should have been daunted by this. It was essentially the same dilemma as that faced by the famous Jamaican bobsled team – absolute lack of supporting infrastructure or, to put it another way, no snow. However, I was still sufficiently naïve to think it didn't really matter. What I needed to do was work on consistency

2. Like dog years, but stupider.

in my putting technique, which I could do anywhere, not worry about the intricacies of the layouts, or so I thought. It wasn't useful or practical to base all my practice on seaside courses. A little bit of the promenade would have to come to our house.

So for my birthday I asked for, and received, a Perfect Solutions™ Battery Operated Putt Returner and a Masters Deluxe Putting Mat. These were to be my secret weapons, the climbing frame and vaulting horse of my personal minigolf gym. The mat was bright green and twelve feet long, made from 'specially selected synthetic matting to ensure consistent roll'. It came with a flag, two bunkers, 'a selection of foam wedges which can be placed under the mat to create cambers and dips', and instructions in English, French and German. It was great. *Versuchen Sie Es Selbst!*

I would set up the putting mat so it ran the entire length of the sitting room and while Tina tried to watch TV, putt all nine of my special balls, then retrieve them from the side of the mat, under the sofa and, every so often, the cup. Once I had mastered a particular combination of foam wedges, I'd lift the mat up, rearrange them and start again. My wife's beady and reproachful stare added to the challenge.

The Putt Returner, however, was not quite the perfect solution I had hoped it would be. I had had visions of something neat and efficient, Jack Lemmon in his office in an early sixties metropolitan comedy, but the Perfect Solutions™ Battery Operated Putt Returner was a bulky, plasto-metallic box, shaped like a flipper. We grew quickly to detest each other. If you struck the ball too hard, it simply bounced off the back of the Putt Returner's collecting tray; too soft and it never made it past the lip. Should you be lucky enough to pop the ball right on to the sensitive spot, it was punched back to you by a small metal arm, which then retracted itself with a horrible drilling noise, like a skull being trepanned. And that was when it worked. Half the time, the ball just sat there. After a couple of days, I didn't bother with it and it squatted in the corner, gathering dust and sulking. But I persevered with the mat and the trips to the seaside.

'You know the European Championships are taking place in Latvia in August?' Peter had told me, when I'd last seen him. 'I was thinking about going, if you're interested. I don't know if I can get the time off work but if you want to go, I can sort it out for you.' I nodded and smiled. Of course I didn't want to go to Latvia! Latvia? Are you mad? I said I'd think about it.

But now I was spending all this time practising and the idea of going to Latvia began to appeal to me. Denmark would be good practice, and why stop there? Denmark was essentially a friendly; Latvia was the real thing. What other sport was going to afford me the opportunity to compete at the top level, to play against the best in Europe, and probably the best in the world?

I decided I'd do it, conditional on my performance at the Danish Invitational Open. That would be the control. I could always pull out. If Denmark was a disaster, I just wouldn't show up in Latvia. Who was going to come after me? The minigolf police?

Six long weeks after that first trip to Clacton, I made my way to Southend-on-Sea for an afternoon's practice prior to the Main Event – the BMGA British Masters. According to Peter's directions, the course was to be found on the seafront, part of the Peter Pan Adventure Island amusement park. I walked down from the station through the middle of Southend, ball bag in one hand, swinging my brand-new putter with its bright blue sock in the other.

The course, when I reached it, was across the road from a pub offering non-stop karaoke from eleven in the morning to eleven at night, and lap-dancing at lunchtime, possibly combining the two during Happy Hour. A large yellow plastic sign hung by the admissions gate: 'ADVENTURE ISLAND WELCOMES THE BRITISH MASTERS MINIGOLF TOURNAMENT.' I couldn't see any BMGA members. Perhaps they were in the pub.

Ignoring the temptation, I began my first practice round. The Lost City, like the Lost World in Croydon, offered adventure golf, eighteen holes divided into two nine-hole courses – Aztec

Adventure and Inca Challenge. They featured all the by now familiar props and sound effects – a crashed two-seater aeroplane, an abandoned jeep, the chirruping of crickets and the distant howl of hungry wolves (all quite convincing, this being Southend). The first hole was best played with a rebound shot off the back boundary. I opted to use one of the bounciest balls in my bag – the red Fun-Sports number 4. Because the ball was heavier than the similarly bouncy blue 8, it would roll further on the carpet. I played the hole a few times to find the right line and moved on. I no longer felt self-conscious: I was absorbed in the task of learning how to play the holes, a sensation I might almost have mistaken for pleasure.

In general, long straight putts or short connecting putts into tunnels were best served by the heavy dead balls – green 1 or black 3. Long rebound shots like the first needed the red or blue ball: either would bounce and keep running, even if a double rebound was required. As for the rest of the balls – who could tell? Certainly not me. I stuck with the three or four balls whose primary properties I understood.

As I climbed the 'rock' steps to the fourth hole, a long curving run through a cave (red ball 4), I saw Peter coming through the turnstile and on to the course. We waved to each other. He looked very pleased about something.

'Good news!' he said, when he arrived at the top of the steps. 'It looks like Sky Sports will be covering the tournament tomorrow.'

'Sky Sports!' I said, amazed. 'Pressure's on, then.'

'Yes,' said Peter. 'I haven't had as much time as I'd have liked to practise. But the staff here are being very helpful.'

I offered to play a practice round with him later on, and he went off to consult with the owners of Peter Pan about the timetable for tomorrow. Sky Sports . . . Just as I had with the radio student, I felt slightly worried for Peter. The prospect of a stitch-up seemed likely, especially given the surroundings. But Peter could look after himself. And satellite and cable channels did have a lot of airtime to fill. You could watch all sorts of niche sports on those channels. And they were internationalist in their outlook, weren't they?

From a speaker above my head, a monkey hooted and screamed its little hairy head off.

Sky Sports arrived mid-way through the opening rounds of the tournament. There were three of them: a couple of sturdy men with cameras and mics, and a stern woman with long hair and sunglasses who seemed to be running the show. They had a job to do and were no friendlier than they needed to be. They prowled the course under the woman's direction, collecting shots of the jeep and the aeroplane, and conducting an interview with Peter from the spot where he and I had spoken, above the course, looking back over the greens and the seafront road lined with Vegas arcades. Peter, I noticed, removed his glasses for the camera.

I'd arrived at about ten o'clock. It was a beautiful day. Competitors, unaccustomed to sunshine on such occasions, bought ice lollies and sun cream. I felt anxious but excited as we waited to start. I had played a couple of good practice rounds yesterday, level pegging with Peter, and I was determined to keep my cool and enjoy myself today. I felt I knew how to play each hole and that all the practice over the last few weeks had to count for something.

'Ah,' laughed Lionel, when he saw my Fun-Sports kit, 'they got you too, then.'

We discussed the merits of our specialist equipment. Lionel, too, had difficulty distinguishing between the different balls. 'I just use the heaviest ones or the ones with the most bounce to them,' he said. I confided that I thought we might have been sent the kiddies' version. Lionel agreed. 'I was suspicious as soon as I saw the putter. Would you have chosen pink, given the choice?'

'No,' I said, 'I wouldn't.'

'I think Peter's German contact has a job lot of pink putters that he saves up to send to England.'

'Why?'

'To demoralize us,' he said, poker-faced. 'To keep the British players on the back foot.' Lionel, I realized, had a drier sense of humour than I'd credited him with.

I chatted with Tim Davies and Vicky, and a couple of their Hastings friends, who were competing today, Ted and Mark. They had come up the afternoon before and had had a few problems finding their guesthouse. As a result, the BMGA Players Champion and entourage had only managed to squeeze in one quick practice round before the tournament. 'Oh dear,' I said meanly. 'That's a shame.'

'Is that a special minigolf putter?' asked Ted.

I showed them the putter and the bag of balls. Vicky laughed but the men were fascinated. Tim examined the head of the putter, pressing the rubber in with his thumb, a rollie hanging out of the side of his mouth. 'Ooh, nice colour, Andy,' he said, and took a couple of experimental strokes.

'See, I'd rather just use a normal putter and a dead ball,' he said finally, handing back the club. 'Anyway, you're taking this a bit seriously, aren't you?'

I told them about going to Denmark and the European Championships in Latvia. Vicky laughed even harder.

'I've been to Latvia,' said Ted. 'Where are the Championships? Rīga?'

'Yeah, that's right,' I said. 'Why, what's it like?'

Ted rubbed his chin thoughtfully. 'Yeah, it's all right. Very poor. All run by the Mafia too.'

I laughed.

'No, it is,' said Ted. He wasn't joking.

I wished them luck as sincerely as I could manage and went to talk to the Vallorys, who had arrived *en masse*. Five of them were competing – Gary, Steve, Martin, Robert and Joe – and they were accompanied by a mixture of wives, girlfriends, kids and toddlers in pushchairs.

'It's a day out, isn't it?' said Steve Vallory to me. 'Here, is that a minigolf club?'

I commiserated with Robert over his defeat at the last tournament, but he was his usual affable self. 'Never mind. I just couldn't keep it together at the end. Should have brushed all that crap off the carpet. Terrible weather. This is a bit better, isn't it?' he said, meaning both the sunshine and the course. 'Mind you,' he continued, 'some people went down the rankings after that tournament.'

'What do you mean?'

'Well,' said Robert conspiratorially, 'if you turned up and played badly, by Peter's reckoning you could go down the rankings. I think you did – and I did too. The scores were so big 'cause of the weather that people who didn't turn up, it didn't affect their scoring average or something. I couldn't work it out. Seemed a bit unfair, though, being penalized for turning up. It's this system Peter's got.'

'I bet Peter went up the rankings,' said Joe Vallory. He was wearing a smart Kangol cap, backwards.

'Yeah, that's right!' snorted his dad. 'He doesn't look much, Peter, but he's a sharp mind.' There seemed to be some rivalry between Peter and the Vallorys.

I told them that he'd got Sky Sports down here. That had been quite sharp.

'Really?' said Joe Vallory, adjusting his cap. 'Sky Sports? Why are they here?'

'To film us,' I said.

'Putting like puffs,' said Joe.

'Er, yes,' I said.

'Bloody hell,' said Joe ruefully. I was not alone, it seemed, in fearing a stitch-up.

The Masters had attracted a field of thirty or so brave souls, brave not only because of the presence of the cameras but because the tournament was being played on a sunny Saturday afternoon on Southend seafront and was therefore fully exposed to the attentions of the passing crowds. Local lads barked with laughter when they saw the welcoming banner and the motley collection of contenders. 'Matt!' they shouted. 'Matt! Come and look at these wankers!'

Some of these lovable maxi-urchins were even competing in

the tournament, non-BMGA members but local qualifiers. Scott was forced to play his first round with one of them, a Southend geezer called Steve. Steve was followed round by his mate, also called Steve, and their respective girlfriends. Steve the mate mock-commentated the whole match, cheering on Steve the player ('Oh, he's hot! He's the kiddie!' etc.), who strutted like a cock, and needling Scott ('Oooh, an elementary error!'), whose game went to pieces accordingly. Steve was a moron and a bully, and so was Steve, but who was going to stop them? Scott ended his round with sixty-three and looked thoroughly miserable.

Meanwhile, I was on a roll. I had been teamed with a friendly native called Neil and Tim's friend Ted, and I was playing the round of my competitive minigolf career to date.

'Blimey!' said Ted, after a fluky hole-in-one on the long fourth hole. 'You're on form!' He was right. I was on form: three twos and an ace. For the first time I had connected.

The combination of the new club, change of ball from hole to hole, some decent homework and, I believed, a much improved and practised stroke proved sustainable over the full eighteen holes. I kept my head down and ground out the putts. I finished the first round with a confident forty-three, in joint third place and just one stroke off the leaders, Joe and Steve Vallory. I was ecstatic.

'What did you get?' said Scott, as I finished.

'Forty-three, I'm afraid,' I said.

'Well done,' said Scott quietly, and turned away, betrayed by the one man he'd thought he could rely on to mess it all up.

While scores were registered and second-round groupings worked out, I traded scores with the top flight of the BMGA, trying not to look smug. Most hovered around the forty-five, forty-four, forty-three mark, and looked surprised but pleased to welcome me into their midst.

'Forty-three?' said Tim. 'Good stuff!'

'Forty-three?' said Peter. 'Really?'

'Congratulations, Andrew,' said Robert Vallory.

'It's those bloody little balls,' said his son.

For the first time, I was going to make the cut. In the second round I was drawn with Robert and, worryingly, Southend Steve. And the camera crew were at large, recording the players in action. Still, I thought, all I have to do is play safe, not get intimidated, grind round the eighteen holes again and I'll be home safely. I'm really going to have to go some not to make the cut.

Well, I did go some. My second round was a disaster, a risible fifty-four. How could this happen? I dropped from joint third place to joint twenty-second, twelve places and a good seven shots off the cut. I couldn't believe it, I felt sick with the unfairness of it. And the problem, I realized, was that I had felt like this from three or four holes into the round. My game had collapsed because early on I had given up: I had become paralysed with self-pity.

At the fourth hole, the scene in the first round of that lucky ace, I took four. At this point in the first round, I had taken a total of seven shots. But on this round, I had taken a three, another three, a four and another four – fourteen! I felt the familiar hot flush of embarrassment, the frustration once again of screwing up in front of my peers. 'Come on, Andrew, what's happening?' said Robert Vallory, after another fluffed putt. But it was no good. I had stacked up fourteen already without trying. I played resentfully, angrily, badly.

At the eighth hole, I played the blue 8 round against the border of the hole so that it would scoot off about half the way round and end up near the cup. It didn't. It bounced off too early, didn't keep its line and came to rest a good five feet from the cup and right against the border. Great. Steve's mate Steve had, thankfully, got bored and gone off to paw his girlfriend, but had he been there he would have said something like, 'Oh, no! These tactics have bitten his butt! It's a disaster! What an arse!'

But it got worse. As I turned the corner from the tee, there was the camera crew, waiting to record this tricky putt for posterity.

'Look,' I said to the producer, with as much politeness as I could muster, 'would you mind not filming me? I'm not playing very well and you're just making it harder for me. I'd really appreciate it.'

She didn't even bother to answer, just looked at me and shrugged. The cameraman showed no sign of turning his attention elsewhere.

I stalked indignantly back to the tee. We were just there as a bit of fodder to fill up a few minutes of satellite airtime, in the 'And finally . . .' slot, no doubt. It didn't matter to them if I sank this putt or not. But it mattered to me.

Mercifully, I did sink it. It looked like the ball might lip to the left but it decided to spin and drop, and as it did so, I raised an index finger to the camera and winked in triumph. I couldn't stop myself. Then I walked on to the next hole.

As soon as my round was over (me fifty-four, Robert Vallory forty-one, Southend Steve forty-one), I said a few farewells to whoever was passing and virtually ran back to the station. I had been given a glimpse of the top flight but then the elevator doors had whooshed shut and I had plunged back down to where I really lived: the basement. I didn't want to stick around to see who won: whoever it was, it wasn't going to be me.

A couple of days later, I received Peter's e-mail notification of the result. Robert Vallory was the Masters Champion, having beaten Joe in a play-off, an Oedipal drama I had missed. I felt a pang of remorse. It sounded like a great contest.

Peter's e-mail contained the expected date and time of the Sky Sports coverage. It was about ten days away, as part of a golf show called *European Tour Weekly*. I made a note to tune in to see the play-off and if they would broadcast my super putt.

They did. I watched the report with a growing sense of indignation, which quickly turned to outrage. As I had feared, the BMGA British Masters filled a chortling three-minute slot after the main tour news of the week, Lee Westwood's victory at the Deutsche Bank-SAP Open ('Tiger tamed by Worksop Whippet!').

And finally . . .

*(Establishing shots of Southend seafront, accompanied by the
rinkiest, dinkiest seaside music in the Sky Sports library.)*

VOICEOVER: 'Last weekend, Southend-on-Sea in England hosted
the British Masters – the minigolf British Masters, that is!'

*(Shot of roller-coaster full of screaming children, with large
goofy alligator as figurehead.)*

'Played out on the magical Peter Pan Adventure Island Lost
City course, the event is one of several tournaments on an
increasingly popular circuit.'

*(Shot of course with caption: Lost City Course, Southend-on-
Sea, 18 Holes for the Price of 9.)*

'Competition was fierce on the traditional seaside course,
voted one of the best in England, where hazards include
aeroplane wreckage, Augusta National speed greens and some
wickedly narrow fairways!'

*(Montage of missed putts from Peter, Tim, Scott and South-
end Steve, watched by Steve Vallory and me, wincing. The
'wickedly narrow fairways' line is accompanied by a shot of
a red ball rolling down a narrow wooden ramp. The next shot
is of a white ball emerging from a tunnel on a completely
different hole.)*

'Televised events offer five-figure prize funds in America and
minigolf is booming in Europe, even if the stakes are a little
more modest.'

PETER, WITHOUT GLASSES, WITH COURSE BEHIND HIM: 'Well, minigolf's a sport for all really. I mean, anybody can play, regardless of age, men and women. You don't have to be particularly
fit, you just need to be able to concentrate on your shot, hit
precise putts – good putting ability!'

And to prove Peter's point that absolutely anyone can play
minigolf, however unsporty, unsuitable and unfit, there was my
super putt, me slouching over my putter, the ball just about
curling into the cup, and me walking away, winking and raising
a triumphant digit, looking idiotic. And the truth was, the shot

wasn't even proof of good putting ability. Seen from this angle, it was obviously a stroke of luck. My posture was awful, my shoulders hardly moved and all the motive force came from the wrists. Any real golfer or minigolfer would look at it and snort with derision.

The music accompanying the report now changed to the sort of comedy musical quacking that accompanies clowns.

> VOICEOVER: 'Although the stakes won't break the Deutsche Bank – or even Monty's piggy bank! – and although clothing contracts are in short supply – no spikes please! – these guys are deadly serious.'
>
> PETER: 'We're trying to get away from the phrase "crazy golf", 'cause that implies a sort of luck-based course where, you know, it doesn't rely so much on putting accuracy. The courses we play our tournaments on are a true test of ability.'

Peter was right, of course, but who was going to listen? The report sniggered on, including some shots of a faked ace, complete with dubbed-on cheering and applause ('Are you watching, David Duval?') and a futile attempt by Peter to steer the interview towards the pressures of international competition.

> PETER: 'The hardest hole I've played has obviously been on one of the championship courses that they use for the world championships, one of the standardized courses, and there the margin for accuracy is minimal. You have to hit the ball within, sort of, half a centimetre of the correct line, er, and exactly the right strength of putt, otherwise you'll hit the obstacle and you could end up taking seven.'
>
> VOICEOVER: 'And unfortunately for Peter, he wasn't able to keep his charge going, and he couldn't squeeze his way into a play-off.'
>
> (Shot of Peter and Tim shaking hands.)
>
> 'And in the end, a two on the first extra hole was good enough

for Robert Mullery to take the first prize, and be crowned British Master for 2000.'
(*Shot of Robert's final putt and the crowd applauding, before cutting to the presentation.*)
THE COURSE OWNER: 'And the winner of British Masters minigolf and a cheque for two hundred and fifty pounds is . . .'
THE MAYOR: 'Robert Vallory. Is that right?'
ROBERT: 'Yes.'
THE COURSE OWNER AND MAYOR: 'Well done, Robert.'
VOICEOVER: 'So, an English double at the weekend for Lee Westwood and Robert Mullery. Straight into the winner's speech – Disneyland, here we come!'
ROBERT (*grinning*): 'Shall I hold up the cup?'
VOICEOVER: 'Makes you proud to be British.'

You miserable sods, I thought. You couldn't even get his name right.

I felt affronted by the facetiousness of the Sky report. It showed a fundamental lack of respect for the skill and sincerity of those involved, and their ability to reproduce that skill under pressure. I knew it was a skill because I didn't have it. I had practised, I had improved – at least I thought I had improved – but when it came down to it, I had gone to pieces. I had failed, and the reasons I had failed were in my head.

Things were changing. I had the equipment. I had the will. For the first time since childhood I had a suntan. And another thing. For the first time in my life, I believed.

8

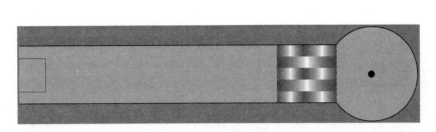

Unregelmässige Passagen – irregular passages

Here is an old Marxist joke:

Q. When is a sport not a sport?
A. When it fails to function profitably within the parameters of the commercial-industrial complex, while at the same time neglecting sport's role in maintaining and reinforcing systems of male hegemony!
(Exit Harpo left, head drooping, tooting horn – toot toot! – to little or no comic effect.)

The humour of the Marxist has not worn well.

However, while we wait for the tumbleweed to finish blowing across the page, consider this. In an inversion of the first rule of comedy, the reason this joke isn't funny is *precisely* because it's true. A sport isn't a sport until it's been enthusiastically embraced by money and men.

Functionally, all sports do more or less the same thing. A ball must be thrown or hit or pushed with a hand or foot or some kind of stick. Two individuals or groups of individuals compete against one another on land or water or even in the air. They must ensure that they perform this activity within some designated lines or on a table or in a ring. In general, they must try not to fall over.

The red team plays the blue team plays the red team, and so on.

But some sports are bigger than others. Hegemony makes the world go round. So here is the Marxist joke again, retold in the manner of a saucy postcard:

Q. When is a sport not a sport?
A. When it's only got a tiny wad!

Not much funnier, but still true. Proper sports are measured in money and men, in worth and girth.

Using these double standards (and *entendres*), you can see why so few people think minigolf is a proper sport. Football is proper because it's engorged with hard cash and blokes just can't leave it alone. Cricket is a long, slow screw. Darts has the stamp of a very weird fetish. But miniature golf is . . . well, miniature. No one spends and makes piles of money on it. No one uses it to explore and express his masculinity – it's just too small. As a result, the belittling of minigolf, my sport, was really beginning to rankle. It was a modest enough game already without being diminished still further by comedians like the Sky Sports gang. Size might not matter to them but it did to me.

A few weeks after Southend, however, I took part in a non-BMGA miniature-golf tournament that offered a glimpse of what life might be like in a world where minigolf was considered a proper sport, bulging and tumescent. And it was horrible.

At the Glenlivet Office Putting Championship in London, golfers from blue-chip companies, many of them men, were taking their miniature golf very seriously indeed. They practised alone, or stood around in twos or threes, swapping jokes like they were grooming one another. Although there was a free bar, with a plentiful supply of the Glenlivet single malt to sample, most of the blue chips stuck to soft drinks.

'Dear, oh dear, look at this lot,' said a woman called Ann-Louise, waving a beer bottle in the direction of a troop of baseball-capped and balding sports-baboons. 'What a state.'

Ann-Louise was the events manager for a charity that helped

the elderly. Although the charity ran an annual celebrity golf tournament at the Belfry, and although Ann-Louise's husband was 'dead keen' on golf, she didn't know much about the sport and she certainly didn't play it.

'Haven't you been practising?' I asked her.

'Practising?' replied Ann-Louise dismissively. 'No! God, I haven't even got me own putter!'

In order to make it to tonight's Glenlivet grand final, all the contenders had taken part in heats, most of which were conducted in their own offices. Ann-Louise's had been fiercely contested. 'We had a couple of real golf pros in our qualifying thing – well, not actually pros but they think they could be, you know – and both of them went out in the first round, which they weren't happy about.' She took a triumphant swig of her beer. 'Then *I* won it, so they were doubly gutted. Ha!'

Ann-Louise had been magnanimous in victory. 'Well, I just told them, don't be so daft. It's only a bit of fun.'

Other female competitors I spoke to told a similar tale: the men in their offices who had failed to qualify sulked at their workstations for days. Bad enough to be beaten by a woman, but to be beaten by a woman *not taking it seriously* . . . Around us, males who had reached this level clutched their orange squash and prepared to fight for dominance of the group. A couple ate the bananas they had brought in their briefcases, for energy.

Office putting is an American invention, which involves using the terrain of your office as a crazy-golf course – filing cabinets for obstacles, wastepaper baskets for windmills, and so on. The Glenlivet Office Putting Championship was taking place in the company's headquarters but, like most crazy-golf courses, the setting soon faded into the background. All that mattered was the terrain. How were you going to negotiate that pot plant, say, or this specially constructed boulevard of whisky bottles, especially with the distraction of those few employees who were still at their desks trying to work?

I asked the Glenlivet's global marketing director, whose name was Geoff, what the thinking was behind the championship.

'We've been looking for concepts for PR ideas and innovation on the Glenlivet brand,' said Geoff. 'The broader idea is something I've always called "Mixing Business With Pleasure". Office putting is a concept that works within that.'

Geoff told me that he and his team had experimented with corporate softball and something called touch rugby before alighting on the notion of office putting. He spoke evangelically of the game's potential. 'One of the things with the idea of office putting that has evolved as we've developed it,' he said earnestly, 'is that it's an extremely powerful tool for team building and for organizational harmony. In many ways if we talk about Outward Bounds as the team building apparatus of the nineties, I actually think potentially the concept of office putting is an interesting way of taking Outward Bounds into the new millennium.'

I thought Geoff was serious – mad, but serious – until I read the exact same thing in the press release handed out to journalists before the tournament started. Geoff was simply putting the Glenlivet spin on office putting, which was, after all, his job. But office putting was also surprisingly responsive to being spun.

The Glenlivet had invested around £100,000 in the Office Putting Championship. That figure included mentoring, trialling, tastings, self-starter kits, advertising, PR, and polo shirts and baseball caps with Geoff's 'Mixing Business With Pleasure' motto embroidered on them. The Glenlivet is one of the many brands owned by Seagram, the multinational corporation whose portfolio also includes Absolut vodka and Sandeman port, and the Oddbins chain of off-licences, as well as Universal Music and Universal Films.

The building in which the championship was taking place was huge, a fearlessly modern office complex that was home not just to the Glenlivet but also to all the other Seagram brands. It was a powerful statement of corporate intent. I stood on one of its flawlessly appointed balconies and marvelled at the ways in which the organizers were extracting maximum value out of minigolf. The main putting area, an irregular patch of green felt surrounded by a white picket fence, was at the centre of the proceedings.

Above it stood a large electronic screen on which the tournament action would be relayed and on which, currently, the Glenlivet's head distiller was discussing just what it was that made the Glenlivet so *smooth*. Down by the bar, a jazz band extemporized tastefully, while employees gave interviews to national newspapers and a Japanese TV crew collected footage for a news channel back home. The blue chips mingled and admired the building, whose atrium afforded superb views of all the departments representing Seagram's many and diverse interests. You had to admire the ingenuity of the event. It was a perfect physical manifestation of vertically integrated marketing; £100,000 well spent.[1]

Geoff believed it was happenstance that the offices doubled as the Seagram HQ. 'The fact is that it's the perfect forum for office putting,' he told me, straight-faced. 'It's coincidental that Seagram own it. Even if Seagram didn't own this building, it would be fantastic as a platform for running the event.'

Be that as it may, I put it to Geoff that utilizing minigolf was a particularly astute move on his part, given that golf was a game for blue chips and many of those taking part tonight probably played quite lot of golf themselves.

'Sure,' said Geoff, 'but also it sort of captures the innovation design thought, which I think is underpinning the idea of office putting, which is all about designing holes and getting people to use their imagination.'

I think Geoff was floundering.

Among the various film crews, I spotted a couple of the Sky Sports team who had come to Southend, including the producer who had ignored my request for the cameras to be turned off. 'Hello,' I said to her. 'You won't remember me.'

She didn't.

---

1. It was well spent at the time. A few weeks after the Glenlivet Office Putting Championship, Seagram was swallowed up in turn by Vivendi, another multinational, who announced they intended to sell off the drinks business, including the Glenlivet.

'You filmed a miniature golf tournament I took part in the other weekend,' I said. 'In Southend . . .'

'Oh, that!' said the producer, and raised her eyebrows. She was employed by the PGA European Tour, not Sky, and was planning to use the Glenlivet Office Putting Championship in the same way she had used the British Minigolf Masters on *European Tour Weekly* – as a bit of light-hearted filler between the serious items on proper golf. I sensed she felt all this frontline putting reportage was a bit beneath her. When I told her how much I liked minigolf as a sport in its own right, she laughed. 'God,' she said, rolling her eyes, 'you don't call it a real sport, do you?'

But look around you, I thought. It might be for one night only but look at this place. Look at how much money Glenlivet and Seagram have spent. Look at all the blue chips jostling for supremacy. They're all treating it like a real sport. This is a powerful tool. Geoff said so.

When is a sport not a sport? The more you think about this question, the harder it becomes to answer. You can have money and men in abundance and still struggle to get your sport treated properly. Synchronized swimming? Much too girly. Chess? Too brainy, attracts the wrong kind of men. Dog-fighting? No, too cruel (but see me in the car park later).

And then there's wrestling. Wrestling is arguably the biggest sport in the world today, the most powerful tool in the global sports box. The World Wrestling Federation is a billion-dollar business and has made superstars of its hyper-masculine fighters – The Rock, The Undertaker, Stone Cold Steve Austin – and of its chairman Vince McMahon who, as WWF *aficionados* will know, likes nothing more than to climb into the ring himself, stripped to the waist, and smash one of his employees over the head with a chair. From the boardroom to the mat, WWF has the worth and the girth.

But very few would consider wrestling of this sort to be a proper sport, not least the WWF themselves. It's much too enjoyable for that. Backstage, but always on camera, wrestlers swear dramatic vengeance on one another or conspire to overthrow the

McMahons. Scores are settled in the ring; championship titles are bestowed and taken away with bewildering speed. Linda McMahon, chief executive of the company and Vince's wife, describes the WWF as 'top-quality action-adventure soap opera'. If pushed, the organization will describe itself as providing 'sports entertainment' and with good reason. The WWF is better than sport.

The writer Simon Garfield, whose book *The Wrestling* definitively chronicles the somewhat gentler era of Big Daddy and Adrian Street, describes the WWF as 'sport to the power of ten'.

'The thing the WWF realized,' he told me, before Insurrextion, one of the year's two British WWF events, 'is that what you need are big stars. And they have to be big enough to transcend the sport. Other sports are belatedly catching on to this too – it's clearly the case in football. One star player will give you ten thousand extra season tickets. The difference is that sport needs stars like David Beckham or people who misbehave, like Alex Higgins, but also players like Steve Davis or Gary Neville, who just play. In wrestling they all misbehave and they are all stars.'

The supposed barrier to thinking of wrestling as a proper sport is, of course, the ancient complaint that wrestling is fixed, but since the WWF started to admit in the mid-1990s that, yes, we decide the results of the bouts in advance, wrestling's popularity has soared. Wrestling fans don't really care who wins as long as they get to see the stars knocking the crap out of one another in a suitably acrobatic, and entertaining, fashion. It's strangely inspiring to think that in the WWF it is genuinely not whether you win or lose but how you play the game that counts.

The only people who still seem bothered about this are a few disgruntled sorts who see the WWF's popularity as an insult to other, nobler pursuits – boxing, for example. Boxers are warriors, knights of the canvas, whereas wrestlers are little more than clowns, tumbling bozos in rubber pants. Boxing is rarely dismissed as trashy or pantomime, although in the words of that great panto favourite Frank Bruno, it is in reality 'just showbusiness with blood'. Boxing isn't fixed, not quite, but nor are the fights always fair: such was the money riding on Audley Harrison's professional career that if the promoters could have arranged for him to box a succession of one-armed kangaroos they would have done so.

Simon Garfield thinks the closest comparison to the WWF in terms of an organization is the World Snooker Association. 'That's a real sport but it's totally self-contained too. In a way, snooker would do a lot better if they developed great story lines. The characters are there. Jimmy White – the people's champion who's never really fulfilled his promise. Ronnie O'Sullivan – a brilliant player with this incredible Essex lifestyle and a dad who's serving a life sentence for murder. If they fixed the results, it would go through the roof.'

And even if Mick Foley – Mankind to his millions of fans – knows in advance whether he is to be the victor or the vanquished, he still has to step out into the arena and do it. And it still hurts. Anyone who doubts the utter physical commitment of wrestlers should watch Foley having his skull stitched back together while his wife and young children look on, in Barry Blaustein's documentary *Beyond the Mat*.

'The function of the wrestler is not to win: it is to go through the motions which are expected of him,' wrote Roland Barthes, fifty years ago in *Mythologies*. It's a pity Monsieur Barthes isn't around to enjoy the WWF. Tickets for Insurrextion sold out within half an hour of going on sale and it cost me nearly a hundred pounds to get in. But I got my money's worth.

Insurrextion had the best atmosphere of any event, sporting or not, that I attended in the course of writing this book. There was a sense of real anticipation in the crowd, seemingly every single one of whom had brought a large sign or placard they had made at home. Some of the messages painted on the signs were straightforward ('Stone Cold Sucks!'), some were the catch-phrases of favourite wrestlers ('Shut the Hell Up!') and some were downright bizarre ('I Smell Weasels'). My favourite was the completely incomprehensible 'I Love the Hardy Boys!' So did I – when I was ten. It wasn't until I read the programme that I realized the Hardy Boys was the (quite possibly satirical) name of a tag team duo who, to judge from their sneering mugshots, looked more likely to commit crimes than solve them.

The Hardy Boys placard belonged to a teenage girl in the row in front of me. She and her boyfriend had illuminated the slogans on their cards with pictures torn from a newspaper and the *TV Times*. As the Hardy Boys' bout approached, the girl grew increasingly excited until, when Jeff and Matt Hardy finally appeared in a shower of fireworks on the platform ahead of us, all she could do was scream and bury her head in her boyfriend's shoulder. The bout was a four-way tag team contest between Edge & Christian, the Hardy Boys, the Dudley Boys and X-Factor.

'Jeff! Do it! Do it now!' implored the girl, as the sides of ham started slamming into one another.

But after all the build-up, the main event was brief. The Hardy Boys, despite the rapturous reception they had received from the arena, were scheduled to be in and out of the ring in under five minutes, and so, after a few daredevil swoops, smashes and dives, Matt Hardy was quickly pinned by Christian and the Boys were dismissed. As soon as the Hardys withdrew, the girl and her boyfriend ran outside for a post-grapple cigarette.

'The public is completely uninterested in knowing whether the contest is rigged or not, and rightly so,' said Barthes, 'it abandons itself to the primary virtue of the spectacle.' At a WWF event, the public are encouraged to be part of the spectacle, a waving backdrop of signs – if you're really lucky, yours will be one of those shown on TV. The only disadvantage to this was that whenever a camera swung past our seating, all the placards shot up in the air, blocking my view of the action.

While the wrestling itself was impressive, what I could see of it, what I enjoyed most about Insurrextion was the sheer grandiloquent scale of the thing. It was like a rollicking send-up of proper sport. From the bombast of the show to the larger-than-life heartlessness of the wrestlers to Vince McMahon's inevitable appearance in the final bout (where, for a change, someone smashed him over the head with a chair), everything was exaggerated to the point of ludicrousness. And yet there was a sort of perverse integrity to it. The WWF was upfront in its intentions: to entertain the paying customer and to make money for the McMahons.

(For the record, Insurrextion also featured the most mixed crowd I saw in nearly two years of being a spectator. All ages were present; there were lots of couples and families; every ethnic group seemed to be represented in large numbers; and there was an even split between men and women, cheerfully yelling and gesticulating and demanding awful and gory retribution. It was nearly poignant.)

In early 2001, the WWF and NBC joined forces to create the XFL – the Extreme Football League. NBC hoped McMahon's populist savvy would attract young male viewers, the ones advertisers love, and give the network huge Saturday-night ratings. NFL rules were relaxed to allow for more 'action'. Footballers were given nicknames like Deathblow and miked up so that every crunching tackle could be heard on air. Trailers showed towel-wearing cheerleaders lounging around a steamy locker room. Stars of the WWF like The Rock and The Undertaker made guest appearances to pour characteristic scorn not on one another or on Vince McMahon, but on the NFL, whose restrictions on tackling quarterbacks McMahon dismissed as 'pantywaist rules'. You could be forgiven for thinking they might fix the results.

The XFL was an unconditional disaster. After a successful start in February – sixteen million viewers for the inaugural game between the Las Vegas Outlaws and the New York/New Jersey Hitmen – ratings swiftly plummeted to little more than two million. By the end of March, XFL was reckoned to be the lowest-rated prime-time show ever broadcast on a major US network. Sponsors fled. 'If they had pitched it closer to football, they would have lost the wrestling audience,' former CBS Sports president Neal Pilson was quoted as saying. 'If they had made a burlesque out of football to conform to the expectations of the wrestling audience, they probably would have lost NBC, which as I understand it wanted to play quality football.' NBC pulled out anyway and in May the WWF shut down the XFL after just one season.

The reasons for the XFL's collapse would seem to be straight-forward. By all accounts, the football was poor. More import-antly, it seems that people want the sports they consider 'real' to be handled 'realistically'; your sport must have the appearance of authenticity, a bit of sports-think that led one commentator to make the unintentionally droll observation that 'The XFL's dis-mal failure is evidence that a distinction still exists between sport and entertainment.' Amen to that.

Will the McMahons care? Not much. The WWF lost about fifty million dollars on the XFL. That represents just under half their revenue from WWF-branded merchandise alone from the previous financial year. It's a blip. With typical chutzpah, they have licensed a posthumous XFL T-shirt. It poses a simple, if ungrammatical, question: *'If it was shaped like a football, and it smelled like a football, and grown men in tight pants chased it around a football field while fans drank beer and cheerleaders danced?'*

And then, beneath a red XFL football, the answer: *'It Must Have Been Real Football!'*

Back at the Glenlivet Office Putting Championship, a one-night-only bout where men were men and minigolf was rich, I was not enjoying myself. I didn't like minigolf being 'pimped' like this. It felt wrong.

Of course, I was also playing badly again, which didn't help. After a couple of misjudgements, I stopped trying, gave up, just as I had in Southend. I glowered at my playing partners, Mike, an account manager for a frozen-food company, and a barrister called Tim. I resented being so effortlessly outclassed by begin-ners. This was supposed to be my sport.

And there was something wearily familiar about all this jocking about in the office. It reminded me of the period when Fantasy Football first impinged upon British cultural life. I was working in a bookshop at the time. It used to be the case that the written word existed as a refuge from sport. Not any more. Every morn-ing, lunchtime and afternoon, the staff-room reverberated with pretend tactical discussions, team selection, all the useless know-how of the pub, the pitch and the playground. Oh, do be quiet, I used to think. I came in here – this room, this building, this job – to get away from you lot.

But there was no escape, ever.

I consoled myself with the thought that money raised from the Office Putting Championship was being donated to charity. In the run-up to the tournament, the Glenlivet had collected £12,000 for the Great Ormond Street Children's Hospital.

'We got a lot of response from the companies on that,' Geoff told me matter-of-factly. 'We asked for a donation of twenty pounds. Companies clearly stated that the value that they got from the event was significantly higher. Therefore the opportunity to raise more money for charity next year is greater. So next year we'll put an even greater degree of charity focus on the event.'

Geoff was honest about the value of this activity to his own company: 'It's not just about an event, it's about how you can spin an event. It's like any sponsorship. It's as much about how you use it as the event itself.'

At least someone was feeling the benefit. I let my irritation get the better of me, eliminating myself in the first round by hitting the ball with such ill-tempered force that it nearly shattered a bottle of whisky. Demonstrating the *sang-froid* required by his day job, Tim the barrister coolly aced the hole and went through instead.

'Well done,' I said, relieved it was over.

As the rounds proceeded, and more and more contenders fell by the wayside, so a crowd began to grow for the grand final, and the mood grew more boisterous. People clustered behind the white picket fence, looking up at the big screen, cheering on the survivors. In contrast to their earlier abstemiousness, many blue chips were now sampling the complimentary booze as speedily as they could.

Geoff was acting as master of ceremonies for the grand final, and his commentary was being relayed through the public-address system. He did not shirk his duty and mentioned the Glenlivet every thirty seconds.

'I think we'd all agree that, thanks to the Glenlivet, this has been a terrific evening,' said Geoff. He congratulated the two finalists and turned to look for his assistant. 'We need to toss a coin to see which one of you goes first. Where's the guy with the coin? Where's the official tosser?'

'He's holding the microphone,' said someone behind me, to loud guffaws.

The dazed and delighted champion turned out to be Lee, a computer programmer from Crewe. Lee won a holiday for two to Chicago and a 1972 reserve bottle of the Glenlivet, with which he was photographed extensively.

'Does it get any better than this?' Geoff asked him.

'I'm just speechless,' replied Lee.

'Great,' said Geoff.

Some weeks later, I asked Geoff if he felt the evening had been a success. 'Absolutely,' he said. 'I think you can only measure success on feedback, and people have told us they genuinely enjoyed it. Fun is quite a consistent word. It's a bit of a cliché but the evening really wasn't about winning, it was about participation.'

Geoff clearly hadn't been talking to the same people I had. At the end of the night I'd bumped into Ann-Louise the events manager again. Earlier in the evening she had seemed to be enjoying herself but now she looked upset about something. 'What's the matter?' I asked. 'Disappointing second round?'

But Ann-Louise hadn't made it to the second round. When the start of the competition was announced, she had gone to the wrong floor. By the time she realized her mistake, had run downstairs and found her group, they had started playing the first round without her. 'Two of them were from some bank or other,' said Ann-Louise. 'They were mates, you could tell.'

Ann-Louise had asked if they would mind waiting while she played the first hole and then they could all carry on together. The two boys from the bank refused and informed Ann-Louise that they had disqualified her. She was late. They couldn't let her play. 'You would have lost anyway,' said one.

'But you can score if you want,' said the other.

'They were bastards,' said Ann-Louise. She sounded furious.

There was something inevitable about Ann-Louise's run-in with these bankers. It was dismal proof that once you turned minigolf over to proper sport, it was as susceptible as any other game to the big boys' affluence and arrogance.

Things changed in the nineties, but not as much as you might have been led to believe. For all the inroads women have made into sport in the last ten years, especially football, many men still resent their presence, or refuse to take it seriously. 'When middle-class people and women started going to matches, I thought it's a shame that hooliganism has stopped,' said Frank Skinner, in a recent interview, 'because that used to keep them out.' A lot of men would prefer to keep sport for themselves.

But money changes everything. The bigger the sports industry grows, the more it's going to need the indulgence, and income, of women. And as digital and satellite channels multiply, there will be more and more airtime to be filled, so more and more sports will have to be presented seriously, whatever the participants' allocation of chromosomes and however miniature their choice of sport.

For better or worse, we may find that the question of what constitutes a 'real' sport becomes easier to answer than ever before:

Q: When is a sport not a sport?
A: Never.

9

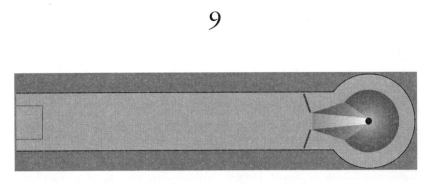

Vulkan – volcano

In his landmark study of the Beatles and their records, *Revolution in the Head*, Ian MacDonald describes the effect of repeated heavy doses of LSD on an increasingly psychedelicized John Lennon: 'Gradually fatigue and sensory overload conspired with [Timothy] Leary's prescription for voluntary ego-death to dissolve his sense of self.' This is what sport was doing to me. I was dissolving.

Far from building my character, sport was breaking it into little pieces. An intensive diet of minigolf, bolstered with shots of whatever other sports I could lay my trembling hands on, was wearing me down. 'Luckily,' continues MacDonald about Lennon, 'his constitution was robust enough to avert physical collapse, while the scepticism that balanced his questing gullibility warded off a permanent eclipse of his reason.' I dared make no such assumptions for myself.

The strain began to manifest itself in uncharacteristic bouts of temper. Impatience bubbled into resentment. Two incidents in particular alerted me to my pressing need for professional help. The second was, shamefully, ignominiously, on a crazy-golf course. But the first was at the Lawn Tennis Championships at Wimbledon.

I had been to Wimbledon once before, as a young teenager. I

had gone with a friend called Matthew King. I could remember hardly anything about the day, apart from the fact that, in the car on the way home, Matthew King's dad had got very angry with us for being unable to give him a full run-down of what we had done and all the famous tennis players we had seen. 'I don't know why I bother!' he kept shouting, as he drove us home. He seemed irritated beyond all common sense.

But standing in the queue at half past seven in the morning, having already queued for nearly two hours, and unaware that much of the rest of the day would be spent in other queues – queues for food, queues for the toilets, queues for return tickets – I began to wonder whether there was something about Wimbledon that drove otherwise reasonable men to distraction. I wanted to kill someone.

There is something very British about Wimbledon: you queue for ages to get something expensive, which, when you get it, is not quite the thing you wanted in the first place. Like the Boat Race, the sport comes a poor second to the event. Who do you know who follows tennis throughout the rest of the year?

An afternoon at the All-England Club is like spending an afternoon in a shopping precinct in Guildford, with the option, if you can be bothered, of watching some tennis. It really is like a Guildford shopping centre too; pedestrianized in red-brick, with fast-food concessions and fashion boutiques. The Boat Race is – supposedly – upper class. Likewise, football is – supposedly – working class. But Wimbledon, with its bargain-hunting Hen-maniacs, the armed forces acting as stewards and its self-sustaining, never-ending queues is – triumphantly – middle class. It was pleasant at first. But gradually it became a killing field.

I got up at half past four for my day at Wimbledon. It was the summer of Anna Kournikova. She could be seen all over London, on billboards advertising sports bras ('only the balls should bounce') and in the pages of newspapers, tabloid, broadsheet or sports supplement, all extensively illustrated with action/glamour shots of the blonde beauty. 'Why Anna Kournikova is bad for women's tennis' ran one particularly shameless example, next to a picture of the athlete at her most winsome and nymphet-like.[1] Many carried stories of the supposed lengths to which her young male fans would go in order to ogle her. Anna would be appearing at Wimbledon today. And, you had to keep reminding yourself, she would probably be playing some tennis.

The platform at Southfields tube station had been made to look like a tennis court, with a big IBM-sponsored screen showing highlights of old matches, tall IBM Perspex pillars full of tumbling tennis balls, and a green felt surface, which would be just right for playing minigolf. It was just before six a.m. I followed the crowds down the road and into a field. 'Merton Council welcomes you to Wimbledon Park.' I felt bleary but optimistic. Five hours later I fell through the gates of the All-England Club in a barely suppressed rage, and considered calling it quits on the spot.

The crowd was as cosmopolitan a mix of jovial sorts as you could wish to find anywhere – half-wits of all ages, creeds and colours. Behind me was a bright and cheerful family, all save the dad, whose name was Steve. He walked with a limp and looked shattered. His wife was wearing a curly comedy wig, bearing the cross of St George. She kept up a constant stream of chatter, based on the newspaper she was reading – 'Henman: I Am Heading For Glory' (accompanied by picture of Henman heading a tennis ball); '£750,000 House Not Good Enough For Anna'; 'Are the powerful Williams sisters forcing the more tactical players like Martina Hingis out of the game?' – which she punctuated with requests for items from their car, a sandwich or a jumper. And off Steve would hobble, gratefully.

People ahead of us had camped out overnight. As the queue inched forward, we passed the remains of their temporary settlements: abandoned tents, smouldering fires. Someone had even built a proper barbecue out of bricks, with a grill on top.

1. The article, by Jon Henderson, is a thoughtful piece on the tendency in coverage of women's sports to favour beauty over excellence. But, as one correspondent subsequently noted, the magazine 'put the beauty on the cover, not the excellence'.

At about six thirty, a man appeared selling copies of the *Daily Express*. If you bought one you got a free England T-shirt. The bewigged mum bought two, a T-shirt for each child, although neither seemed to want them. She kindly gave me their spare copy of the paper. In it was an interview with Boris Becker, mostly concerned with Anna Kournikova: 'Anna is good news for tennis. We need more Anna Kournikovas and André Agassis on the tour.'

I was beginning to understand that my chances of seeing either of these players were growing increasingly remote. I now knew Agassi wasn't even playing today. Kournikova was due on Centre Court at about three o'clock this afternoon. But any Centre Court tickets would be long gone by the time I reached the turnstiles. Never mind, I thought, last time I came here, we queued for a standing place and saw – funny, I could now remember at twenty years' distance what had eluded me and Matthew King just hours later – Chris Evert. I just have to do the same today. Once I'm inside, I'll get out of this queue and join the one for standing places.

By now, we had crawled out of Wimbledon Park and on to the road leading to the All-England Club gates. We were passed by five or six butlers, carrying silver platters, distributing cards advertising an Internet search engine. Across the road, local residents had rented their driveways to stallholders selling unofficial Wimbledon souvenirs: sweatshirts, tote bags and teddy bears. But no one was buying. There was no need. There was so much free stuff.

By eight-thirty, I had accumulated two T-shirts, a pair of binoculars, a fistful of the butlers' cards, a plastic bowler hat bearing the cross of St George and the logos of the *Sun* and the *News of the World*, a fan to cool off with, sponsored by Perrier and pressed into my hand by a girl in a green Perrier jacket and green Perrier baseball cap, two boxes of Mr Kipling's Strawberry Sundaes, and a sticker bearing the legend 'I've queued at Wimbledon!' – a gift from the Wimbledon Lawn Tennis Association.

It was perhaps too early in the morning for Mr Kipling's Strawberry Sundaes. I kept seeing them lying in the gutter or shoved into bushes next to the road. A steel band drifted by on the back of a float, surrounded by miniature palm trees, sponsored by another Internet start-up company. In fact, many of the free gifts and costumed characters were sponsored by Internet start-up companies. In addition to the butlers and the steel band, there were also Eurobet.co.uk glamour girls in matching outfits and out-of-work actors dressed as bananas or dogs. The slowdown in the global electronic economy would clearly affect not only the prospects of many of these companies but also the opportunities for gaining Equity cards.

The poor sod in the dog suit did his best to amuse the queue, waving and pointing like Jude the Stadium Cat, and pretending to cock his leg over somebody who had fallen asleep in their deckchair, which raised a laugh from almost no one except my neighbour, who had now wrapped herself in an England flag. When the dog reached us, she jumped up to give him a hug. Her family ignored her. Steve was doing the crossword and the two kids were attempting to grind Strawberry Sundaes into one another's hair.

At eleven forty-five, tired, hungry and on the brink of homicide, I finally gained admittance. There were no tickets for Centre Court, No. 1 Court or No. 2 Court. The daily allocation had already disappeared. The rest had been distributed months earlier to county associations and overseas lawn-tennis associations, and to the public in a postal ballot six months ago. The only ticket I could get was a Peasant's Rover, a ground-only pass that entitled the bearer to go anywhere and watch whichever matches they pleased, as long as they could get in and didn't mind standing in dung.

I queued for a sandwich, then made my way to Centre Court, to join another queue for standing places.

But there was a problem. Although I could see terraced standing areas around some of the outer courts, I couldn't locate the entrance to the standing area of Centre Court. After a fruitless couple of circumnavigations, I stopped to ask a soldier where the standing area was.

'Standing area?' said the squaddie. 'I don't think there is one.' He called over a superior officer. 'Is there a standing area at Centre Court?'

'Not at Centre Court, no. There's limited standing space on some courts, but not here.'

'But there used to be, didn't there?' I said, an edge of frustration creeping into my voice. 'I need to get into Centre Court.'

'Well, years ago there was standing room,' said the older soldier, while the younger assessed my admittedly limited potential for troublemaking, 'but that disappeared about ten years ago.'

In the wake of Hillsborough, the Taylor Report had called for the removal of all terracing in all stadia, not just football grounds. And that included Wimbledon. You had to be seated to watch the tennis, and to be seated you had to have a ticket. And I didn't.

'But I have to get in,' I whined. 'I got up at half past four. I've been queuing for *six* hours.' The two soldiers, who clearly thought they had a prime example of one of the Anna Kournikova saddos they had read about in the papers, just shrugged.

'You might be able to pick up a used ticket from the booth,' said the senior serviceman, 'but people don't tend to hand in their tickets till they leave for the day.' There were red boxes dotted about, in which holders of tickets for reserved seats – if they felt like it – could place their tickets, and from where they were collected and resold from a kiosk for another five pounds.

'Well, where do I go?' I asked desperately.

The younger soldier walked me over to one side, or possibly escorted me away from the entrance. 'You see that queue?' he said, pointing to the top of a hill that overlooked the main courts. 'You want to get up there now if you're going to get in this afternoon.'

In a state of mind somewhere between unthinking acquiescence and turbulent, corrosive rage, I climbed the hill and joined the straggly line to wait for a ticket, where I was reunited, just minutes later, with Steve, his wife and their two children.

'Ooh, hello again!' said the woman, when she saw me. 'Would

you like one of these strawberry things? We can't eat any more.'

I began to pray, fervently, for rain.

There were approximately – no, exactly – twenty-five people in front of me in the line. Not everyone was waiting for Centre Court seats: Steve's wife patriotically wanted to see Greg Rusedski on No. 1 Court, even though he was neither very British nor very good. Nevertheless, it was going to be a long wait.

During the first hour, the queue did not move at all. No tickets were returned. Pete Sampras was playing on Centre Court. Surely a handful of people would leave after seeing the reigning champion? And surely they'd be the kind of people conscientious enough to surrender their unwanted tickets?

Although there was a huge screen showing the BBC's coverage of the day's play to all those on the hill, I couldn't be bothered to watch. I was too tired. I lay on my back in the sun and drifted in and out of sleep. I missed Richard Krajicek's four-set thriller against the German Michael Kohlmann. I missed Serena Williams' easy dismissal of Asa Carlsson, and Venus Williams' even easier victory over Kvetoslava Hrdlickova. I raised my head occasionally to see if the Sampras game had finished. On screen, Centre Court appeared to be far from full; not everyone, it seemed, was considerate enough to deposit their tickets in the red boxes.

Gradually, tickets started appearing in ones and twos at the kiosk, as corporate guests began to float off after lunch. By the time I finally got hold of my Centre Court pass, some three and a half hours later, I'd almost forgotten what I was queuing for. Then I remembered. Oh, God, I thought, as I plodded down the slope, now I'm going to have to watch some tennis.

And yet, when I finally took my place in the historic surroundings of the All-England Lawn Tennis and Croquet Club Centre Court, a warm and beatific calm swept over me. I felt light and absurdly happy. At first, I thought the fatigue and attrition of the day had acted like brainwashing and that, if the umpire suggested it, I would obediently marry whoever was sitting next to me. However, I quickly realized that the happiness I felt was genuine, and was the result of my surroundings. It really was rather civilized. By British sporting standards, it was a symposium.

Anna Kournikova, seeded fiftieth, was playing the French number ten seed Sandrine Testud. The first thing you noticed about Miss Kournikova was not that she was strikingly attractive – she wasn't – but that she was very good at tennis. In 1999, she had finished as the top-ranked doubles player in the world. That this should be a surprise was, I suppose, partly the fault of Anna Kournikova herself, or at least her career advisers, but also the result of coverage that resisted the idea that beauty and excellence could co-exist. It was a simpler story to highlight one or the other, for or against. Looking around, I could see a few sweaty-palmed boys, but I could also see a few sweaty-palmed old journalists, scratching furtively in notebooks, probably writing stories about Anna (19) and her travelling army of spotty and besotted admirers. But the crowd gave them nothing to work with. No one wolf-whistled. No Anna acolytes, crazy with frustrated desire, tried to distract Miss Testud from her game. Good play was applauded generously, regardless of player. No one, to my knowledge, had a wank.

Additionally, the sense that Centre Court at Wimbledon was as special a place as everybody said it was was heightened by the near absence of sponsorship or advertising. There were no billboards to catch the eye. It was wonderful. It preserved the venue's history, allowing you to draw a line from the present to the past. If Fred Perry had been able to perform his feats of heroism without the assistance of, say, Dew Valley, the Cooked Bacon, why shouldn't Tim Henman (aside from the obvious)? The focus of the match was the match, and within this unique space, nothing except the minor presence of Robinson's Barley Water and Slazenger tennis balls could distract from that. For the first time that day, something had gone right. I settled down to watch – and even enjoy – the match.

But, carelessly, I had forgotten my earlier prayer.

After two games, the heavens opened. Fat, providential drops of water spattered the empty seats around me. The match was suspended. Miss Kournikova and Miss Testud returned to the changing room, and the grass was swiftly covered with the historic Centre Court tarpaulin. The drizzle became a downpour. I turned my back on the All-England Club and tramped through the gathering gloom back to Southfields station, my fragile sporting life crumbling and decomposing like a Strawberry Sundae in the rain.

There was no eruption today. But it was coming.

Back on the tour, things went from bad to worse. In all my recent matches, I had folded. I had done it in Southend. I had done it at the Glenlivet Office Putting Championship. But now I started to do it in practice too, ever more quickly and with ever more bitterness. A few bad shots and I blew up. It wasn't just that I wasn't improving. I couldn't understand why sport – even the sport of my choice, so obscure and with so little competition, into which I was sinking so much time and commitment – was steadfastly refusing to yield *anything* in return. And Denmark was creeping ever nearer.

In Liverpool for a wedding, we drove through the Mersey Tunnel to New Brighton. New Brighton is what the seaside would look like after a nuclear war. There is no beach: it was long since washed away by changes in the tidal flow of the Mersey. The resort's amusements are clustered together in giant concrete bunkers, painted council mint green. The day I was there, early in the summer holidays, it was almost completely abandoned, and battered by wind and sleet.

Britain's Worst Crazy Golf Course[2] is located just back from the seafront, with a row of houses running behind, and a brick colonnade carrying a blizzard of graffiti: 'If you want a shag call this number', 'Jenny N. sucks her dads dick' and, mystifyingly, 'Barney was here, 20%'. The only thing Crazy about New Brighton's Crazy Golf Course were the concrete paving slabs it was made from, and which rendered it effectively unplayable. The

2. Status confirmed by several experts in the field.

eleventh hole, for instance, consists of two dozen cracked, uneven slabs and demands you send your ball round a corner, over a humpback bridge with no edges, through an obstacle (the grate from a fire, turned upside down and painted red) and into a cup with half a broken beer bottle in it. The beer bottle was not affixed, and might have been removed since my visit.

Not so long ago, I would have found Britain's Worst Crazy Golf Course funny, or sad, or appreciated it as a metaphor for this area's decline into poverty, a gritty if kitschy modern tableau. But now it irritated me. It was a waste of time. I didn't even bother to play it.

The dam finally burst on the Isle of Wight. A trip to the island in the company of Paul and Mike turned sour when I had a huge temper tantrum over a missed putt. By the Esplanade Gardens in Shanklin, I threw down my club and stormed off the course. It was shameful behaviour and even writing about it makes me cringe.

The plan had been to play every course on the island, in a clockwise direction, for money, with numerous side bets to liven things up – a separate match-play wager between me and Mike, a tenner to the winner of each eighteenth hole and so on. Things started well, but after a few courses our initial high spirits had dissipated. Puckpool Park in Rye, an adventure course on Sandown Pier, the Needles Pleasure Park at Alum Bay, we played them all, each more grudgingly than the last. At Alum Bay, with its Isle of Wight-themed obstacles (thatched cottages, car ferry, castle), its invigorating breeze off the Solent and its impressive view of the Needles, all I could do was complain about the leaves and bits of bark that speckled the playing surface and express disbelief that its originators should have been so thoughtless as to build it under trees. The mood began to darken.

It was my fault. I could no longer play crazy golf for fun. The introduction of money only made things worse. I needed to be a better player this weekend, not to put one over on old friends but to feel I was improving. But because most of the courses we played were concrete, the three of us kept cancelling each other out. No significant bundles of cash changed hands. Skill didn't come into it, and without skill I couldn't see the point. Betting just seemed to emphasize my insecurity over not only my own ability but also the credibility of the game itself.

After losing the fifth match of the day to Mike with a fluffed two-footer at the last, I wanted to quit. But neither he nor Paul would hear of it. They were enjoying themselves. I should have been pleased. The weekend was a success. But I was tired and hungry and I couldn't face another arbitrary eighteen holes.

On the twelfth, I suggested we stop playing and go to the pub instead.

'OK,' said Paul. 'Let's just finish up these few holes and then we're done.'

I bit my lip.

I really didn't want to do this any more. Really.

'Just six more holes and that's it,' said Mike reasonably, reasonable to anyone listening in a reasonable state of mind. But my reason had nearly gone.

I lined up my putt at the thirteenth with the last dregs of my concentration. Just grind it out, I thought, and then it'll be over.

Instead of following the path along which I had hit it, however, the ball bounced away to the left, and became wedged between the obstacle and the wall.

But it wasn't the putt that tipped me over the edge.

'OK,' said Paul, ever the teacher, 'try that again but this time give it a bit more pace.'

That really was it. Whose game was this anyway?

'Fuck it!' I yelled. *'I've had it!'*

And I had. I threw down my putter. *'This isn't going to help me for Europe!'* I shouted, insanely, and stalked off to sit on a wall, looking out to sea and feeling very, very stupid. Paul and Mike ignored me and finished their game. I think they thought I was just a bad loser. But I didn't envy them their victory. I envied them their fun.

*

One week later, a few days before I was due to fly to Denmark, I stood nervously on the doorstep of a terraced house in a quiet street in Henley-on-Thames. I'd made an appointment to see Dr Kirsten Barnes, the sports psychologist who had worked so successfully with the Oxford Boat Race crew earlier in the year. It wasn't just that I hoped she would be able to improve my game and stop me imploding under pressure: I was looking to her for The Answer. I rang the bell.

The door was opened by an attractive woman in her early thirties, with dark bobbed hair and, I couldn't help noticing, very broad shoulders. Kirsten Barnes had won two gold medals in rowing for Canada at the 1992 Olympics in Barcelona and still rowed for pleasure now. Her husband Terry had rowed for Great Britain for nearly ten years.

We went through to the living room, and I expressed surprise at the lack of rowing paraphernalia in the house.

'We do find other things to talk about,' said Kirsten Barnes. 'Tea or coffee?'

Dr Barnes's manner was friendly and supportive. The first great thing she did was to take me seriously. As we sat in her living room and I confessed that the sport I required help with was miniature golf, she didn't even blink. Did she think miniature golf qualified as a sport?

'Yeah.' She looked at me as if to say, Why wouldn't it? 'It's skill and it's ability, and it's movement and thinking. There's a start and finish. I'm not going to get into a philosophical debate on how you define sport.' She laughed. 'Whether it should be an Olympic sport might be a different question.'

In the kitchen, I could see the front page of *The Times* from the morning of the Boat Race framed and hanging on the wall. There was Kirsten's photograph. 'We thought it was very amusing,' she said. In fact, she was modest about her achievement with the Oxford crew. 'The result of the Boat Race was a result, but the thing is, it wasn't *my* result, it was the rowers' result. I've been on those starting lines. I've had coaches and support staff. I couldn't have done it without them – especially my coach – but at the end of the day it was down to me. And we could have gone through all the mental preparation, but if the crew didn't believe they could do it, they still wouldn't have done it.'

There were certain common ailments Dr Barnes dealt with, whatever the sport. She had worked with international squash players and the England women's rugby team, an ex-Cart driver who was now driving mini Formula One cars in France, and a young three-day eventer, and the things that united them were the different demands of competition and training.

'In the training environment, the big thing is motivation,' said Dr Barnes, cupping her hands round a mug of tea. 'You're doing the same thing day in day out, and it can be boring. But in the competition environment, you only get one chance to do it. You've only got one chance to walk on to that court or on to that pitch, or stand and putt that one ball. So, I help people handle pressure in the competition environment – turning nervous energy into positive useful energy, being excited rather than scared or worried – but I also try to work on training, dealing with the boredom and fatigue of a routine.'

In fact, Dr Barnes preferred to think of herself as a performance consultant rather than a sports psychologist. 'I like to be athlete-driven. I'll very rarely, if ever, come in with an agenda of what I think they should be doing. But if people are coming in learning stuff, I'll be a bit worried. The learning should be done, you should be just fine-tuning and tweaking things. I support the final preparations.'

Ah. I decided, under the circumstances, that it would be better not to tell Dr Barnes the whole truth *vis-à-vis* my level of skill. After all, I wasn't so much fine-tuning my minigolf game as trying to turn the key in the ignition and get the damn thing started. Instead, we discussed certain techniques I could use to combat the specific problems I had with concentration, and with giving up.

Kirsten Barnes listened carefully, asked me a few questions about environment, technique and so on and jotted down a few notes. First, she suggested I set myself goals that were achievable, rather than aim for outright victory or bust. I nodded. That seemed straightforward enough. Next, she thought I should give some consideration to planning not only the day of the tournament but also the period running up to it. 'If you're really prepared, you can just concentrate on the competition itself. Give yourself an extra half an hour to get to the venue or the course or whatever, so you don't get stuck in traffic and get stressed. With the three-day eventer, we've looked a lot at planning for the day, because it's so jam-packed. And that's with a horse too. If you're nervous, the horse is going to get nervous, so then it becomes a two, um, person situation.

'And keep a diary. Write down after an event what you did that whole day. What's overlooked so often is that attention to detail. When people have a good day, often they don't make time to debrief and evaluate afterwards, so when they do it again a month later, they can't remember *why* it was such a good day. It doesn't have to be beautifully written, you just have to create a log of information. Then you can set yourself some targets and measure them.'

Finally, we discussed how to combat nerves on the course during the tournament itself.

'You need to work on a pre-putt routine,' said Kirsten Barnes, 'something that allows you to focus on each putt separately. Take your time. Take a deep breath. Shake your arms. Look up at the treetops. Anything that gets you into the right frame of mind to compete. That should help with the nerves, and it should also help you deal with this problem of expecting to play badly. Don't allow yourself to get into that frame of mind. If you play a bad shot, don't dwell on it. Leave it behind. And likewise a good shot, actually. Stay focused.'

I wrote it all down in my notebook: the goal setting, the diary, the – dynamic words! – pre-putt routine. In retrospect, I realized that these tips were the sports-psych equivalent of 'Take two aspirin and see me in the morning', but at the time they seemed less like aspirin and more like tablets of stone, handed down.

But what was most inspiring was Kirsten Barnes's attitude.

Her background was in sports rather than psychology. From the age of fifteen, she had been preparing for gold. After the 1992 Olympics, she had entered a period of de-training and decided that, whatever she did with the rest of her life, she wanted to stay close to sports people. 'I can't reproduce the success of winning an Olympic gold medal but, I tell you, I was in tears when I watched a squash player win a world championship title back in the autumn. I was so happy for her. The emotion and the passion that I get as an athlete I try to take into my work.'

That she was prepared to think of my chosen sport – to think of me – in this way was infectious. For the first time in my life, somebody was treating me like a sportsman. It was liberating to discuss minigolf so seriously. I knew how difficult the game was, and here was someone who believed me. Someone who had won gold medals. I asked her if she kept them in the house.

'Yeah,' said Kirsten Barnes, smiling. 'You wanna see one?' Nearly ten years on, and the thrill had not yet worn off.

I had never examined an Olympic medal up close. It was attached to a long multi-coloured ribbon, with the year inscribed on one side and on the other an athlete being carried on the shoulders of a jubilant crowd. It was heavy and very golden, surprising in both cases since, of course, there isn't much gold in an Olympic gold medal. None the less, it was an object that, whatever it was made of, rebuffed scepticism.

'What was it like to win this?' I said, awestruck.

'It was a relief,' said Kirsten Barnes.

Our time was up. In a few days, Kirsten was flying out to the Gold Coast to the Team GB holding camp, where she was one of two sports psychologists helping British Olympic athletes acclimatize to Sydney-like conditions. 'I'm kind of on call,' she said.

I thanked her profusely for her help.

'That's OK,' she said. 'Good luck. Let me know how you get on. Remember, realistic goals.'

I understood.

'Stay there and I'll print you out some training goals and match-evaluation sheets you can take with you to Denmark.'

I waited until Kirsten Barnes was upstairs, and then I took the gold medal out of its box and hung it carefully around my neck, jubilant crowd side out. Realistic goals. I closed my eyes and tried to imagine, for just about the first time ever, what it might feel like, realistically, to be a winner.

IO

Brücke – bridge

There's something intangible that makes contests between great teams or gifted individuals not just beautiful to watch but profoundly meaningful, even though in the overall scheme of things they are demonstrably meaningless.

WOODY ALLEN

Day One – Tuesday

In Denmark. I am keeping a diary as per Kirsten Barnes's instructions. 🎐

(🎐 Although this chapter is based on the diary I kept in Denmark, by necessity I have omitted much of the technical material and some of the more distressing swearing. I have also tidied up the text – corrected minor errors of punctuation, reinstated personal pronouns, incorporated insights and observations that did not occur to me until many months later, etc., etc.)

I nearly missed the flight this morning due to an argument with the check-in clerk over my putter. Passengers were not permitted to carry blunt instruments on to the plane. I wanted to keep it with me but she insisted on stowing it in the hold. I spent the flight fretting that sub-zero temperatures would crack the shaft,

179

leaving me putterless before my first big international tournament.

Tearful reunion with putter on the Tarmac at Copenhagen, apparently unharmed. Perhaps deep-freezing will have had beneficial effects . . . ?

I connected to Odense on the train. There are lots of windmills in Denmark, of the turbine variety. According to a report in the paper, Danish firms control over half of the global market in turbine windmills, worth in excess of £2.5 billion, and there are now more people employed in the Danish wind-energy industry than in the British coal industry. The trains run on time too. We arrived in Odense exactly when we were supposed to.

I'm staying in a recently refurbished hostel next to the station – up some steps, through a shopping centre, down some more steps, past a McDonald's, along a stretch of noticeably clean pavement, round a corner and home. My room has a shower, four bunks and is even cleaner than the pavement outside, breathtakingly clean. You could eat your crispbread off any one of its gleaming surfaces. The hostel has a breakfast bar, a washroom, a games room with TV and Internet and e-mail access. It costs the equivalent of just under twenty pounds per night. It is, and this is a point worth repeating, very, very clean.

Odense is Denmark's third largest city. Its name translates literally as 'Odin's shrine' but I've seen little evidence of wisdom and war. The whole place is a shrine to considered urban planning, with plentiful cycle paths and designated pedestrian thoroughfares. It is overwhelmingly pleasant and hygienic, and certainly uncontaminated by people. When I went into town for supper, there was hardly anyone around save the odd cyclist and, in one of the smart precincts, a few drunks and punks. But even they looked wholesome and fresh.

Passed a sports shop. In the window were last season's Manchester United strip at half price and Peter Schmeichel's autobiography in the original Danish, or translated into Danish (I wonder which). But crossing the road, I noticed a familiar logo. The traffic lights were made by Ericsson. Come on, you Rs! Come on, you traffic light!

I had a beer in Froggy's Bar and wandered back to the hostel, across a park with some modern art in it – a collection of metallic discs that talked to you. Unusually for Denmark, they only spoke Danish so the impact of the piece was lost on me. I tried to call the tournament organizer, Steen Handberg, from the hostel payphone, but his mobile was switched off. Retired to my spotless cell to write this and prepare for minigolf tomorrow. It's half past ten and still light outside. Focus. Focus.

Day Two – Wednesday

I woke up at four o'clock this morning with light blazing through the curtains and no indication that the sun had actually set. This is Denmark, not Iceland – what's going on? I was in the middle of a dream about the Williams sisters. They had switched from tennis to minigolf and were dominating the game with their power putting. In my dream, I couldn't understand how this could possibly work. 'Minigolf is about finesse, not brute strength,' I said to the annoying woman in the comedy Cross of St George wig. 'I know,' she replied. 'Think how Martina Hingis feels. Those girls drove her out of tennis and now they're driving her out of minigolf!'

I couldn't get back to sleep so got up, had a shower, and reread the notes that Kirsten Barnes had given me.

At eight o'clock, already feeling jaded, I went down to breakfast. I tried calling Steen again, but without success. I still wasn't sure of the location of the minigolf course and couldn't find it on any map. I asked the receptionist but she had no idea. Hmmm. The possibility of an elaborate hoax presented itself, an obscure prank by Peter. Perhaps Steen Handberg didn't exist. Perhaps the name was a telltale anagram. I dawdled over breakfast and came up with 'Send there, bang!' and 'Danger, he's bent.' An hour later, optimistically clutching my putter, I set out to find the minigolf.

'*Jeg leder efter* Odense Minigolf Club?' I inquired carefully at the Tourist Information Centre.

'Well done!' said the woman behind the desk, and drew a cross on my map.

The minigolf course was right over on the other side of the city, along Vestergade, into Vesterbro and then Middelfartvej, and then right into Christmas Møllers Vej – miles away, in other words. In keeping with the general orderliness of Odense, it's part of a dedicated sports area on the outskirts of the city. Alongside the minigolf course are a football stadium, an ice-hockey rink, a bowling alley, and a cycle track. How civilized, I thought. And how far away.

I walked right through historic Odense and out the other side, past garages and warehouses, into the identikit industrial surroundings of a typical European town, and then further into the suburbs. Finally I saw a blue road sign pointing right – MINIGOLF.

The course is up a track between some trees, past a couple of small tents and a caravan selling beer and Jolly Cola. One of the tent-dwellers was playing loud psychedelic rock on a cassette player at consciousness-expanding volume. He was a middle-aged man with a neat beard, wearing an embroidered cap and smoking what looked like a joint, a bag of minigolf balls scattered out in front of him. I nodded at him and he slowly bowed his head to me, the sorcerer acknowledging the apprentice. I had arrived.

At the top of the hill stood the OMC clubhouse. As I climbed towards it, a young man wearing shades and a baseball cap hailed me. 'Hey!' he said. 'Are you Andy Miller?' He spoke excellent English with an American accent.

'Yes,' I replied, marvelling once again at the ease with which Danish people spoke English.

'I'm Jon Drexler,' he said, shaking my hand. 'Really good to meet you. I saw your name on Steen's website.' I had seen his name on the website too. He spoke English with an American accent because he was from America not Denmark.

Jon told me that Steen and some of the other guys had been up playing cards and drinking until four in the morning and we shouldn't expect to see them until dusk. If I wanted to make myself known to the organizers, then Morten was up in the hut and I could register with him. 'He's a nice guy. Good player too,' said Jon. 'Doesn't speak much English, though.'

Jon was right. Inside the clubhouse sat a portly man in his late thirties with a paintbrush moustache. He had very round shoulders, his spine transcribing a ninety-degree arc from his neck to the small of his back. It was obvious he had played a little too much minigolf.

'Hello,' I said. 'My name's Andy Miller.'

'Yes,' he replied, standing up to shake my hand and nodding.

'From the UK . . . ?' I continued, after a long pause.

Morten nodded again and laughed but said nothing.

'Right,' I said, after another awkward pause. 'Right, well, I'll come back later when Steen's around.'

'OK,' smiled Morten.

I trotted back down the hill to the beton course. It looked close to crazy golf, but was obviously designed for real competition rather than mere fun. White lines and metal rails bounded its brick-red playing surface. The Wizard had discarded his cap of meditation and his special cigarettes and was practising on the third hole of the course. It was a dog-leg, interrupted by an obstacle; a concrete block approached on the south side by a narrow ramp, whose exit was on the east, a good nine or ten feet from the cup. From the way the Wizard kept cursing and shaking his head, the hole was obviously causing him to stray from the path of Zen clarity and calm. He appeared to be deliberating on how best to approach the narrow ramp, either by shooting the ball straight ahead or bouncing it off the metal rung that surrounded the hole. Whichever method he used, only very occasionally did his ball fail to make its way safely into the tunnel at the top of the ramp. Straight up or on the rebound, the Wizard putted with enviable accuracy. Yet still he muttered and swore and flung resentful glances upwards to whatever deity or giant hogweed lived in his sky.

I realized that the Wizard's curses were connected not to clearing the obstacle but to whether or not the ball ended up in the cup. He wanted a hole-in-one every time and was attempting to hit a specific spot on the tunnel wall. Slightly left, and it lipped the cup. Too hard and it just kept running. But if the ball hit exactly the right bit of concrete, it was guaranteed an infinitesimally accurate rebound, which would scoot past the cup, bounce off the back rail and drop safely home.

'Hans has got a good line here,' said Jon Drexler. 'Pretty close to mine. I play it off the rail. I figure it's safer than going up the middle. You want to play a few holes?'

We played. The course was more difficult than it looked and it looked difficult enough. Jon was generous with his advice, free with the information he kept jotting down in a notebook and modest about his own considerable skill. I applauded when he effortlessly aced the second hole, a long straight run, the cup guarded by four metal blocks, but he shrugged it off. 'Even a blind squirrel will find a nut eventually,' he said. 'Let me show you the line.'

Jon's line required three rebounds. He pointed to one of several dinks in the concrete. 'Play it from there, and roll it gently across this mark here so it hits the rail just about here.' He indicated another mark about three feet from the tee and a nondescript bit of the steel rail. 'If you're looking for the point on the rail, just work it out from the paving slabs here. It's just about at the end of the fourth full slab along. The idea is to come off the rail and hit one of the blocks at about seventy-five degrees, so the ball makes a third bounce off the rail up there and comes back into the hole. That's about the simplest way to do it,' he concluded, apparently without irony.

'Wouldn't it be simpler just to go straight down the middle?' I asked.

'Sure,' said Jon, 'but that's a long putt to find that little gap at the end there. You're going to find it hard to do that every single time. But you come in off the side and over these marks and you're breaking it down into shorter putts. In theory, it's easier.'

He consulted his notes for the next hole. His thoroughness was slightly alarming, but finding the right combination of ball and speed of stroke and telltale marks on the concrete are all part of the serious miniature golfer's game, I suppose. Not to prepare in this way, not to carry out a full reconnaissance, is not to play the game properly.

'You're going to want some more balls,' Jon informed me. 'There's a guy called Svend who's selling them. We can get what we need from him.'

The most difficult hole is the seventh. Using a special club, you have to chip the ball, actually drive it, from a raised mound over a thirty-foot stretch of grass and on to a circular concrete 'green'. Worse, the 'green' has been constructed with a number of slopes and dips that are invisible to the naked eye. The only way to navigate it is by reading a topographical map that dangles on a piece of string from the metal fence behind the hole. It's like looking at an artist's impression of the moon's surface, and about as easy to play on – or, for that matter, breathe. I didn't know whether to laugh or hyperventilate.

'You know,' said Jon, 'I'm not even gonna play this today. There's no point.'

'Absolutely,' I replied. 'It's absurd.'

'No,' said Jon, 'I just don't have the right ball. I need to see Svend.'

'Right,' I said. I wondered what Jon had in mind – a jet-propelled ball or some kind of James Bond remote-control device presumably. They were probably legal here.

The course concludes with what looks like the hut from a cuckoo clock, stuck on top of a tall pole and accessible only via a long metal slide. 'This can be a one or this can be a seven,' said Jon. I took seven and finished my first round on the international stage with a side-splitting total of fifty-eight.

'It'll be a lot easier for you once you've seen Svend,' Jon reassured me. 'He'll have lines that I don't have. And I think the tournament's going to start on Saturday, not Friday. Steen didn't get as many people signing up as he wanted. So we've got an extra day's practice. It's not so bad.'

'Hey!' exclaimed a large guy striding towards us, shaking

me out of my reverie and startling a hare, which bounded out
of the long grass and shot across the first tee. 'Hey! You Andy
Miller?'

The man was grinning broadly. He was wearing shorts and
a Danish Invitational Cup commemorative polo shirt. It was
Steen.

'Sorry I wasn't here. We were up till late, playing a bit of poker
and having a few beers, you know.' He turned to Jon. 'How are
you this morning, my friend?'

'Good, thanks,' said Jon. 'Is Svend here yet?'

'Yeah, he's around here somewhere,' replied Steen vaguely.
'He was up with us, you know, and he was really having a few
beers, you know?' He laughed uproariously, before becoming
suddenly grave. 'But you need to sort your balls out, right? We'll
go find him.'

Steen had been accompanied from the hut by the lugubrious
Morten. Like Morten, he had a droopy paintbrush moustache.
Standing together, they looked like the shield-carriers from
Asterix.

'How is the hostel for you, Andy?' said Steen, turning to me.
'It's really good, isn't it? *Jolly* good! *Bloody* good!' Steen, I soon
learnt, was proud of his English and his grasp of traditional
English slang.

'You want something to eat? We have some food up in the
office, a *jolly good spread*!' He turned to Jon. 'If you want
pancakes, we can get those done for you! Ha ha ha! And, Andy!
You can get a beer from the office, you can get a beer from the
trailer there. Maybe we play a round for a few beers – well, a few
beers from you! We give you a hard time, me and Morten! We
thrash your bloody pants! Ha ha ha!'

Morten said something in Danish and laughed too.

'Morten says us two should play you two, the Danes versus
the Yanks! Better keep a few dollars back for the beers! Ha ha
ha!'

I pointed out to Steen that America was a British colony, not
the other way round – well not quite.

'Oh, sorry, Andy! *Dreadfully* sorry! We don't want to get you too angry. You know, we don't want to beat you real bad on the beton and you have a few beers, go into town, get real angry, kick some tables over! We don't want you to riot! *You Danish bastards! Fuck the IRA!* Ha ha! Ha ha ha!'

It was only a month since riot police had battled traditional British hooligans in the streets and squares of Copenhagen. It was good of Steen, I felt, to see the funny side.

At this point, the mercurial Svend joined us. He was a giant, tall and broad with dyed blond hair. He was also very hung-over, his eyes red-rimmed and tired. However, he was even more jovial than Morten and Steen, heartily slapping their backs, shaking my hand and nearly wrenching it off. The three Danes conversed for a while, before Steen turned to me and said, 'OK, Jon, Andy, Svend is just going to get a beer and then he'll make sure you get your balls and, Andy, he will play a round with you and show you what you need to do.'

'Hello, Andy,' boomed Svend, much to the amusement of Steen and Morten.

Svend and I raced round the course. There were cards to be played and beers to be drunk and he didn't want to waste time on minigolf. He aced most holes, bellowing in triumph when he did so. Whenever he felt especially pleased with a shot, he would flap his arms and make a noise like a chicken, and other players would respond in kind, like *Spartacus*, starring Foghorn Leghorn. Everyone knew him and everyone liked him.

At the end of the round, I gladly handed over five hundred kroner for all the balls Svend had chosen for me, and felt like I'd secured a bargain. They included a heavy black number for the first and second holes, a small white ball with a picture of a hedgehog on the side for pitching on to the eighth (very little onward roll, should you be lucky enough to hit the 'green'), a huge brown Deutschmann o81, which hugged the bumps in the concrete and which I christened the Egg, and a scarred and pitted burgundy bullet ball to aim at the cuckoo clock at the end of the course.

Jon Drexler had been right. This wasn't so bad. The company was good. The sun was shining. This was a pretty meadow in a pretty country. And I did want to play again.

At the end of the day I walked back into town with Jon. As we made our way down the path to the main road, we passed the Wizard, who had resumed the lotus position outside his tent and was enjoying a hand-rolled cigarette. Once again we exchanged nods.

'See you,' said the Wizard.

'Hans is German,' said Jon to me after we turned the corner, 'and he's a really good player. He should do well on Saturday. But he's more laid back than a lot of other German players. Much more.'

We had dinner at a busy pizzeria in the centre of Odense. The streets were all but deserted, yet the restaurant was full of people. Where had they all come from?

Over dinner Jon told me about his experiences at the World Championships in Holland. Team USA was split between dedicated miniature golfers and a few friends and associates press-ganged into representing Uncle Sam by the dedicated miniature golfers – 'Two people from the military, another quantitative number geek like myself, a trucker ... And we practised hard,' Jon told me. 'Nobody practised harder than us. We were out on that course from seven in the morning until eleven o'clock at night. We practised in the dark. You couldn't even see the hole, you could only hear the ball hit the side or rattle up the ramp.'

But it was not enough. Team USA finished last. In spite of this, Jon felt it had been worth the effort. It showed that the US was prepared to take such competitions seriously: at a previous world championship, the American squad had given up and gone home before the tournament had even begun.

'You know,' said Jon, whose high-school reunion was imminent, 'at least I'll be able to say I've represented my country.'

'Will you tell them what at?' I asked.

'Sure,' said Jon confidently, leaning back in his chair.

'And what if they don't believe you?'

But Jon had already given this some thought. 'I'll say, "Well, now, who's being jealous?"'

Jon's goal this trip was straightforward – to make the cut on Saturday. By doing so his would be the first American name in living memory to appear on a European minigolf leader board, restoring a little US pride. Jon played a lot of sports and reckoned himself to be competitive in all of them. He wasn't particularly athletic, he just liked to play. He was an enthusiastic fan of the Chicago Cubs (the hapless baseball team who had last won a World Series in 1908). And he liked chess. He was thinking of taking up archery.

'So why minigolf?' I wondered aloud.

'To meet women,' said Jon Drexler. 'Why else?'

Day Three – Thursday

Exhausted. Will try to make this a shorter entry than yesterday.

I managed to drag my score down to the mid-forties today, but that's in practice rather than competition. Kirsten Barnes told me to set realistic targets, so here is my target for Saturday. I don't expect to make the cut but my target is to break forty every time I play. Forty is the magic number. You can play bet on for percentages. It's a glory bypass, but I'm not after glory. All I want is to preserve a bit of dignity.

Before commencing his first practice round this morning, Jon Drexler walked me round the OMC eternit course. We're not playing eternit in this competition but in Latvia we will be. As usual, most of the little concrete runways and loop-the-loops were beyond my meagre abilities. It's like snooker or billiards, played on a bumpy table, with bricks in the way, and a potentially infinite number of cue balls. In an act of real kindness, he has suggested I borrow his bag for Latvia.

'You know,' said Jon, as we stumbled to the end, 'you can really improve on this in just a few days. We did.'

But you still came last, I thought. I don't want to come last.

Jon told me that before going to sleep last night, he had

visualized each of the holes on the tournament course and the ball dropping easily into the cup. 'But it only works if I know the exact line of the ball,' he said. I must try this tonight.

Jon was also becoming more methodical in his practice methods. At every hole, he would stand, legs apart, holding his putter horizontally in front of him, and creatively visualize the shot he was about to take. His eyes followed an imaginary line from the tee to the cup, his body completely still while his head turned slowly and methodically. It was a pre-putt routine of robotic intensity.

I worked on my own pre-putt routine: I shake my arms and hands and try to loosen up my shoulders; I take a deep breath and, just as Kirsten Barnes suggested, gaze up at the treetops to find some clarity and stillness. It works. The routine enables me to distance myself quickly from bad putts or bad luck, and not carry them with me to the next hole. And it's just as important to move on from good putts as bad ones. Every shot should be its own challenge. Bad play breeds frustration. Good play breeds complacency.

This would sound ridiculous at home, but I feel able to concentrate in this way, to think like this because I'm not at home. I'm free. There's no embarrassment about this being 'crazy golf', because 'crazy golf' doesn't exist here. And there's no embarrassment about being cack-handed, self-defeating Andy Miller because that Andy Miller is back in the UK. This Andy Miller can do whatever he wants to do.

'Crazy golf' is a state of mind whose boundaries I no longer recognize.[1]

Under the trees by the eternit course, I had a long conversation with Steen. His best score on the beton was thirty-three and on the eternit a jaw-dropping twenty-two, but he had a problem with consistency. 'I have a little ping-pong going on,' he said. 'A little yin-yang. I'm not stable, that's my problem.'

Minigolf in Denmark received the support of the government.

1. I did actually write this.

The Dansk Minigolf Union became a full member of the Danish Sports Federation in May 1995, with full national sporting rights and co-operation with the organization overseeing all national sporting efforts, Team Danmark. This meant financial support for the national team and the payment of salaries to national coaches.

But, according to Steen, minigolf was still some way from being fully embraced by the Danish people. 'I would like it to be. The problem is that people here in Denmark consider this as a beer drunken sport. "Let's go camping. Let's get *a pint*, you know, and let's fool around and go crazy."' Steen shook his head. 'And there is general prejudice. People think it's weirdos who's playing it.'

Steen and Morten had devised the tournament, which they called the Di-Cup, as a way of reviving the fortunes of minigolf, and maybe their own fortunes as well. 'In the eighties,' Steen told me, 'there were tournaments like this all the time. There were a lot of Germans, Norwegians, Swedes, even American and Japanese players – not so much UK, of course. Denmark is relatively small compared to the other minigolf nations, but basically we talked about doing the big tournament, PGA Tour, something like that, to make it kind of a – how do you say? – trademark tournament, very exclusive and high profile.'

The trademark of the Di-Cup was very straightforward: it was supposed to be Europe's richest tournament. They had advertised originally for 256 players but ended up with just fifty-four. This meant that not only was the event now a one-day competition but also that the projected first prize of thirty thousand kroner had been drastically reduced, largely because it was drawn from the competitors' entrance fees. 'But, you know, we're gonna get a hundred and fifty players next year, so the money will be really good.'

Steen informed me that I would be playing on Saturday with Morten. 'He's a strong contender. He's been playing since for ever. You're gonna get your butt kicked!'

'And Svend?'

Steen pulled a face. I think he felt that Svend, for all his un-doubted talent, was part of the fool-around-and-go-crazy image problem that afflicted minigolf in Denmark. The Di-Cup was designed to be a prestigious new fixture on the international minigolf tour and the hard-drinking, cock-a-doodle-doing Svend didn't fit that profile.

As the day wore on, I played again with Jon and received some help from three Norwegians, one of whom, confusingly, was called Finn and lived in Sweden. Finn appeared at my shoulder from time to time, corrected my line, and rummaged through my bag, testing the properties of various balls by rolling them against his cheek or under his nose. For some reason, he was very taken with the Fun-Sports 8.

'You must keep these cool,' said Finn, picking up my bag and moving it out of the sunlight and into the shade under a bush. 'Too hot and . . .' He mimed the balls bouncing high above my head and out of control. He held up the 8. 'Even this one!' he said, and laughed heartily.

Peter Soerensen, meanwhile, gave me some useful assistance on the driving range of hole number seven, getting me to stand so far back behind the ball that my initial shot couldn't fail to scoop the little Hedgehog high into the air and, smack, down on to the lunar 'green'. It felt a bit unnatural but it seemed to work. When I had managed to land the ball three times in a row, Peter Soerensen slapped me on the back and said, 'OK, that's it. You do that from now on.'

Peter is a member of the World Minigolf Sport Federation's technical committee. He'll also be accompanying the Danish squad to Latvia as one of the tournament's official invigilators. Here in Odense, however, he is employed in an exchange scheme, coaching two players who have come from Latvia – Dace and Ilze Kupce, who are sisters. They are very pretty, very thin, and very intense. Ilze has long dark hair, while Dace's is cut into a boyish crop. She is twenty; Ilze is seventeen. Under Peter's tutel-age, they practise all day, spending up to an hour on particular holes until they get them right. I haven't seen them smile once.

One reason for this may be the constant presence of their parents. Mr Kupce is tall, with thick-framed spectacles and a moustache, and follows the girls round with a notebook – the Richard Williams of Latvian miniature golf. Apparently, the Kupces drove here from Latvia. They don't have much money to spare and Steen tells me that these are competitors for whom the big prizes are far from symbolic. They have come all this way to win.

I wanted to speak to the Kupce family but they were rather intimidating, the girls unsmiling, Mr Kupce standing behind the mesh fencing at the back of the seventh 'green', quietly recording every one of his daughters' tee-shots. They were busy. I'll speak to them tomorrow.

There is little in the way of etiquette when it comes to practising the hole you want to practise. You just push in. The younger Danish players share Svend's habit of making animal noises whenever they play a good shot. It doesn't have to be a chicken – you can bark like a dog or howl like a hyena. One young guy called Vincent screams like a chimpanzee at moments of great excitement, for which I'm told he's been cautioned several times.

I ended the day with a round against Steen and Jon. Under pressure, I slipped back to a fifty, but Jon was only three shots ahead of me and Steen came in with a forty-three, a fairly awful score ('*Bugger!*' said Steen).

As I've been writing this, loud music has started blasting from the park opposite the hostel. They seem to be having a rock festival.

Just been to look. On the pedestrian crossing I was nearly run over by a motorbike, driving *over* the crossing and right into the crowd. A really bad sort of electric hard-rock polka group were on stage but the crowd were going berserk. There was a big crush at the front, bare-breasted teenage girls sitting on their boyfriends' shoulders. A lot of Danish drunks knocking back the Elephant beer. One boy urinating on the talking sculpture. This is more like it. I bought an Elephant beer for myself and piously returned to the hostel.

Apparently, Danish people have one of the lowest life expectancies in Europe. They like to drink and smoke, eat plenty of meat, and generally have a good time, after a few decades of which they drop dead, used up but happy. I can hear them having a good time from my window.

I'm going to have an early night, get up tomorrow morning and really concentrate on getting my score down. Forty is the magic number.

Imagine the first hole. You are in control. You have the right ball. The putter head connects with the ball. A slow, graceful stroke. Of course. Hitting the mark by the fourth full slab, proceeding unmistakably towards . . .

A Queen tribute band is on stage now. They're playing 'I Want To Break Free'.

Day Four – Friday

Woke up late. Hangover. Made mistake of returning to rock festival. Trampled by Elephant.

45; 43; <u>35</u>; 45; 43

Bed. More tomorrow.

Day Five – Saturday – Di-Day

MORNING

Although I don't play until this afternoon, I got to the OMC just before nine to hear Steen run through the tournament rules. He had shaved off his handsome moustache overnight. 'This is a big deal here today,' he told me, 'and we want everything to be very, you know, professional.' Clearly, facial hair was for amateurs.

I also wanted to offer Jon some moral support. He's one of the first to play and has been drawn against Dace Kupce who, of course, has her own considerable back-up team. Must speak to the Kupces today.

'I'm feeling pretty good,' Jon told me, when I wished him luck. 'I'm playing pretty good and I really think I can make the cut.'

One person who wasn't feeling pretty good was Svend. He had stayed up late, drinking beer and playing cards again – so late, in fact, that rather than go home to bed he had spent the night under a bush. I stood next to him during Steen's opening remarks. His eyes were even more bloodshot than usual and he had twigs in his hair.

'Good luck,' I whispered.

Svend gave me a slow, solemn nod in return. He was still drunk.

Though Steen might not approve, I could sympathize with Svend. After the surprise rock festival, I felt terrible for most of yesterday morning. I overslept and didn't make it down to the club until nearly lunchtime, with a splitting headache. The first round of the day was torture, but I finished with a not-bad forty-five. I played again and this time took forty-three. My head was clearing. Forty was still my target. Was there, I asked myself, anything I could change about my routine to shed a few more strokes?

I bought a Jolly Cola and sat on a bench by the eternit course, watching the Wizard play a round on it for relaxation, the sick bastard. He, like all the European players in Hastings, putted with his legs far apart and a grip that extended much further down the shaft than the standard overlapping golf grip I had been using.

And I suddenly realized where I had been going wrong. I had been under the impression, somewhere deep in my sports psyche, that what I had been doing over the last few days and months was playing some kind of golf. Like all British people, I had assumed that crazy golf was simply a stupid and diminutive version of what went on on putting greens and that therefore the same skills were required and the same methods could be applied. But that wasn't the case. You could learn very little from the similarities between golf and miniature golf: it was the differences that were instructive. Real miniature golfers – it seemed so obvious now – drew on a full range of equipment and techniques specifically geared to miniature golf, and which had little or nothing to do with golf itself. They responded without embarrassment to the specific demands of their sport.

In other words, what was the point of a new putter and new balls if you carried on using them in the same old way – or, rather, if you played the wrong game with them? Yesterday, I had enjoyed the freedom of being an Andy Miller far from home, taking minigolf as seriously as he wanted to. So why not go native? Why not adopt the European stance and the European grip? It was against all good advice, not least Kirsten Barnes's, to make such drastic changes just before a tournament, but if not here and now, when?

I approached the first tee. Shake arms, gaze at treetops. Legs wide apart, unclasp hands and extend index fingers to form straight line on the grip. Feels OK. Try a few exploratory swings from the shoulders. Also OK. Select correct ball, long-running black one. Place ball on correct spot and aim for rail. Check to make sure nobody's looking. And swing.

Needing only the gentlest of putts, the ball glided swiftly and easily off the rail and into the cup. An ace.

I repeated the procedure using the same ball at the second hole. It rebounded exactly where it was supposed to, off the rail and again off the metal block. Another ace.

As this miracle round progressed, the challenge was not to replicate the same formula every time, but not to get distracted by my own mounting excitement. I wasn't going to just break forty; I was going to smash it.

And I did. On the eighteenth, I slammed the bullet ball so hard up the metal ramp, it nearly shot out the back of the cuckoo clock, an emphatic final ace bringing my eighteen-hole total to thirty-five.

Of course, there was quite a bit of luck involved – I had fluked a two on the driving-range seventh – but it proved to me that I could do it. My new stance and new grip lowered my centre of gravity and stopped me from cocking my wrists, making it more difficult to pull shots. I knew I could break forty easily. I had the mental game. I had the technical expertise. I was in control.

I felt like a robot encountering human emotions for the first time. Was this . . . sport?

Then I shot another forty-five and another forty-three and quit the course in a foul mood. But I need to remember how that thirty-five felt if I'm going to get anywhere near it this afternoon.

LUNCHTIME

To kill time before my bit of the tournament, I walked into Odense's old town to see some of the tourist attractions, the majority of which are connected to the storyteller Hans Christian Andersen, who was born in Odense in 1805.[2] You can tour the tiny house he was born in, learn about his life and triumphs at the Andersen Museum and take your children to the Andersen-inspired children's cultural centre, the TinderBox.

You can also shop. The great fabulist left Odense aged fourteen to join the Royal Danish Theatre in Copenhagen (or, as my guidebook puts it, 'Andersen got out of Odense as fast as he could'), but no matter – his fellow Odensers have found it in their hearts, and wallets, to forgive him. The streets of old Odense are lined with Little Mermaid tea-shops and Thumbelina boutiques selling Little Matchgirl candleholders and Brave Tin Soldiers to hang from your Christmas tree. There is even a men's outfitters called the Emperor's New Clothes, whose racks were completely empty.

I ran through my pre-tournament routine in my head and tried not to think of myself as an Ugly Duckling. Be positive. Be focused. In the museum cafeteria, I attempted to relax and simultaneously locate the Zone. I retrieved my putter and balls from the cloakroom and I walked out into the sunlight and on – along Vestergade, into Vesterbro, down Christmas Møllers Vej – to meet my fate.

---

2. There is also an Elvis Presley museum in Odense for some reason, but it was shut when I was there. Perhaps a reciprocal arrangement exists and there is a Hans Christian Andersen museum in Tupelo, Mississippi.

I broke forty. Twice. Thirty-eight and thirty-nine. When I walked away from the eighteenth, I cried. I really did. I was elated. It was fantastic. I am a swan.

Of course I didn't make the cut. I went round with Morten, who was as good as Steen said he was. He shot thirty-one and thirty-two without a visible pre-putt routine of any sort: no deep breathing or self-mesmerizing voodoo. But he was playing his game and I was playing mine.

At the final hole, I knew that I needed to ace the long metal ramp to keep my score below forty. The eighteenth could be a one or a seven. Right now, it had to be a one. I ran through the routine: shake the arms, take a deep breath, find some stillness in the treetops. I rechecked my new grip, visualized the line, took a couple of preparatory swings. A small crowd had gathered. To these expert onlookers, it must have seemed like an awful lot of bother to go to just to scrape in under forty. But nobody laughed. And when the ball hit home first time – a little softly, in fact, only just dragging itself into the cuckoo clock – there was a little round of applause. And I cried.

Morten made it through to the final four, along with the Wizard, Martin Nevers and a visiting player from Aalborg, Bjarne Hansen. The still worse-for-wear Svend won his initial group with thirty-one and an amazing twenty-seven. He flapped his arms and posed for photos by the leader board. But subsequently his hangover got the better of him. He struggled through another round, unusually silent, but couldn't hold it together, and after the final hole he disappeared to find somewhere to pass out.

I couldn't find Jon Drexler, but to judge from the results posted on the leader board, he didn't make the cut. By one shot. I hope he hasn't gone home.

In the final round, Morten had some unlucky breaks and the Wizard's composure finally deserted him. At the eighth hole, a volcano, he threw down his club in despair, and was transformed back into plain old Hans Knut Martin from Germany. He sat defeated in the grass, and his wife hugged him and comforted him by rolling his ear between her thumb and forefinger, which seemed to revive him a little. That left Martin and Bjarne, who frittered away his three-shot advantage at the eighteenth, which led to a play-off. It was very tense.

While we waited for the play-off to begin, I noticed the Kupce sisters in the crowd. Neither Ilze nor Dace had made it to the final stages of the competition and for the first time in a week, they were smiling. I was just about to go and talk to them when Steen announced we were starting again. I can talk to them in Latvia . . .

The play-off continues until one player makes a mistake. In the end, Martin's luck holds good. Both players take two at the first, and Bjarne takes another two at the second. But Martin's first putt on this hole is a good one. He knows it, the crowd knows it, and Bjarne Hansen knows it, practically conceding defeat before the ball is in the cup. The crowd roars its approval. A little girl next to me, wearing a bootleg Andy Cole T-shirt (*Goal King Cole!*), screams Martin's name like he was, well, like he was Andy Cole. Martin hugs his girlfriend, takes off his baseball cap and wipes a hand across his eyes. Bjarne shakes the victor's hand and sits by himself, looking devastated. Hans Knut wanders over to offer his condolences. Would Bjarne like his ear rolled maybe . . . ?

At the prize-giving ceremony, Steen hands out cheques to those who made the cut, all thirty-two of them. He then gives Morten, Bjarne and Martin their medals and trophies. They stand on the winner's rostrum and Martin lifts the Di-Cup itself (actually a rather beautiful blue glass vase) above his head. The crowd gives a mighty cheer and Bjarne looks like he wants to swallow his own face.

'I think it was really exciting,' said Steen. 'Can I say on the website that you're coming back next year?'

'Of course,' I said. I had had a great time. Maybe I would come back.

'You don't have to,' said Steen, 'but it's good for our publicity.'

Steen and Morten are planning to attend the Open in Hastings in September.

'I think we'd do pretty well, right?' said Steen.

'I think Morten will win,' I said. Morten smiled confidently. He thought so too.

I said my goodbyes to Finn, the Wizard, Peter Soerensen and some of the young Danish players. 'See you, Andy,' said Vincent the chimp. 'See you in Rīga!'

See you in Rīga.

For the first time, I feel enthusiastic about going to Latvia. This trip has been a real breakthrough. I have the mental game. I have the right equipment. I have the right grip. I have international experience. It's been a lot of effort – time, money, personality realignment – for two over-par rounds on a provincial Danish minigolf course. But just like a real sport and just like a real sportsman, I believe it was worth it. I have achieved what I wanted to achieve.

I am ready to take it to the next level.[3]

I took one last tour round the eternit course. It was no easier than when I'd tried it with Jon. After four holes I gave up. There will, I'm sure, be plenty of time to master it in Rīga. And why spoil an otherwise perfect day?

EVENING

I found Jon back at the hostel. He was still smarting at missing the cut. He works for an airline, which was how he could afford to fly to Denmark. However, to save money, he'd had to wait for spaces to become available on scheduled flights. It had taken him forty hours to get to Odense, and the prospect of the return flight wasn't making him feel any more cheerful. 'All I need,' he said morosely, picking at his salad, 'is for Baggage Handling to break my club. That'd be a great end to this trip.'

'You've already got rid of your balls to me,' I said.

'Keep 'em,' said Jon. 'Actually, no, don't. It'll pass. I get very frustrated when this kind of thing happens.'

---

3. I wrote this in the diary too. Jesus.

I told him I understood.

Jon had played well initially but after a few unlucky shots in the back nine found himself head to head at the eighteenth with Dace Kupce and her whole family. Like me, he needed to make his first putt his last putt. But it didn't happen.

'I hit a great shot, I had the right speed, I hit it off the rail exactly where I ought to have done, and you know what? It just hit the barrier. And I made the exact same putt second time round and it went in.' Jon shook his head. 'So Dace has to get it first time. And she does. Straight up. She goes through and not me.' He stabbed an olive through the heart. 'And then she gets knocked out in the next round. Not that I'm a sore loser . . .'

I informed Jon that the exact same thing had happened to Martin Nevers and Bjarne Hansen on the eighteenth. A shot they thought was safe had inexplicably failed. Maybe it wasn't nerves. Maybe it was sabotage. Dace's father could have gone to the course the night before and bent the rail or something . . .

'No,' said Jon magnanimously, popping the olive into his mouth, 'I choked. It happens to everyone.'

Not me, I thought, not any more. Bring it on.

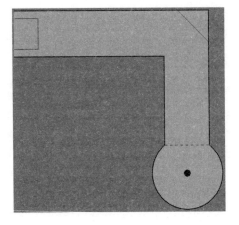

Rechter Winkel – right angle

What does it mean to be a man in the UK when you don't like sport?

It means you cannot be entirely trusted.

It means that there's something not quite right with you. Men think so. Women think so too.

It means you do not share common assumptions about clothing, beauty, patriotism, and the merits of spitting.

It means you are probably homosexual.

It means always having to say you're sorry.

You learn all this at school, because school is where the lifelong bonding of sport and masculinity really begins. I can't express it more succinctly than the great Vivian Stanshall, so I won't try:

> *The odd boy lay down by the football field,*
> *Took out a slim volume of Mallarmé.*
> *A centre forward called him an imbecile.*
> *It's an odd boy who doesn't like sport.*

MALE CHORUS: *Sport, sport, masculine sport,*
Equips a young man for society.
Yes, sport turns out a jolly good sort,
It's an odd boy who doesn't like sport.

At least, that's how it used to be. But Viv was writing in the sixties. Recently, another group has usurped the Jolly Good Sorts. These days, Lads make the rules. Lads rule the school.

The story of the 1990s was the story of the Lad, and how everyone – pop stars, stockbrokers, prime ministers – wanted to be just like him. A Lad is either a boy pretending to be a man, or a man pretending to be a boy. Not only has he not put away childish things, he has found new things to be childish about – fast cars, beer, a lady's breasts. He has also carefully nurtured and sustained certain childhood obsessions into later life – the breasts, of course, but chiefly sport, sport and more sport. In the nineties, sport was the Lad's rallying call. Were you an Odd Boy (or Girl) in your youth? Here, beneath the banner of sport, was a chance to forget all that and finally fit in. Cast your difference aside! Untuck your shirt and join us!

Millions did, of course. We called these conscripts New Lads, and their female counterparts Ladettes.[1] But the few remaining Odd Boys who resisted did not forget, or forgive, so easily.

Mark Gatiss, of The League of Gentlemen, describes their career as 'our revenge on double PE'; Chris Lowe, of the Pet Shop Boys, says, 'I think Neil [Tennant] probably wanted fame and success to make the point to his school or whatever . . . a triumph of his type over your footballing type.'[2]

Sport is how we teach young boys, and girls, what 'real masculinity' is; it's how we give our children something to kick for or

---

1. Like New Labour, New Laddism peaked some time between Euro 96 and the release of *Be Here Now* by Oasis.
2. Chris Lowe is a famous Arsenal fan. He describes the adoption of 'Go West' by football crowds in the 1990s – a Village People song covered by the Pet Shop Boys – as 'our greatest achievement'.

against. This isn't just my embittered opinion. Well, it is, but there is considerable academic evidence to back it up.

For example, in 1998 Jon Swain from the Institute of Education at the University of London began a study of the construction of boys' masculinities at a junior school in southern England. He focused on the playground behaviour of a year-six class of ten- and eleven-year-olds:

> The subordinate group of boys were barely granted a look-in during the games of playground football, and were also conceptualized as 'other' by the dominant group. Although they were sometimes allowed to occupy the same space on the pitch, they were not really part of the game: they were largely ignored, hardly got a kick of the ball, and were frequently publicly derided and ridiculed for their lack of skill and prowess . . . In fact, in many ways, this group of boys became feminized and subjected to various types of homophobic commentary in the form of name-calling such as 'Gaylord' and 'Poofter', and remarks like, 'Why don't you go and play with the Brownies?'

Even allowing for the constraints of academic style, Swain is moved to remark at this point, 'and this is despite the fact that professional footballers seem habitually prone to kiss, cuddle and lie on top of each other pretty much every time a goal is scored'. Quite.

He concludes: 'Although the boys in the subordinate group were already stigmatized in other school contexts, football seemed to reaffirm and emphasize their subordination.'

How do you feel about the games teacher played, brilliantly, by Brian Glover in Ken Loach's film *Kes*? One national newspaper recently rated him as one of the funniest cinema characters of all time. Danny Baker wanted to write a sitcom based on his adventures. But he always seems like a bastard to me. Don't people watch to the end of the film?

As you know, I still bear a grudge against Mr Jackson, he of the disastrous hockey practice. My friend Mick cannot recall the death of his games master, face down in the school swimming-pool, without laughing. 'No one forgets a good teacher,' said the government's multi-million-pound recruiting campaign. And no one forgives a bad one. Why?

Research suggests that games teachers unwittingly collude with the Lads in their classes to create and reinforce male-pattern behaviour, assisting the process of subordination identified by Jon Swain and others. For an essay entitled 'Exploring the Everyday "Philosophies" of Physical Education Teachers from a Socio-logical Perspective', Ken Green of Chester College of Higher Education interviewed thirty-five PE teachers in secondary schools in the north of England, *Kes* country:

> What PE teachers articulated was typically a kind of check-list of aims and practices frequently centring upon words and phrases like 'enjoyment', 'health', 'skills' and 'character' . . . The overt emphasis upon enjoyment, the unusual justification for activity choice, and the emphasis upon sports performance (presumably one of the things which discourages some pupils), amongst other things, suggested that teachers perceived PE as somehow different from the rest of the curriculum.

He goes on to define the teachers' views as 'justificatory ideologies; that is to say, ideologies that served to vindicate teachers' preferred conceptions of PE . . . Much of the "knowledge" incorporated into, and thus constituent of, PE teachers' "philosophies" appeared, in fact, ideological: that is to say, it was by degrees more or less mythical, more or less false, more or less distorted.'

In other words, that's football. It's common sense to believe in the universal beneficial properties of PE and sport – enjoyment, health, skills, character – but what is common sense if not a ragbag of 'justificatory ideologies' that allows you to do what you want to do, based on what you've always done?

Ken Green sums up his study with a flourish. PE teachers' 'philosophies', he says, are 'sometimes overlapping, sometimes contradictory, frequently ill thought-through and typically confused'. (Did you fail to make the hockey team, Ken? Write and let me know.)

Odd Boys will not find any of this surprising. That games teachers believe their lessons are breaks from the boredom of other lessons, that they buddy up with the first team and forget the rest – we all know this. We learnt it young, and so did they. Games teachers are never Odd Boys; they might conceivably be Good Sorts, but they are almost certainly Lads, and Lads stick together, 'sticking together' being a central tenet of the Lads' code. Sugden, the character played by Brian Glover in *Kes*, is one of the Lads, a grown man who talks and plays football like a boy, and who picks on boys who are not like him. And so it goes.

Or does it? I hadn't knowingly met a games teacher since I left school in the mid-eighties, but I couldn't believe the species had evolved much from Woody Allen's 'those who can't do, teach; and those who can't teach, teach gym' model. Still, feeling strong after Denmark, I thought I should at least do the (cough) profession the courtesy of bringing myself up to date.

I was shocked by what I discovered, shocked and delighted. Rejoice! It turns out that school sport has been in decline for years.

Why did nobody tell me? Many commentators portrayed this decline as a crisis, but I don't agree. Do today's more sensitive young people realize how lucky they are? They are living through a golden age of idleness! Soon, no one will care if you play sport or not. No one! Forging a sick note will become a dying art, like drystone walling.

And I wonder where that will leave the poor emasculated PE teacher. I made an appointment to see one, to gloat.

Dave Jacobs has been a PE teacher for eighteen years. Currently he teaches PE three days a week at a comprehensive school in North London. He runs lessons across all age-groups, and manages the school's six football teams, one for each year, arranging fixtures, booking pitches, organizing minibuses and so on. For the last five years he has worked part-time. The rest of the week, he's a personal trainer, with private clients in Hampstead and Highgate.

I'd arranged to visit Dave's school during one of the few lunch-breaks when he wasn't supervising a practice of some kind. As I walked through the gates and up to Reception I had to keep reminding myself that I was a grown-up now so there was really no need to feel sick, but I did anyway.

I was supposed to meet Dave in the staff-room, but I couldn't find it. I stuck my head round the door of a dingy sixth-form common room. It was a tip. Cigarette smoke hung in the air like dust. Two students were practising French with one another; a boy lay across three chairs, his muddy trainers on the cushions, shouting into a mobile phone; a girl with lank blonde hair sat with an exercise book open, looking dejected and text-messaging someone.

'Excuse me,' I said to the girl, 'could you tell me where the staff-room is?'

She looked up from her phone. 'This is it,' she said.

No wonder morale was low. I sat down on a cracked red plastic chair to wait for Dave. A set of disturbing paintings hung on the wall: a horse's skull rendered in hallucinogenic colours, two drab, shadowy abstracts in green, grey and black, and a portrait of what appeared to be some wire-cutters. Opposite me was a bulletin board, at the centre of which someone had pinned a large printed sign. It said 'CRISIS? WHAT CRISIS?'

On my way to the school, I had read an interview with Trevor Brooking, the ex-West Ham and England footballer, BBC pundit and chair of Sport England, on the state of school sport. Sport England, formerly the English Sports Council, is jointly funded by the government and the Lottery and is involved in supporting and developing sport in schools. 'There's an apathy towards sport among many young people these days,' Trevor Brooking was quoted as saying. 'There has been an extremely significant decline in the traditional "British fighting spirit" in sport, which is famous around the world.'

They've certainly heard of it in Denmark, I thought, remembering Steen Handberg shouting, 'Fuck the IRA!'

'That spirit has been diluted by too many people saying "Don't worry, at least you tried,"' continued Trevor, 'and too many years of non-competitive sport in schools, where everyone was congratulated simply for turning up and taking part, and exceptional performance was not rewarded with prizes because some teachers felt that was unhealthy and would put some kids off from playing. That created an environment of average output in sport.'

Sitting in this dingy staff-room, I read Trevor Brooking's words again. What Trevor seemed to be saying in essence was, it's not the taking part that counts, it's the winning. But these were children. What was wrong with telling them, 'Don't worry, at least you tried'?

'Andy?'

I glanced up. It was Dave. He was a stocky man, about forty, who had come to our meeting dressed as a games teacher. I fought the desire to address him as 'sir'.

We walked through the school to the office Dave shared with the other games teachers, just past the sports hall. A handful of boys played a ragged game of basketball, every slam and dunk echoing off the walls. The office was cramped and smelt of unwashed games kit. Dave perched athletically on a stool and I read him what Trevor Brooking had said in the newspaper about non-competitive sport being responsible for a decline in national standards.

Dave was a West Ham fan. 'Trevor Brooking's my hero,' he said, 'but that's a bit of a sweeping generalization.' He looked crestfallen.

He outlined a few other possible reasons why sport in schools had dwindled to its current sorry state – chronic underinvestment in facilities; the teachers' strikes of the 1980s, which destroyed the goodwill needed to run after-school coaching; the ongoing sale of school playing-fields by local authorities; a National Curriculum that specified a compulsory PE period of a mere hour a week; OFSTED; the bureaucracy afflicting all areas of teaching, not just games; and, most significantly, the apathy of kids themselves. Why would you want to get sweaty and dirty, unless somebody made you, when there were so many TV channels and video games to enjoy?

'Sometimes competition is appropriate, sometimes it isn't,' concluded Dave. 'But it *has* to be participation PE for all, so you're not getting a kid standing on their own, not touching the ball, thinking, 'I'm rubbish! What a waste of time!' You've got to make sure that each child is involved and not excluded. You've got to try and make the lesson a good atmosphere.'

I boggled at Dave. He might look like a games teacher, but he was talking like a considerate human being.

On the wall of Dave's office was a QPR poster. The club had written to the school, he told me, offering cut-price tickets to the next home game against Grimsby – just five pounds. It wasn't the first time QPR had done this. Cheap tickets had also been available for a fixture against Huddersfield earlier in the season. 'We had a little bit of uptake for that game, but nobody's come to see me so far regarding Grimsby,' said Dave.

I told him I wasn't surprised.

'It's not so much QPR,' he said. 'The kids are so into the Premiership, they can't really be bothered with first-division football.'

In addition to the Premiership, Dave told me, his kids liked basketball and the World Wrestling Federation; anything, in fact, closer to showbusiness than sport. It was a big problem, said Dave.

This made sense. The sport gold rush of the last few years hadn't just coincided with a decline in kids' willingness to play sport, it had contributed to it. Provided you wore a football shirt, did it really matter that you didn't play football in it?

So how do you motivate kids to take part? I asked.

'The key is to give them as much opportunity as possible,' said Dave. Pupils at the school could try gymnastics, volleyball, badminton or swimming as part of the PE curriculum, then football, basketball, rugby, hockey, netball or cross-country as part of the games curriculum; PE and games were taught separately. 'You've got to encourage them, try to build up their confidence,' continued Dave heretically. 'If a pupil wants to take it further and be really competitive, there's the after-school clubs where they can play really competitively, and then they can play against other schools as well.'

And what about the real objectors, I persisted. What do you do with them?

Dave laughed and told me about one boy who had come to Sports Day dressed in a T-shirt that said 'Sometimes Life Seems Just Like Walking Around In Circles'. 'I thought that was quite funny. He really could not see the point of PE or sport. But hopefully, there are so many things in the curriculum, there will be something they enjoy.'

Was Dave trying to wind me up? If so, he was succeeding. His sheer reasonableness was beginning to irritate me. I clung to the thought that he was probably a real bastard out on the football field.

'Dave,' I said, 'have you ever seen *Kes?*'

'Yeah, I'm a bit like that sometimes,' he replied.

Aha!

'For a laugh, you know. Scoring the Bobby Charlton and all that. The kids quite like it.'

'But games teachers are all sadists, aren't they, Dave?'

'Perhaps people who say that were at schools where the teachers were sadists. I don't think you'd get past OFSTED if you taught like that now. These days, you probably spend more time with the weaker pupils than the stronger ones.'

I tried to detect the smallest note of disappointment in Dave's voice, but there was none.

'Look, I'm biased,' he said, 'but I think sport gets you to work as a team, which has got to be good. You can get leadership qualities. You've got to show some character sometimes if you don't want to play, which I think is a good thing all round. There are the obvious fitness benefits. And when you leave school, you'll have a lot of leisure time, unemployment. If you get to enjoy sport, if you like badminton, for example, that's a good way of socializing and meeting people.'

These were the old 'justificatory ideologies', of course, and yet, sitting in this ratty office in this underfunded school, it was hard not to feel that Dave was entitled to them. He deserved, in the words of his football hero, to be congratulated simply for turning up.

'It's a nightmare trying to book a pitch, these days,' said Dave. 'Red tape. It's just very difficult. People aren't helpful. If there's an option of calling it off because there's been a slight downpour, they will do. Everything seems to be difficult.'

No! I thought. Don't feel sorry for him! He's the enemy! 'I hated sport at school,' I said. 'You'd have had your work cut out with me.'

'Well, there's always going to be one or two that really detest a certain subject,' replied Dave. 'I wasn't too keen on maths.'

'But some people just don't like maths,' I said desperately. 'You didn't change your mind about maths after trying a few rounds of equations or logarithms, did you? And, anyway, aren't you more exposed to ridicule in PE?'

'What about drama?' countered Dave. 'If you're a particularly quiet, shy kid, and you're forced to act in front of people, perhaps you hate that. I would have thought there are times in English or maths, say, when a kid makes a mistake in front of the class, the brighter kids snigger at them or condescend.' He crossed his arms and grinned at me. 'Wouldn't you?'

A bell rang. Lunch-break was over.

'Dave,' I said meanly, as I got up, 'does it ever worry you that some kids might leave here and hate you for the rest of their lives?'

'No,' said Dave Jacobs. 'I've never thought of that, never thought of it at all.' I believed him. 'Hopefully, most people will remember me as being OK, a laugh and a joke. Hopefully.'

I was going to have to revise my opinion of games teachers. After talking to Dave, rejoicing at the collapse of school sport seemed rather decadent. He appeared to be a decent man who was doing his best under difficult circumstances and so, no doubt, were many of his colleagues. Suddenly, bearing a twenty-year grudge against an entire profession seemed, well, pathetic.

The Lad's view of school sport I'd expected to hear from Dave was better articulated by Trevor Brooking. It was a disconcerting inversion. The games teacher favoured sport for all; but the head of Sport England wanted winners, and blamed teachers like Dave for the lack of them. It made my schooldays seem very far away.

At the school gate, I told Dave I was off to Latvia shortly, to represent the UK at the European Miniature Golf Championships. He nodded his approval and, for the first and only time that day, I got a glimpse of another Dave Jacobs. 'We should have a game sometime,' he said. He shook my hand a bit too hard and winked. 'I'll have that UK place off you!'

The following Saturday my schooldays came back to me with a thump. I'd been invited to a friend's birthday party, which was fine, but it was taking place in Regent's Park and revolved around a laid-back, just-for-fun game of competitive softball, which wasn't fine. Why couldn't we all have a nice picnic?

This birthday softball match is an annual event. Every year, my friend books a softball square (or pitch or court or whatever it is) and invites all his friends along to the park to play softball, just for fun. I don't know why he does this, but it always leads to another annual event – the argument he and I have when I tell him I'm not coming. This is selfish behaviour, I admit. It's his birthday, after all, and he should be allowed to choose how he celebrates it. But, of course, I never do sport, not for birthdays and certainly never for fun. My friend has right on his side, but I have *absolute* conviction on mine.

However, this year I decided I should go to his birthday party, partly out of affection for him, partly out of a new respect for Britain's PE teachers, but mostly because I thought I might do OK. Thanks to minigolf, I had my new healthy attitude. I had more control over my limbs than ever before. I felt like I could avoid a complete humiliation. I was not a kid.

We met in the park after lunch, about thirty of us. It was the hottest day of the year, just right for staying indoors and watching a film or, at a push, sitting under a big umbrella in the beer garden of a pub. But we weren't indoors and no one had brought an umbrella or even a can of shandy. A softball *habitué* explained the rules of the game to me, or tried to. I threw the softball experimentally from hand to hand. It was disconcertingly heavy and hard.

'Someone broke their thumb on that last year,' said my tutor.

I tried not to let any of this deter me. I was going to enjoy myself today, just like other people did.

'Happy birthday,' I said to my friend. 'I'm going to enjoy this.'

'You aren't,' said my friend. 'But thanks for coming.'

He was right, I didn't enjoy it. I volunteered to loiter deep in the outfield, out of the way. I tried to pay attention to the game and shout hearty encouragement to my teammates. But every time the not-so-softball was pitched, I experienced an old and familiar dread.

Fuck, I thought, I hope that doesn't come over here.

It was a reminder of how far I still had to travel on the path to sports enlightenment. It was also a reminder of how difficult it can be to leave school.

'My view is that physical education is a curriculum subject, and as such we have an obligation to deliver physical education in a way which provides a positive learning experience for every child.'

Shortly after Softball Saturday, I found myself sitting in the poky offices of the Youth Sport Trust, listening to its chief executive, Sue Campbell. She is a Jolly Good Sort and a modest sports evangelist.

'You know the expression "Sport builds character"?' she asked me.

'Oh, yes', I said, 'I know that one.'

'Well, I don't actually go along with that. I think sport reveals character. Sport is the vehicle, but what happens around it is what changes kids' behaviour.'

I nodded mutely and stirred my coffee. First Dave Jacobs, now Sue Campbell. For the second time in a fortnight, I had the uncomfortable feeling I was being outmanoeuvred by a games teacher. Wookie was never this cunning.

'Oh, I think sport is one vehicle,' said Sue Campbell, when I pressed her on it. 'I wouldn't claim it's *the* vehicle. But because it contains passion and emotion and expression, as well as scientific rigour, something about that art and science stuff together, it's an experience that's very difficult to replicate anywhere else, except probably music. It touches the emotions and challenges your skill.'

Sue Campbell came to the Youth Sport Trust after eleven years as the chief executive of the National Coaching Foundation, having trained as a PE teacher, lectured at Leicester and Loughborough, and represented her country in netball as a player, coach and team manager. In 1991, she was awarded the MBE. She is the games teacher's games teacher.

'At school, we didn't need you to feel like you were a failure or a success at games,' she told me, 'but that you enjoyed it. The bottom line would be for me that whoever manages that sporting experience for you, whether it's a teacher or a coach, they are the person who make it either a good or a negative experience. They make it either a character-building experience or they make it a character-destroying experience.'

I couldn't imagine Sue Campbell destroying anyone's character. She seemed so reasonable.

The YST's centre of operations is situated above a Euston sandwich shop, just round the corner from the somewhat grander headquarters of Sport England. The charity was formed in 1994, in their words, to 'build a brighter future for young people in sport'. Since January 2000, Sue Campbell has been seconded three days a week to be the non-political adviser to the Department for Education and Employment and the Department for Culture, Media and Sport. She works specifically for the Minister for Sport and the Minister for Schools, in an attempt to create 'some joined-up thinking' between physical education and school sport.

She listened while I relayed Trevor Brooking's comments on the supposedly detrimental effects of non-competitive sport in school, which I now knew practically by heart. She was emphatic in her response.

'If we really evaluate how many young people enjoy what we might call the traditional way of playing sport, I'd say it's the minority rather than the majority. In my era, if you were good, PE was great, after-school sport was wonderful, you played for the school team and you were off. That's the traditional route. But for those who weren't, it was a horror show. In this country, we kind of swing from "it's all about excellence" to "it's all about participation". But somewhere in the middle is right. Trevor's perception is one end of it. But we need both.'

I told Sue about the problems Dave Jacobs had with apathy among his kids. The YST had recently completed a two-year research programme to explore participation issues for girls. It had been part-funded by Nike.

'We turn down most sponsorships,' shrugged Sue, 'but Nike were willing to go through a very lengthy, high-quality research programme to get to the end conclusion. I'm not underestimating why for their purposes, but we didn't go for the short-cut, high-profile, you know, let's-throw-some-posters-into-schools approach. And Nike is a cool brand. PE teachers are telling us they no longer have to fight kids to get them into kit. They say this has got girls more interested than the activity alone. You have to recognize the brand has brought us something we couldn't have done on our own.'

As a child, Sue had needed no encouragement to get into kit. She had been a big football fan. 'Still am. I used to go with Dad to the Trent End at Nottingham Forest every Saturday. I'd spend hours kicking the old football against the garage door and thinking I'd won at Wembley and all that stuff, scoring the winning goal, you know how it goes.'

'Not really,' I said.

'But that football thing of coming off the pitch on Tuesday and being manager by Friday has not been good for coaching in this country. Coaching is not about your ability to play, coaching is about your ability to communicate, motivate, empathize, think creatively, devise and structure practice and training, understand the balance of human behaviour and human performance – it's a heck of a lot more than "I know how to kick a ball, so I can teach this other guy to kick a ball." '

Sue felt football's rapid growth had had other detrimental effects outside football. 'Football's good and bad and ugly bits have become people's perception of what sporting culture is and should be,' she said. 'It's unfortunate. I think sporting culture is much more – what's the word? – egalitarian, empowering, exciting than that.'

I told Sue about my experience in Denmark and my forthcoming visit to Latvia. I wondered if she'd include minigolf in that sporting culture.

'Yes,' she said instantly. 'It's a test of skill. It might not conform to the rigour some would put on it, but I can't see that it's fundamentally very different from many other sports we take part in. It requires co-ordination and it requires decision-making and analysis to do it well, presumably based on where the sunlight is at that moment and the shadows it's casting and the way the water is falling . . .'

I was impressed. 'You seem to know a lot about minigolf,' I said.

'I've got some friends in Florida. They play it very competitively. I've had a go.'

'Are you any good?' I asked.

'No, I'm hopeless,' said Sue.

I let this obvious lie pass, but I could understand why Sue Campbell was so in demand. She was inspiring to talk to.

'Sometimes it isn't the activity that puts you off, it's the manner in which the activity is delivered,' she said, as our meeting drew to a close. 'OK, perhaps when you were younger you did not have great physical attributes, or felt you didn't. You've pursued minigolf and you've clearly got a buzz out of that and you've pursued it to a very high level. I don't trivialize that at all – I don't trivialize anybody pursuing anything to a high level, because to me, that's following your star. I did that in sport. That makes a difference to your life and how you feel about yourself. That's what good PE should do. It has nothing to do with sport. It has everything to do with achievement. It has everything to do with finding a medium through which you can make a difference, not just for yourself, for things around you. If sport can be used as that kind of vehicle, medals aren't important. I don't care if it's minigolf or what it is. What matters is you've pursued a little dream and you've made something happen.'

Blimey. I left the Youth Sport Trust feeling empowered, excited, and if it's possible for a person to feel more egalitarian, that too. This was how kids should feel, I thought, like anything is possible.

I passed the offices of Sport England. A large TV screen in the foyer was tuned to Sky Sports. Maybe I've judged Trevor too harshly, I thought. He might be an ex-footballer, he might have a skewed view of sport as a result, but having been so pleasantly surprised by my meetings with both Dave Jacobs and Sue Campbell, I had real hope that things were changing.

So, when I got home, I rang Sport England.

'Good afternoon,' I said. 'I'd like to request an interview with Trevor Brooking, please.'

'Yes,' said the woman from Sport England. 'Can I ask which publication you represent?'

'I'm writing a book,' I said, 'about what it means to be a man in the UK when you don't like sport. I'd like to talk about the crisis in school sport.'

There was a brief silence at the other end of the line.

'You're a man,' replied the woman, puzzled, 'and you don't like sport?'

'That's right,' I said. 'Sorry.'

There was another pause and then the woman laughed. 'You must be really angry about this Section 28 stuff too!' she said. 'I'll put you through.'

I never did speak to Trevor Brooking so, Trevor, if you're

reading this – encouragement is not a bad thing. Sometimes consolation helps. I'm sorry you played for England in the ten years they weren't good enough to qualify for the World Cup, and when they finally did qualify in 1982, you only played for fifteen minutes because of a groin injury.

Don't worry. At least you tried.

12

Liegende Schleife – flat loop

I returned from Denmark with my head held high. By breaking forty twice in the tournament, I felt I had conquered the more erratic elements of my mental game. Thanks to Kirsten Barnes, I now had a means of dealing with my own short fuse. But with less than a month to go until the European Championship in Rīga, I knew there was a drastic shortfall in my level of technical ability. I still wasn't very good at hitting the ball.

In desperation, I turned to golf. This was not a perfect solution. As I'd come to realize in Odense, minigolf is not golf, it's another sport entirely. But in the absence of any serious practice opportunities – the UK, remember, has no beton courses and its eternit courses are not of a tournament standard – I had little alternative. There was putting in golf, and putting was my problem. I didn't know where else to go.

Putting is often referred to as golf's 'game within a game' or, in John Updike's phrase, 'the sick man of golf'. Does anyone actually enjoy it? Driving the ball is much more exciting; lifting it out of a bunker a greater challenge; but putting is all fuss and frustration. To reach the green in two, only to take a further three to reach the cup – who needs it? Often, the secret of a great golf game, of a great golfer, is the patience required to work on putting technique. You heal your game by tending its sick man.

At the Woburn Golf and Country Club, I had a consultation with Harold Swash, the man they call the pros' Putting Doctor. 'Oh dear, oh dear,' he tutted, as I spread my legs and hunkered down low over the ball, minigolf style, 'that's not right at all.'

We were out on the practice green. Harold Swash gave me a few useful pointers – posture, putting arc – but I liked my new specialist grip and stance and found I was reluctant to change them back to a golf-based model. I hit a few practice balls until one finally dropped, and we both breathed a sigh of relief.

'And that's how you do it!' said Harold Swash. We went inside.

To be fair to Harold Swash, he had made it clear in advance that he would probably be unable to help me. 'All I know about miniature golf,' he had said to me in the clubhouse, 'is that it's a totally different game to putting out on the golf course. You're using walls, obstacles, bouncing off them, so different side spins are something you have to contend with. You don't meet that on the golf course because, fundamentally, you're only talking about one surface. Yes, you might have little problems now and again when the greens are spiked up, or very nappy against the grain of the green, but nothing like the ball on a minigolf course. And, let's face it, you have to go round corners on those!'

Nevertheless, surely at least a little of the technique was transferable? Harold Swash had worked with a number of famous golfers on their putting, including Darren Clarke, Sam Torrance, Mark James and Nick Faldo. He believed there were four basic elements that made a good putt.

'One, the blade of the putter needs to be square to the target at the address and strike position. Two, the blade needs to be square to the path of the stroke through the hitting area, so as not to put a slice or a hook spin on it. Three, it's important to hit the ball with a slight upstroke, a *tangential strike*, which assists forward roll and accuracy. And four, you should have a smooth, controlled acceleration through the hitting area, in other words, good rhythm.'

I smiled and nodded. What was he talking about?

'If you've got the slightest little bit of negative thought going through your mind as you're addressing the putt, you're going to take two. At least. Walk away and start again. You've got to believe in yourself totally. When I was playing golf regularly, I was the world's greatest putter and believed it.'

'What was your handicap?' I asked. He was giving me a free lesson.

'My wife and two kids,' said Harold Swash, and chuckled.

'Ha,' I said politely.

Harold Swash described his golf technique as 'shunt, shunt, shunt and putt'. He believed putting to be a quantifiable mechanical skill, and referred to himself as a 'creative engineer'. He had designed both putting aids – the 'Hold Rite' Training Glove, the 'No Ifs' Green Reader – and some putters, the Supaline and Supafeel ranges for Dunlop, the Swashbuckler (described by the *Mail On Sunday* as 'revolutionary') and most notably the Rhythmiser, which had a bendy rubbery shaft and looked like something the Chuckle Brothers might use, but helped develop 'a smooth, pendulum-like putting action'. At sixty-seven ('five under par,' joked Harold Swash) he still travelled the world, giving lessons and working with professionals in Atlanta, Denver, Las Vegas, LA . . . In 1997, he had survived a quadruple heart bypass, and the following year a ruptured aortic aneurysm on the practice green at the Augusta National Golf Club.

'I'm very lucky to be alive,' he told me. 'Some people say I'm lucky, some people say I'm blessed, but some people say, "That old guy up there doesn't want you yet – there's a lot of guys down here still want putting lessons!"'

Once again we both laughed.

'These are all my pet sayings,' said Harold Swash. 'They drive my family crazy.'

Among the many professional golfers Harold Swash knew was Jarmo Sandelin, the Swede who had been in the Ryder Cup team at Brookline. 'He's very tall but he's someone who has the best posture on the tour for his putting. He started his career playing miniature golf. He's here somewhere. You should try and have a word with him.'

It was a few days before the Victor Chandler British Masters, and the pros were arriving at Woburn to practise, perhaps to consult with Harold Swash. I spent an hour or so waiting to see if Jarmo Sandelin turned up to buff his already excellent putting, but there was no sign of him.

Just a few weeks later I got close to Jarmo, along with about a hundred thousand other people. It was at the 129th Open Golf Championship at St Andrews in Scotland. I arrived at the Old Course just before nine o'clock on the second day of the tournament. The sun was out and a breeze was blowing in from the bay. I had come to see this great putter putt. Jarmo had teed off some fifty minutes earlier so, rather than race round the outskirts of the course – the Red Route – trying to catch up with him, I took a seat in the rapidly filling grandstand by the seventeenth hole.

The seventeenth hole at St Andrews is known as the most difficult par-four in the world. It is called the Road Hole, or just Road, because of the road that runs closely parallel to it. Like the House of the Rising Sun, it has been the ruin of many a poor boy. If you don't drop your ball on to the road, there is always the Swilcan Burn or the abscess-like Road Bunker to explore, or out of bounds in the Old Course Hotel's back garden. The Road Hole always draws a large crowd of gawpers because, just like a real road, there are occasionally some horrific accidents on it – gruesome triple-bogies and the like. The grandstand was packed.

It was windy up there and people around me were rubbing on sunblock. I pulled on my Glenlivet Office Putting baseball cap and waited for the first players to appear. Shortly afterwards, a trio of golfers, with entourage, could be seen way, way down the fairway – the Road Hole is 455 yards long. I checked the daily drawsheet. This was Colin Gillies and Jamie Spence of the UK, and Wei-Tze Yeh from Taiwan.

Watching them tramp towards us, I couldn't help thinking that the topography of the Road Hole was like that of an enormous crazy-golf layout. The player had to steer his ball round an elongated dog-leg, taking into account not only the cavernous bunker, a water hazard (the Swilcan Burn) and the undulations of the green, but even a giant novelty obstacle – the replica train sheds that stand in front of the tee, blocking the golfer's sight-line. It was really so difficult, I mused, as Colin Gillies thrashed about in the sand of the bunker, as to be plain silly, another hallmark of the crazy-golf experience. You could even argue that, given St Andrews' fondness for marketing itself as the home of golf both royal and ancient, it had a historical theme not so very far from Aztecs and Pirates. Not that that would be much consolation to Colin, who double-bogeyed.

By the time Jarmo Sandelin came through an hour or so later, we had seen all manner of disasters and just one birdie. I was eagerly anticipating how Jarmo would play the hole. I was also looking forward to getting my first real glimpse of him. Apart from his putting skills, he had a reputation, I'd discovered, as one of the game's more colourful characters, with a taste for flashy clothing – expensive hand-made belts, crocodile-skin boots turned into pointed-toe golf shoes by a cobbler in Stockholm, the $6,000 see-through Versace shirt he had worn at the Portuguese Open. Press reports used words like 'flamboyant' and 'contro-versial'. In 1998, *Golf Magazine* described him as the Dennis Rodman of European golf. There had been well-publicized spats with other professionals, like Mark O'Meara and Phil Mickelson. His captain in the Ryder Cup, Mark James, said 'He has taken the normal parameters of eccentricity and pushed them to new limits'. And then there was the minigolf.

So there was a double disappointment in store when Jarmo appeared. First, he was dressed soberly and appeared to have fallen out with no one on his way to the green. And second, although he birdied the Road Hole, it was by landing his ball just two feet from the cup with his approach shot: incredibly skilful but leaving him a disappointingly easy putt. What an anticlimax. Fortunately, one of his playing partners, Mark Calcavecchia of the USA, also birdied with an uphill putt of nearly fifty feet, but I felt obscurely cheated. It was the right putt from the wrong player. I descended from the grandstand and discovered that the early-morning sun and wind had burnt the tops of my ears.

I ambled down past the village of corporate hospitality tents and bought a bacon sandwich from a van. I wondered if Dad had ever come to one of these big events. He'd played golf here, when I was a child, I remembered that, but I couldn't recall a visit to a big championship. He would have loved it.

As I strolled down behind the eighteenth green towards the club entrance, Jarmo Sandelin strode past. I made to hail him, but I still had a mouthful of bacon sandwich and he had just finished his round (two under, four under for the championship), so he ignored my muffled exclamation – 'Mfftr Thwndlinn!' – and kept going. It probably wasn't the right moment to ask for minigolf tips anyway.

That morning, an important piece of putting research of the kind Harold Swash would approve was made public. Using infra-red cameras capable of taking two hundred pictures a second, researchers from universities in Edinburgh, Strathclyde, and Marseille & Grenoble had studied the putting of ten golfers with handicaps under five, in order to calculate the mathematical formula for the perfect putt:

$$Vc = 2D\,(1/T)\,(PT/k)\,(1 - PT2)\,(1/k) - 1\,[1]$$

As befits a breakthrough of this magnitude, the formula had been published in the *Sun*. 'And with the Open Championship starting today at St Andrews,' reported the paper loftily, 'experts say Sunday's winner will be the man who best masters the equation.'

In a way this was true, although none of today's competitors seemed to be using calculators. I had come to see Jarmo Sandelin, but most of the 99,999 other spectators were here for just one man. As I crossed to the first tee, I saw a group of fat, middle-aged sales executives, pasty and hung-over in the mid-morning sun-

1. Where Vc represents club velocity, D is amplitude of forward swing, T is time of forward swing, PT is proportion of time before the ball is hit from the top of the swing, and k a figure used by psychologists to denote how golfers' internal guide couples with the timing of the shot. Happy now?

light, and the fattest and pastiest of them was silhouetted against the leader board. He stretched out his arms. 'I am Tiger Woods!' he shouted.

Everyone agreed that if Tiger Woods was going to win this Open, it would be with his putting. Actually, that's not quite true. The wide-open terrain of the Old Course, with its lack of rough, was so suited to Woods' prodigious long game, it was more accurate to say that he could only be let down by his putting; but no one seriously thought that that was going to happen. Woods was clear favourite to win the Claret Jug, and if he won, he would once again make history – at twenty-four, the youngest ever winner of all four Grand Slam events (the Open, the US Open, the Masters and the PGA).

Tiger Woods is arguably the greatest sportsman in the world today. Those who try to argue that he isn't either don't like golf or don't like Woods. He is also rich on an industrial scale. It is estimated that his most recent deal with Nike, signed a few months after the Open, will net him $100 million over five years. The deal will expire in 2006. Woods will be thirty. As a golfer, he will not yet have reached the peak of his game.

I planned to follow Tiger Woods around the Old Course. I'd asked Harold Swash how he rated Woods' putting ability.

'Tiger Woods is a very good putter,' he said. 'He has this wonderful ability to concentrate and his rhythm is a young man's rhythm. But his technique does have the opportunity to be improved. But he's going to get better is what I think.'

Well, he seemed good enough to me. As we slowly progressed round the Red Route, I witnessed one inspired shot after another. It wasn't always easy to see Woods putt, what with the crowds, the stewards, the camera crews and Tiger's 'people', but, oh, my, only a fool would deny that they were in the presence of greatness. Harold Swash was right. It was the ability to concentrate that seemed remarkable, that despite the maelstrom around him, Woods apparently saw nothing but the game. He parred the Road Hole, even though he was nearly in the road. He shot sixty-six, six under for the day. It was a tutorial in brilliance.

There is nothing naff about Tiger Woods, nothing parochial, as there is perhaps about other golfers, and probably some aspects of golf. He is dignified in victory and never graceless in defeat. In his method and his athleticism, he has taken the game apart and put it back together in his own image. He doesn't dress like a slapstick comedian.

Two days later he won the Championship, eight shots clear of the nearest challengers, with a four-round total of 269, nineteen – nineteen! – under par, beating the previous record for the Open at St Andrews.

Do I sound like a fan? I suppose I do. But to see such a display of ability up close was, truthfully, awe-inspiring. The idea that surfaced in the days after the tournament, that Woods is in some way bad for golf, that his style of play and his dominance of the game are boring . . . I suppose you might think that if you believe sport isn't sport unless somebody loses. But what should Woods do? Be a little less great? Go put some money on the snail-racing.

Standing at the first tee on that second day, waiting for Woods to tee off, there occurred a much-reported Historical Moment. Jack Nicklaus walked up the eighteenth fairway in his last Open, and as he walked the crowd rose to its feet and gave him a huge and heartfelt ovation. Nicklaus stood on the bridge across the Swilcan Burn with tears in his eyes, waving to the crowd, waving goodbye. The baton, it was agreed, had been handed on.

All nonsense, of course, all sentiment and spin, the commercial simulacrum of real feeling. But I stood and observed his departure with tears in my eyes too, remembering my dad watching Nicklaus on TV and him saying, 'The Golden Bear is on the prowl,' and me laughing, a little boy. And standing here, I understood afresh – as you do occasionally, even after half a lifetime – that I wouldn't be hearing that voice again. He should have been there with me; maybe briefly he was.

Bloody sport.

Jarmo Sandelin finished the tournament in joint thirty-first place with 284. The following day, I travelled on up to Thurso, right at the top of the country, just a few miles from John

O'Groats, to play Britain's northernmost crazy-golf course. I can confirm it's still there and that it's a nine-hole eternit course. I could see it through the fence. It was shut.

The following weekend I thought of my dad again. I was at another club for another competition, a Celebrity-Am Tournament to benefit the Variety Club of Great Britain. The event had been jointly organized by the club, near Chingford in Essex, and the Variety Club's Golfing Society. The society's captain for the 2000 season, Sir Henry Cooper, OBE, KSG, had already written to the club thanking them for their fundraising efforts and promising 'bundles of fun and laughter for everyone'.

When I was nine, my dad's golf club hosted a similar Pro-Celebrity Tournament. It remains one of the golden days of my childhood. Jimmy Hill, Lance Percival . . . To a nine-year-old it all seemed impossibly glamorous, especially when Michael Barratt from *Nationwide* signed my autograph book, then grumpily refused to sign that of the girl next to me and made her cry. He chose me!

Later in the day, standing with Dad by the Nineteenth Hole, I was aware of one celebrity in particular holding court, languorously smoking a cigarette, with several empty glasses already in front of him.

'Dad?' I said, fascinated. 'Who's that man there?'

'Peter Cook,' said my father. 'He's a comedian.'

Peter Cook, eh? I didn't really know who he was, but he was famous and I liked comedians.

'Can I ask him for his autograph?' I asked Dad. In addition to Michael Barratt, I had also collected Albie Keen and Johnny Leach, the table-tennis champ.

'Yes,' replied Dad, though I can't believe without a bit of trepidation, 'but ask him *nicely*.' He guided me over to Peter Cook's table.

'Excuse me, Mr Cook,' I said, interrupting a burst of laughter. Mr Cook turned to look at me, cigarette in mouth, one eye half closed. 'Can I have your autograph?'

Peter Cook exhaled a cloud of smoke and smiled pleasantly at my father.

'Of course you can,' he replied, 'but Dad'll have to pay for it.' He signed my book and charged Dad a pound.

'Well,' said Peter Cook, sending to the bar for another drink, 'it is for charity.'

More than twenty years later, here in Chingford, the celebrities were arriving for coffee and biscuits.

'Hello, Gary!' said the woman from the Golfing Society to former Radio 1 DJ Gary Davis. 'Haven't seen you for a while. What are you up to these days?' But then Gary was joined by actor Chris Quinten and I didn't catch his reply. Gary and Chris wandered out to the car park together to get their golf clubs. They seemed quite pally.

At a table by the window, a group of celebs were trading stories about being in pantomime. Jimmy Tarbuck was coming to the end of an anecdote. 'She said, "Don't do that, it'll ruin it for the children!"' he exclaimed, and the whole table, including Russ Abbott and Sir Henry Cooper himself, exploded in riotous laughter. Tarby finished his story. 'They were in it with Humperdinck,' he said.

Sitting alone at another table, rolling a cigarette, was the comedian Mike Reid. I asked him if he would ever consider participating in a charity crazy-golf tournament.

He looked bemused. 'What, windmills and that?' he said.

'That's right,' I said.

'Well, it depends where it is,' he replied.

Mike, by his own admission, was knackered. He was nearing the end of his run as Frank Butcher in *EastEnders* and told me he was looking forward to having 'a bit of quality time for me'.

'Who do you expect to do well today?' I asked.

'Me,' said Mike Reid, deadpan.

I told him I'd seen Tiger Woods play last weekend.

'I've played that course,' said Mike. 'It's crap.'

In all honesty, Mike was pretty scary in real life, so I left him to enjoy a quiet cup of coffee on his own. 'Thanks, Mike,' I said, as I got up.

'Thank you, young man,' replied Mike. 'Make sure you mention the charity.'

At the first tee, the celebrities and their playing partners were moving out, three club members to every VIP. Shake hands, smile for the camera, and off. Some famous faces were more familiar than others. Sportsmen, such as Frank McLintock, were sociable and convivial; the comedians less so. They were there only to play golf.

One comic, however, made the effort to joke with a handful of spectators. It was Albie Keen, whose autograph I had collected in 1977.

'Have you heard?' he said. 'Ken Dodd's dad's dog's dead!'

The spectators, two middle-aged women and a man, looked blank. Albie said it again and laughed, and this time, taking the hint, the two women laughed too. 'Hee hee!' said the comic, and left the tee with a pint of lager raised above his head in farewell.

'I was waiting for a punch-line,' said one of the women when he'd gone.

'He insists on telling jokes, that one,' replied the man beside her. 'I don't know why. He's not very funny.'

On the practice green, I watched Jimmy Tarbuck roll in one putt after another – four feet, eight feet, ten . . . Tarbuck is, of course, one of the country's most famous celebrity golfers. He has written books, fronted videos and even presented a golf-themed TV game show, *Full Swing*. He also has a reputation as the best putter on the celebrity circuit. He and Harold Swash are members of the same club, and the Putting Doctor had vouched for his skill. Twelve feet, fourteen . . . He did, indeed, appear to be a first-rate putter.

I asked Tarby if he'd mind me following him round while he played.

Tarby looked underwhelmed. 'OK,' he said, 'but if you want to ask me anything, you'll have to ask me in the cart.'

And so it was that Jimmy Tarbuck and I rode together down

one of the wide-open fairways of the West Essex Golf Club, him steering and me trying desperately to make conversation.

'The showbiz contingent is fiercely competitive,' he told me, as we trundled along, his pint of lager shandy sloshing about in its plastic beaker. Jimmy plays off a handicap of seven, one of the lowest on the tour. It had been the lowest of all, but Gary Lineker had recently overtaken him. 'But he's a professional footballer,' said Tarby, 'so, you know . . .'

Jimmy Tarbuck had been captain of the Variety Club Golfing Society three times, most recently in 1999. He plays in about thirty events a year. In his golfing life, he estimated the Variety Club had raised in the region of a million pounds from such occasions. 'This club here has done a fantastic job raising the money for two Sunshine coaches, and I think they deserve a great big pat on the back for that.' I really wanted to ask him about his putting but it seemed rude to interrupt.

We pulled up near a tree. Jimmy had struck a powerful drive but unfortunately the ball had disappeared into some long grass.

'Is putting important to your game?' I asked.

'Yeah,' said Tarby bluntly, 'but you've got to get it on the green first. Help me look for this ball.'

After a couple of minutes of hunting I found it, resting deep in the rough in the shade of the tree. 'Over here,' I said: 'I think this is you.'

'Right,' said Tarby. It was a good eighty feet to the green. He addressed the ball confidently, before driving it hard straight into the tree.

'Am I putting you off, Jim?' I asked.

'Yes, son, you are,' said Tarby, with a face like thunder.

On the way back to the clubhouse, I passed Mike Reid again, climbing on to the ninth green and still looking thoroughly hacked off. A blowsy woman ran up to him with a camera.

'Hello, Frank!' she screamed. 'Can I take your picture?'

It occurred to me that, for Mike to enjoy a tournament like this, he must have Tiger Woods-like reserves of concentration. He just wanted to play golf, but the crowd was expecting bundles of fun and laughter, as billed. But, then, it was for charity, and charity facilitated this not-quite satisfactory arrangement, which was just as well since the celebs couldn't quite enjoy their golf, and the spectators couldn't quite enjoy the celebs.

'Of course you can, my darling,' said Mike, producing a Mike Reid grin and a crowd-pleasing dirty laugh. Everyone around the green laughed too. Good old Mike. He might be an amateur golfer, but in all other respects he was a total professional.

It was many months later that I finally got the chance to talk to Jarmo Sandelin. He was in the country again to take part in a tournament at the Belfry. It was the week of his birthday so I had brought him a birthday present. It was a scale model of an eighteen-hole eternit minigolf course made by Faller, the German equivalent of Hornby model railways. I wasn't sure if Jarmo would like the present. He didn't seem like the sort of inter-national sportsman who would spend his free time tinkering about in the loft, painting bits of sponge green, but I hoped it might jog his memory.

It did. On the box was a picture of the course when assembled, with scaled-down trees and some miniature miniature golfers enjoying a game. 'I always have a problem with this one, the tunnel,' said Jarmo nostalgically, pointing at one hole in particu-lar, a curved ramp leading to a narrow tube. 'Is there a course around here somewhere? We should go and play.'

As a former member of the Swedish national youth team, Jarmo's best score on felt was twenty-five and on eternit twenty-one, so it wasn't entirely unhappily that I informed him that there were no courses for miles around.

'Oh, well, that's too bad,' said Jarmo, 'but we should definitely play some time.'

Jarmo Sandelin is a good-looking man with model Nordic blond hair and blue eyes, some way removed from the dandyish figure of his press cuttings. The day we met he was wearing dark, sharply pressed trousers and a not particularly flamboyant blue towelling shirt, which he had designed himself. In conversation, he is thoughtful, funny and charismatic, with occasional flashes of intensity and a fierce belief in himself and his family. His mother had died two years ago, and he fought back tears as he described how hard it had been for him to accept. 'At first I managed to focus on my golf, because I knew how important it was to my mother. But year 2000 was a no man's land. I started to realize she was gone. But, you know, hopefully it's a new generation coming up with my son . . .' Jarmo and his girlfriend and former caddy, Linda, had recently had a baby boy, Lukas.

Sandelin is from a country that in the last twenty years has gone golf mad. When he started in the early eighties there were seventy thousand registered players; now there are half a million. Sweden has produced international golfers of the calibre of Jesper Parnevik, Per-Ulrik Johansson, Pierre Fulke and Jarmo himself, far more than any other Scandinavian nation.

Jarmo was more than happy to reminisce about his minigolf-playing days. 'That was a fantastic period of my life. I had a chance to play competitive miniature golf at that stage around Sweden. It was like a journey in a very small form. If you look at my life today, I do the same journey but the difference is it's New York, Sydney, Johannesburg, Paris . . . Before it was Gothenburg, Borlänge . . .'

He had been supported in his efforts by his engineer father, who was keen for his children to play as much sport as possible. Both Jarmo and his elder brother and sister were encouraged to try ice-hockey, football, ping-pong, even chess. Mr Sandelin was also an enthusiastic follower of English football and the whole family supported Everton. Jarmo, whose English is rather idiosyncratic, told me that this was because they liked to back the underdog – because, in his phrase, 'Liverpool is the big daddy and Everton is the small piece.'

In 1973, the Sandelins moved from Finland to Sweden, settling in Stockholm, where Mr Sandelin had family. They retained their Finnish citizenship. Jarmo only altered his when the Swedish national minigolf team asked him to join the juniors. 'Because my father and my mother thought it was fantastic to be in the national team,' said Jarmo. 'That's the only reason I changed my citizenship.' He laughed. 'I could have been the best golfer for Finland ever!'

'You'd have been a national hero,' I said.

'I could have had a jet plane by now,' said Jarmo, half seriously.

In 1999, Jarmo had won two tournaments and played in the Ryder Cup. This year, he was having a solid but not spectacular season. He believed he had played well in the Open at St Andrews, 'but – oof! – some stupid mistakes. I know I'll make birdies in tournaments, but I got to make extra pars. I got to focus.'

Jarmo was nine when he discovered miniature golf. He and his cousin Marcus had absconded with two hundred Finnish marks from Marcus's mother's purse. On the way back from the amusement park where they had blown most of the loot, they stopped at a McDonald's for something to eat. There was a minigolf course, felt variety, in the basement of the restaurant.

'So we were eating hamburgers and then we took a round. I had sixty. I couldn't understand why I took so many shots, so I said to Marcus, "We have to do it again, I can't be so bad." Next time, I had fifty-five. Good, but I must be better than that.'

The two boys had played a little more, but evening was coming on and Marcus wanted to go home, so he left Jarmo at the course, playing and replaying. 'I stayed there all evening and got home really late. When I stepped through the door they were just going to phone the police. My father was so angry. I'd never seen him so angry before, because he was scared. They didn't see me leave in the morning and they had no idea where I was. That's the only time my father hit me, because he was so scared.'

The following day, in a fit of remorse, Jarmo's father had taken him to another amusement park, a smaller one, to try to make it up with his son. 'And I said, "No, I want to go and play miniature golf." So we went back to McDonald's. And after that, I went there day after day, and I improved quite fast.' He smiled at the memory and shook his head. 'So many rounds, so many rounds . . .'

This intense blond child was soon practically living at the

course, playing in tournaments, often winning them. 'I was very competitive. Winning was the most important thing. I didn't miss a prize for three years, I was always in the prizes, if not a first prize then the second . . .' Jarmo preferred the autonomy of minigolf to team games, and his father approved because his son had found something he liked and he knew the boy would be mentored by older players, and an eye kept on him. And minigolf brought him his first taste of publicity, when a Swedish national newspaper ran a story on the minigolfing *wunderkind*. 'I had a whole page! That was great!'

But when he was fourteen, Jarmo's father died. It devastated the family, and I had a very strong sense that, twenty years later, it is still the defining event of Jarmo Sandelin's life. It was around this time that he started going to the driving range, 'And the same thing happened that happened with the miniature golf. My friends at the club were asking, "Hey, where are you?" And I said, "I'm playing golf now. I need to get better."'

At fourteen, Jarmo was a comparatively late starter. 'I was a hacker. But I believed in myself, and that was thanks to the miniature golf. I knew from the first day I shot sixty, I could shoot fifty-nine. And I saw a chance to be as good at golf as I was at miniature golf. In miniature golf I knew I could never make money. At golf, I knew at least there was a chance.'

He turned professional in 1987. For several years, he worked nights for his brother's cleaning company, and borrowed money from friends. At one point he owed them £30,000; his total earnings in 1992 were £4,531. But he kept going. In 1995 he made it on to the European Tour, where he won his first tournament on just his fourth start and was eventually crowned Rookie of the Year. He had finally become the person he knew he was meant to be. Like Kirsten Barnes in Barcelona, making the tour was 'a relief. I knew what it would mean to my family. It was like thousands of kilos disappeared from my shoulders. It was like, "Thank you, Dad!"'

It was his early days on the European Tour that gained him his reputation as a colourful character, both in his dress sense and in his scraps with other professionals. He wanted to make an impression and in this he was aided by the innate conservatism of the golf world. But it was also Jarmo's belief that the golfers owed it to the crowd to make an effort. 'If we are a hundred monkeys on the first tee, why do we all have to look the same?' he said sagely. 'Who likes to see a hundred same-looking monkeys?'

As for his dust-ups with other golfers, Jarmo referred again to his father. 'I was living with a strong memory of whatever happens in life, if you feel somebody is stepping on you, make sure that they know about it, and if they don't move off, then make sure they move off.'

The belts, the arguments, the snakeskin golf shoes, the fifty-four-inch driver that was now hanging in a sports bar in Monaco ('Oh, God! When I look at it now, I think, Where were my hormones? Were they outside my brain?') . . . After a couple of years, Jarmo realized he was in danger of getting more publicity for his personality than for his golf shots. Fortunately, his golf shots were getting better. In 1999, he won the Spanish and German Opens and, in doing so, earned his place in the team for that year's Ryder Cup.

In fact, Sandelin was somewhat on the periphery of the now infamous 1999 Ryder Cup. He, like Jean Van de Velde and Andrew Coltart, played only in the singles competition on the final day (all three players lost) and was forgotten in the subsequent furore over the American team's bad behaviour.

'If I had scored one point or half a point I would have been the hero, you know? I had my chance, I blew it, and that's life . . . Shit happens. But I don't have to be in the team this time, that doesn't destroy me, because I know there will be another Ryder Cup and I can be better prepared. I was not the hero last time, I might not be the hero next time either, but maybe the next time . . .

'My first dream was to be a professional and after that to be in the Ryder Cup team. My dream is still to be better than one hundred in the world ranking but I've been really struggling. The best I've ever been is sixty-four in 1999. I know mentally I'm capable of being top thirty, closer to top ten.'

So Jarmo persevered on the Tour, hoping for the breaks, and looking for ways to maximize his earning potential. He had recently switched management companies to Octagon, the global sports marketing group whose clients include Anna Kournikova, Darren Gough and Audley Harrison. 'It's a great time to be a gifted athlete,' they tell new clients. 'The world's passion for sport means the opportunities, both within your sport and in the "outside world", are more dazzling than ever.'

Jarmo was aware of the need to be seen as a name that could travel in the 'outside world'. He defined his brand for me as 'personal style and high quality'. Building on his love of fashion, he had plans for a range of clothing he would design himself, and had been to the Paris textile expo some months previously to choose fabrics. I asked him when he planned to launch. 'It depends,' said Jarmo wryly. 'If I win a major or two, it would be good.'

Of course, the golfer winning all the majors was Tiger Woods. Jarmo believed that Woods had mastered every element of the game. 'He was better at seven than I was at fourteen. I am more impressed that he is not fed up with it! He has done it so many hundreds of thousands of times. I can never compete with Tiger Woods at the same level. But he is very good for golf. He is making everyone realize that before him was not the highest level. It was not good enough.'

Did he think he could beat Tiger at minigolf?

Jarmo laughed. 'He would do really good on the minigolf course,' he said. 'His stroke is good, his feeling is good . . .'

Jarmo reckoned that in certain respects golf and minigolf were very similar. The most important thing he had learnt from minigolf, and that I could learn in turn from golf, was focus. 'You have to have concentration. Train your brain just to focus on what you're going to do from the half an hour before you start until you hit your last shot on the eighteenth, one shot at a time.' Jarmo remembered one minigolf tournament where he had six shots to win, but took seven. 'I was ten or eleven years old but I can remember it like it was today, I'd never felt so bad in my life as at that moment. I felt like I was a professional but I'd taken seven and I'd lost. That taught me to be focused. That's the main thing.'

This was what Kirsten Barnes and Harold Swash had said; it was what Mike Reid and Jimmy Tarbuck needed; it was what Tiger Woods had in abundance. And it was what I was going to have to rely on in Latvia.

Despite his reputation, Jarmo Sandelin did not strike me as particularly eccentric, or at least no more eccentric than most successful sports people. His eccentricity, such as it was, lay in an unassailable belief in himself and his own Jarmo-shaped place in the world – Jarmo the athlete, Jarmo the clothes designer, Jarmo the 'golfing entertainer', as he had been known for a while. It was a useful eccentricity to have when you worked in a field of over-achievers even more compulsive than you.

'I've always believed in my destiny. It's my destiny to achieve what I've done to date. I believe my grandfather achieved, and what he did was the first step. My father was born, he stepped out of his surroundings so when I was born I had it a little bit better. And my son is better off than I was. If he really likes to play golf and my destiny is to be around one hundred, then I'm sure his destiny will be greater than that.'

Like a great artist or a visionary entrepreneur, Jarmo Sandelin believed that if he had a bad day, that even if he went out tomorrow and shot eighty, he had done nothing but get in the way of his own destiny. Tomorrow could be different; and, anyway, he would still be Jarmo.

He told me about the days he spent playing golf with corporate clients, or in charity tournaments. 'Sometimes I play with guys and they are so nervous they can't hit the ball,' he said, shaking his head in mild disbelief. 'But to me, it's strange, because I'm Jarmo. I'm just a regular Jarmo.'

I'd brought my putter and bag of balls with me. Jarmo rummaged around, taking out individual balls from Svend's selection and howling with laughter. He picked up my putter and traced the long arc of the expert minigolfer. It was obvious he still had the stroke. There was real grace in it.

'Your putting is famously good,' I said.

'Yeah,' said Jarmo matter-of-factly, 'it's very good. It could maybe be even better.' He took another perfect stroke. 'Maybe I should go back to this. What do you think?'

I liked Jarmo very much. In fact, Jarmo and I shared a birthday. He was exactly one year older than me. 'I'm sorry I didn't bring you a present,' he said, when we parted company, 'but thank you for mine.' The last I saw of him he was striding off across the lobby, miniature eternit course tucked under one arm, to encounter the next inevitable stage in his destiny.

13

Gerade Bahn mit Zeilkreisfenster – straight run with target window

Ten . . .

RAVENSCOURT PARK, LONDON

The countdown to Latvia had begun. In the week before departure I adhered to a strict training regime. Every morning I got up early and walked to the local park, where I'd discovered a disused nine-hole eternit course on a patch of grass near the bowling greens. Clambering over the railings, I would unzip my ball bag, unsheath my putter and, in full sight of the early-morning commuters on the District Line, tackle each hole a minimum of five times. Having accomplished this, I would then continue on my way to work. I felt no shame.

You couldn't hire a club and play this course. It looked like it had lain derelict for several years. It was literally decomposing. There's probably asbestos in it, I thought, trying not to inhale as I putted. But the course was playing a vital role in the UK's bid for glory at the European Championships.

I had no idea which, if any, of these designs – the lightning one, the one with the bridge, the one with the movable pyramids (long gone) – might occur in Latvia. Neither was I particularly convinced of the effectiveness of this training regime; the putting surface was rutted and crumbly and even blebby[1] in places. But I had to do something. I had to feel like these were my final preparations.

Every night after work, I would unroll the practice mat and do battle with the putt returner, whose mechanism now sounded less like a skull being drilled and more like a tremendous mocking raspberry. Putt, bounce, fart.

British medal hopes received a boost, however, when, with a few days to go, the Perfect Solutions™ Battery-operated Putt Returner flatulated a bit too enthusiastically and broke, mid-stream. For once, it was not missed.

Nine . . .

The British Olympic squad were acclimatizing to the heat and humidity of Sydney by training on the Gold Coast. I primed myself for Latvia by spending a weekend in Skegness. The crazy golf would be plentiful, and the conditions would be unpredictable.

I started off at Fantasy Island on the outskirts of town. Fantasy Island is Britain's first themed indoor family resort and Europe's largest outdoor market. It says so on a sign over the gate. It's a concrete acre containing both a funfair *and* a car-boot sale but disappointingly no Ricardo Montalban or planespotting dwarf sidekick. But it does have crazy golf.

It was difficult to know where the outside world ended and Fantasy Island began. In the car park, a woman was selling boxes of washing powder out of the back of a van – if, indeed, it was the car park. Maybe I was already on the shores of Fantasy Island. Further on, possibly inside by now, a stall was offering cheeky replica number-plates: **EURO 2000, DHSS 2**, and perhaps most appositely, **ITS NICKED**.

Sandy Bay was located on the south coast of Fantasy Island,

---

1. Look it up. I did.

just round the corner from the Fryary chip shop. Some thought had gone into its design. It was comprised of nine holes with a sub-aquatic theme, sea-blue felt surrounded by coral and with marine life for obstacles: a turtle, an octopus, a clam. This thematic unity had not extended to the hut, however, which was an oversized woodland toadstool, obviously left over from some other playground with elves and pixies.

Inside the toadstool, with the clubs and scorecards, sat an old man. To enter his place of work, he had to bend down and practically crawl on all fours. It had rained heavily the night before, he told me, which meant the felt was sopping wet and he would spend much of the day trying to stop children treading sand into it, a task of Sisyphean futility. 'Still,' he said, looking on the bright side, 'at least they don't make me wear a pointy hat with a bell on the end.'

I played the course and left, making a mental note to sort out a pension plan when I came back from Latvia.

Directly opposite Fantasy Island is Butlins. There are now only three Butlins holiday camps left in the UK: Skeggy, Bognor and Minehead. They all have crazy-golf courses, truncated Arnold Palmer layouts with a handful of mutilated obstacles. When I went to see June's business partner, the man who had once run the Arnold Palmer franchise in the UK, he took me to see the Minehead course.[2] At Butlins' insistence, he had recently refurbished the course, relaying the felt in fun reds and yellows. Obstacles had been repainted and the sails had been removed from the windmill in case a camper injured him or herself on 'the moving part' and decided to sue.

'What do you think of it?' he asked me.

2. The crazy-golf course at Butlins in Minehead has the distinction of being the only crazy-golf course mentioned by Paul Theroux in *The Kingdom by the Sea*. He describes it as 'not popular', which has a 'mostly harmless' feel to it. If only Theroux had played a bit more crazy golf, he might have had a happier trip.

It was horrendous. It reminded me of what they did to Eva Perón after she died.

'Very nice,' I said.

The Butlins Skegness course looked comparatively intact but it was busy, and to get to it required a day pass, which would be expensive.

'Excuse me,' I said, to the man on the gate. 'Can I have a go on your crazy-golf course? Next week I'm going to Latvia to play in the European Miniature Golf Championships. I'm representing the UK. Look, I've got my own equipment. I've been to Minehead already.'

He wouldn't let me in and I can't say I was surprised.

Eight . . .

ARNOLD PALMER PUTTING, NORTH PARADE, SKEGNESS

More like it. This Arnold Palmer along the prom was in good condition, there were sails on the windmill, and the scorecards still bore the Arnold Palmer imprint. They didn't look as though they'd changed much in thirty years. On the back was a list of the towns in which the franchise once operated:

Battersea	Gt Yarmouth	Sheffield
Blackpool	Hastings	Skegness
Camber Sands	Hornsea Potteries	Southend
Canvey Island	Hove	Tynemouth
Cleethorpes	Leicester	Weymouth
Exmouth	Mablethorpe	Whitby
Goodrington	Margate	Whitley Bay
Gorleston		

The list was seriously out of date but what an empire this had been, stretching from shore to shore, and even annexing Sheffield. I shot a happy forty-one and moved on.

Seven . . .

GOLD MINE ADVENTURE GOLF, PLEASURE BEACH, SKEGNESS

An adventure-golf course with a Wild West theme, situated next to the Cactus Canyon River Ride. Not the most dramatic adventure-golf course in the world – just a few cacti and, incongruously, some Easter Island monoliths – but not about pirates either. I was sick of pirates. The course was all right (nine holes, par thirty, three under) but like Blackpool Pleasure Beach's Alpine Golf and Moroccan Golf at Pleasureland in Southport, it was a treat not to have play surrounded by cannons, cutlasses, yo-ho-hos and a bottle of rum.

Six . . .

JOLLY ROGER ADVENTURE GOLF, OPPOSITE THE CLOCK TOWER, SKEGNESS

No.

Five . . .

THE ORIGINAL CRAZY GOLF, SOUTH PARADE, SKEGNESS

A fifteen-hole course established in 1927, over the road from a row of guesthouses named after royal residences: the Clarence House Hotel, the Windsor, the Balmoral. A Union Jack flew above the hut. It was more charming than playable. The putting surface was made of living-room carpet; the tees were car mats, the cups flowerpots.

I played behind two fat men in England shirts, both of whom had mean-looking dogs with them on chains. The dogs barked and bit one another for something to do. There were a lot of England shirts and a lot of dogs in Skegness. Even the pensioners were animal-handlers. Near the pier, I'd seen an old woman in a wheelchair apparently being pulled along by two massive bull-dogs. And they were on chains too.

They said Skegness was bracing, and it was.

Four . . .

Escape up the coast to Mablethorpe. A pleasant surprise. In addition to a municipal course in Queen's Park and another Arnold Palmer on the cliff top, I found the best crazy-golf course in the country.

Mablethorpe Crazy Golf is on the seafront, next to the Dunes Theatre. It looks out to sea and is bordered with benches and tubs of geraniums. Its eighteen holes are miniature triumphs of ingenuity and make-do. The obstacles had either been restored or made from scratch by hand. There was a windmill, a red and white lighthouse surrounded by rocks, a real cannon newly painted in black and gold. The eighteenth hole was a Fun Castle that rewarded a successful putt by squirting the player with water. The centrepiece of the course was a splendid fifteen-foot replica of the Humber Bridge. You could buy souvenirs from the hut: badges, pens and even a window sticker, 'I've Hit A Golf Ball Across The Humber Bridge On Mablethorpe Crazy Golf.' It was obvious that, unlike so many of the courses I had played in recent months, someone had poured real time and love into the Crazy Golf here.

In the hut was a middle-aged woman with a mug of tea and a copy of the *Puzzler*. I asked her if the Humber Bridge was built to scale.

'Oh, no!' exclaimed the woman. 'It's made from a plank!'

The woman's name was Carol. She and her husband Dave had run the course since 1984, but there had been crazy golf on the site for nearly fifty years. They leased the land from the council, and sold souvenirs instead of ice-creams because the lease didn't allow them to compete with the café next door.

Carol said the crazy golf had really been Dave's baby. He was 'the ideas man'. 'Yeah, he's full of ideas. He'd have me shopping for stuff I didn't know what I was shopping for. He nicked the top off my flower tub. I went out and found my bulbs all over. I said, "What have you done?" He says, "This'll just do for my helter-skelter!"'

They were open from March to October, but Easter and the summer holidays were when they really made their money. They'd also had a shop selling sweets and Mablethorpe rock but Dave had been diagnosed with cancer five years earlier, so they'd had to give that up. The crazy golf was now their main source of income.

They tried to sequence the holes so that players could flow through quickly. 'What we do is have a hard one, then an easy one, then a hard one, then an easy one,' said Carol. Currently, the first hole was the black and gold cannon, but it was causing problems. 'The cannon's actually quite easy, but it *looks* hard. People get in a panic and that can cause bottlenecks. We're thinking of moving it. But, then, you've got to have something on the first hole that makes people go, "Oh, yes, I want to have a go on that."'

Mablethorpe was a quiet, old-fashioned place. Vandalism wasn't much of a problem, Carol told me, not since a few local businesses had clubbed together and had cameras installed. Kids used to come up and throw her flowers around; sometimes OAPs would steal her geraniums. 'And it bugged me because I'd grown them from cuttings. I reckon I spent upwards of forty pounds replacing them.'

From the sound of it, Dave was seriously ill. He wasn't able to devote much time and energy to maintaining the course and devising new obstacles, but he did what he could. 'We were in Scarborough. Up towards the north end of the front, there's one like a Viking ship. I think that rather appealed to my husband. I know he's always had the intention of doing something that ran alongside the hut here, like a ship or a galleon. Obviously that's not going to happen now . . .'

I told Carol about Latvia and to tell Dave that the British Miniature Golf team were giving him and his course the thumbs-up. She smiled and thanked me. 'I'll tell him,' she said. 'He'll be chuffed.'[3]

3. When I was writing this, I learnt that Carol's husband Dave had died. If you're in that part of the country, go and see the course he built. It's unique.

While I was climbing the cliff path to the Arnold Palmer, I thought, I'm going to Latvia. I'm going to play minigolf for my country. For eight days. In Latvia. This isn't funny any more.

The wind was up. I stood by the Arnold Palmer windmill and watched the sand train chugging along Mablethorpe beach, and thought, I don't want to go to Latvia. I want to stay here.

But I knew I was going. It was my destiny.

Three . . .

BROOMFIELD PARK ADVENTURE GOLF, BROOMFIELD PARK, LONDON

Three days to go. I met up with Peter at his house. It was hot, and we played a round at the course that had seen Tim Davies' victory in the rain a few months previously. I shot fifty-one, Peter shot forty-nine. It wasn't for the practice: it was for the company of someone who understood.

Peter was kind enough to accentuate the positive by telling me about his trip to the World Championships. He described his experiences in Holland as 'an adventure'. He said the atmosphere at the tournament was 'competitive but friendly'.

'I was the first British player to compete at international level,' he said. 'There was a huge range of ability and experience. There were players like me who'd never played on eternit or beton, with very little in the way of equipment. And then there were the good players. I knew I was going to be outclassed but they really play to win. The Germans are very good. There are German players who don't stand a chance of being selected who would walk into teams for other countries.'

Peter said that he had been struck by the intensity of it. 'It was serious. It was no less competitive than a football match or whatever you might watch on the telly. I didn't know what to expect, apart from I expected to finish last.'

'And did you?' I asked.

'No,' said Peter proudly. 'In the men's competition I was a hundred and twelfth out of a hundred and twenty-three.'

Peter had beaten competitors from Singapore, Japan and America (not including Jon Drexler).

'I was the worst European, which probably won't give you much confidence for the European Championships,' he said, with a grimace. 'Sorry. I was five shots worse than the worst Estonian. But there was one bad round that I had. If it hadn't been for that . . .'

'Do you think I'll be the worst European?' I said to Peter.

'You never know,' said his mouth, but his eyes told a different story.

This is something you are going to do, I kept telling myself. I asked Peter how it felt to represent his country on the international stage.

'It would have been a lot better if there'd been other British players there, or people I knew,' he said. 'Sorry. And it felt a bit odd carrying the flag at the opening ceremony, I suppose . . .'

Two . . .

MY HOUSE, LONDON

Two nights before flying out, I telephoned my cousin Don. Don had been a long-distance runner for Britain from the late sixties through to the mid-eighties. He had travelled the world in an era when there were still countries, continents even, that only sportsmen could get into. In 1970, at the Commonwealth Games in Edinburgh, he won bronze in the marathon. He recorded top-ten finishes in the first two London marathons too. Dad had been a great supporter of Don, and sometimes we used to go and watch him race up on the downs near our house. It was a family joke that absolutely none of Don's talent or enthusiasm had rubbed off on me.

I told Don where I was going and what I was going to be doing when I got there.

Don was astounded. 'Your father would be very proud,' he said, once he'd got over the shock. 'Mind you, he'd think it was hilarious.'

We discussed how important it was to have a routine. 'But when it gets to within a week of the actual event,' Don counselled, 'you probably won't get any better by doing another week's training. The best thing to do is relax and do nothing. When are you going again?'

One . . .

RAVENSCOURT PARK, LONDON

Putt, putt, putt, putt, putt, putt, putt, putt, putt. No relief.

Buy guidebook, travellers' cheques in US dollars, and QPR replica away shirt, for purposes of sending photo to *Hoops Magazine.*

Pack suitcase. Go to bed.

Get up. Make failed attempt to resuscitate Putt Returner.

Go back to bed. Fall asleep and dream I am in the Portobello Road on a Saturday, buying records and feeling a deep and blissful tranquillity. I find an album I have been searching for for years, a fantastic album by a band I love, the existence of which I really only comprehend when I find it in the plastic crate. The man lets me have it for nothing. I am so happy. I have a sense that I have forgotten something, something important, but in my dream I feel a calm and peace of mind I have not known for months.

Then I wake up.

Zero . . .

14

Sprungschanze mit Reuse – ski-jump with net

If my star would fall
Or disappear at all
I will follow my star till the end of my days,
And my heart's gonna lead me through so many ways,
And if you gonna join me I'll be your guide,
Baby, 'never say never', be my 'Runaway Bride'.

      Brainstorm, 'My Star' (Prāta Vētra, 'Īssavienojums')

It's hard to pinpoint the exact moment when the British campaign at the European Miniature Golf Championships started to go so badly wrong, but in retrospect it was probably when I asked my wife to accompany me to Rīga as the GB National Coach.

'You must be joking,' said Tina.

My wife had watched my transformation from sceptic to obsessive over the year with a mixture of amusement and scepticism herself. She had accompanied me on several weekend seaside forays. On the occasions she played, she usually won. I didn't really want her to be coach, I just didn't want to go to Latvia on my own.

Denmark had been fun, I told her. The people had been hospitable, the atmosphere relaxed. It would be like a fortnight's holiday.

'A *fortnight?*' said Tina incredulously.

The tournament itself lasted only four days, but a mandatory five-day practice period preceded it, which also included the opening and closing ceremonies and a couple of World Minigolf Sport Federation technical meetings that Peter had asked me to attend. Given the vicissitudes of flight timetabling, it looked like I would be in Latvia for nearly two weeks.

We compromised. In order for Tina to be allowed on the course during the tournament, she would have to be registered as a course official, which was some way short of the team coach. And if for any reason she didn't feel like hanging around the minigolf course all day, she was completely at liberty to enjoy beautiful historic Rīga on her own, the new Prague I told her, not that she had ever expressed any desire to go to the old one.

Cracks in this compromise, however, began to appear within hours of landing at Rīga International Airport. Our hotel, an enormous Soviet concrete block formerly known as the Tūrists Hotel, was handily located next to the minigolf course rather than in beautiful historic Rīga. There was nothing wrong with the hotel, which had been recently refurbished by a German chain, except that it was full of very serious tracksuited minigolfers, who barged past us on their way to the course and smiled only at each other. The friendly and jocular atmosphere of Denmark seemed largely absent.

Our room on the seventh floor was small, Spartan and surgically clean, with separate beds and a carpet that appeared to be made from minigolf felt.

'No distractions for the athletes,' I said lamely.

'No distractions for anyone,' said Tina, looking glum.

Next to the hotel was a three-storey wooden house that was falling down. It was a slum. There were holes in the roof and a dead ginger tomcat in the yard. We watched some children playing with it as we descended in the elevator to the ground floor.

The minigolf course was directly opposite the hotel, fenced in at the corner of a rambling, overgrown park. A banner was strung along the fence, which read *Minigolfs, spēle visai ģimenei!* – a game for all the family! Further down stood a display hoarding – EIROPAS ČEMPIONĀTS MINIGOLFĀ – bearing the logos of the WMF, and the tournament's sponsors, most of whom were German or Austrian, including Fun-Sport. Inside the gate was a two-storey white clapboard clubhouse, with a balcony and a kiosk selling cucumber rolls. There was also a trestle table laden with minigolf balls, for sale at nine lati each; about ten pounds.

In front of the clubhouse stood the winners' rostrum. It was positioned next to a display of the competing nations' flags. I was both relieved and slightly unsettled to see the Union Jack. I tried to shake off the feeling that it, like me, was here by default. Although the official period for training did not begin for another twenty-four hours, both the eternit and the beton were fully occupied by players and coaches. I signed in at the clubhouse. Great Britain, it emerged, was the last team to register.

It was early afternoon and horribly muggy. My coach, if I had one, would have advised me to take advantage of this extra time and begin my pre-competition build-up. Instead Tina and I took a decrepit tram over the Daugava River and into Old Rīga, some twenty minutes away.

This part of Rīga, it transpired, was both historical and beautiful, in a ruined, are-they-knocking-that-building-down-or-has-it-just-fallen-over sort of way. Latvia was enjoying only its second period of independence since the thirteenth century. The country was briefly self-governing in the twenty years between the First and Second World Wars, during which time Rīga was known as 'Little Paris', which meant that the buildings were either centuries-old cottages and churches, unrestrained examples of German art nouveau or oppressively functional Soviet cubes. It looked like very few of them, cottage or cube, had been touched since they were built.

However, reconstruction was under way. In the town-hall square, they were painstakingly restoring a fourteenth-century merchants' guildhall that had been destroyed in a bombing raid in 1941; the Soviets subsequently demolished the ruins because they represented 'decadent' German architecture. The hall's resurrection, therefore, was a remarkable achievement, and unthinkable only ten years before. The old merchants whose home this once was had taken their name from St Mauritius, the 'dark-skinned Moor' they considered their main protector, and the hall's reborn opulence was tarnished only by the careless translation of its original name – Melngalvju Nams; the House of the Blackheads.

To emphasize the accomplishment of the venture, the House of the Blackheads was being reconstructed in sight of the Occupation Museum and a statue of the Latvian Red Riflemen, who had fought alongside the Bolsheviks in the Russian Revolution. The statue, like the museum, was a source of some controversy in the new Latvia. Some saw it as a symbol of the old Communist system, but others considered it a memorial to Latvians who had fought in the early years of the First World War. Like Estonia and Lithuania, Latvia had declared independence from the collapsing Soviet Union in the early 1990s and the country was still struggling to reconcile itself to the contradictions of its past. The spate of new buildings was not really reconstruction at all: it was an attempt at reinvention, the careful piecing together of a new national identity from centuries of wreckage.

We wandered down the near-medieval lanes of Old Rīga. They were beautiful. We were both captivated by the outlandishness of the whole thing. How odd, I thought, for us to have been brought here by miniature golf. How strange to be here at all.

We walked to the edge of the old town, looking in shop windows, stopping at a café to write postcards. We were just like tourists. It was a relief. This had the potential to turn into a holiday. Tina might enjoy herself. On the way back, we stopped off at Centrs, a popular shopping centre on one of the side-streets to look for presents for family. The building was large and rambling, but there was a desk where you could leave your bags while you shopped.

We bought a teddy bear for our niece, dressed in the colours of the Latvian national ice-hockey team. Ice hockey is big in Latvia. In May, the Latvians had beaten the Russians at the World

Ice Hockey Championships in St Petersburg, a victory so glorious and symbolic that the country had celebrated for days afterwards, with impromptu parades through the old town.

'Will she know what that is?' I asked Tina, as we picked up our bags from the Centrs counter.

'It's a teddy bear,' said Tina. 'You can give her the fact sheet when she's older.'

We walked back over the river, stopping to take photographs of Rīga's haphazard skyline and agreeing that, yes, this wasn't such a bad place to spend a fortnight after all.

An hour after we left Centrs, person or persons unknown tried to blow it up. Two bombs exploded at the bag check-in, killing one woman who worked there and injuring thirty-four other people. The bombs had been set to go off ten minutes apart, to cause as much chaos and injury as possible. The street outside was full of the wounded and of people hugging and crying. We switched on the TV in our room and there it was, the street we had just walked down, speckled with blood and broken glass.

According to a report in a local newspaper, the police were following up four theories. 'The first theory is business differ-ences,' said a police spokesman, 'second is terrorism, third is a crazy person and the last theory is revenge.' In other words, they had no idea who had done it. The Mafia, political extremists, a customer with a homicidal grudge – no one had claimed res-ponsibility for the bombs. A man had been seen depositing two bags at the Centrs desk then leaving the store. He had not been traced.

The effect of the bombing on the minigolf tournament was immediate. When I came down the following morning for my first practice session, I found that we were under armed guard. The local authorities, obviously worried that such a convocation of nations presented the perfect opportunity for a Munich '72-style terrorist attack, had dispatched police with guns to patrol the perimeter of the course. The policemen wore baseball caps and their guns stuck out from under their ponchos. They stood by the eighteenth hole of the beton, leaning on the fence and chewing gum. Every time a player fluffed their approach shot to the cuckoo clock, the policemen sniggered.

'Wodka?' they enquired, holding out a mock-trembling hand. 'Wodka?'

They said it to me more than most.

It took only a morning for me to realize that I was totally, utterly and hopelessly out of my depth. There was nothing mysterious about this, no slight psychological deficit between me and the rest of the field. It was all about skill or the lack of it. Five days of practice, however committed and correct, were just not going to be enough. I needed years. I was fucked.

Although the design and sequence of the beton course was identical to that at Odense, the balls and lines I had used to play it were rendered obsolete because this course had been constructed from a different kind of concrete and, well, it was just a different course. In addition, somebody had had the bright idea of positioning it beneath some trees, which meant it was always covered in leaves, bits of twig, bird droppings and so on. All the other teams had coaches who knew how to play each hole and teammates who could offer encouragement, guidance and a helping hand when it came to wiping off the bird shit. I finished my first beton practice round alone, walked stiffly past the laughing policemen and essayed the eternit.

This was even worse. The selection of holes was as follows: pyramids; flat loop; truncated cones; waves; somersault; straight run with obstacles; volcano; straight run with target window; sloping circle with kidney; irregular passages; ski-jump with net; flash of lightning; tunnel; double wedges; straight run without obstacles; middle circle; right angle; and labyrinth.

Where to begin? I'd never encountered half a dozen of these holes before, not that it would have made much difference. Unlike beton, which could be played safely for twos, on eternit you were looking for a hole in one every time. On the eleventh for instance, you had to drive your ball up a ski-jump and into a net that looked like a windsock; either it went in or it didn't, and if it didn't, you carried on trying until it did. Most players considered this one of the easier holes, a shot of easily reproduced weight with no surface variables. And it was easy, if you'd done it many thousands of times before as nearly all these players had. I practised the ski-jump. Occasionally the ball flew into the net but mostly it didn't. The noise it made as it hit the metal rim of the net or the boundary fence was excruciating and unusual enough to alert Europe's finest minigolfers to the fact that there was an impostor in their midst.

Of the other holes, I had particular problems with the tunnel. It was this one that even Jarmo Sandelin struggled with. The ball went everywhere except into the little tube. But I also had problems with the flat loop, and the volcano, and most of the back nine. And, unlike the beton, I couldn't play percentages here. It was 100 per cent or nothing. I really was fucked.

Most players seemed to be using one particular ball for the tunnel, a green SV Golf SV 27, without which the hole was deemed impossible, but the ball vendor had sold his last SV 27 two days before. He might get some more, he told me, in very broken English, but not until the tournament was under way. I returned to the tunnel with a sense of futility that was deepening by the minute.

As I was leaning down to retrieve yet another mis-hit, one of the German squad approached me. She was a short girl with a jutting jaw, who barked in triumph every time she scored a hole in one, which was often. I stood next to the tunnel and smiled charmingly, hoping she was about to give me a tip.

She did. 'You must get off the lanes,' she said forcefully. 'Get off them.'

I realized with embarrassment that I had been standing on the playing surface to pick up my ball. This was strictly forbidden. 'Sorry,' I said. 'This is the first time I've –'

The girl ignored me and shrugged. 'It's not my course but these are the rules.'

'Yes,' I said. 'Sorry.'

She returned, shaking her head, to her teammates. She was not interested in my excuses, neither did she find my well-meaning amateurism appealing in any way. I had made an elementary minigolf *faux pas*, like turning up at a water-polo match and carelessly urinating in the deep end. And someone who doesn't know that you don't piss in the pool probably shouldn't be there.

But other competitors were more tolerant and some were even friendly. I received distant smiles of acknowledgement from Dace and Ilze Kupce. The two Italians, Rudy and Al, were garrulous and welcoming. A handful of the Danish squad had been in Odense, including Vincent the chimp, the luckless Bjarne Hansen, and Peter Soerensen who was acting as a tournament official. They greeted me with shouts of laughter and some extensive piss-taking.

'Andy, you won't get the course record,' said one, 'but every time you play – that's the British record!'

Finn the Norwegian was there too, coaching Team Norway's sole representative, a bespectacled and very polite young man called Lars. 'It's hard for him,' Finn told me as Lars wrestled with the flat loop, 'but I think it's harder for you, yes?'

Finn offered to give me advice whenever he could. He asked after his favourite ball, the Fun-Sports 8. When I produced it from my bag, he showed it to Lars and they both laughed. But Finn walked me round the course, telling me which ball to use on which hole. The 8, he said, would be perfect for the somersault at the fifth.

'But, Andy,' said Finn, 'this ball must be right temperature. Quite warmed. Do you have one of these?' From his pocket, he produced a small white sack that he wrapped round the ball like an exposure blanket.

'No,' I said, 'I don't.'

'Then you must keep the ball here,' replied Finn, patting his groin.

It was quite common for players to keep balls warm in their armpits or their pants, stowed in a sling or a sock, said Finn. Many players did this, he assured me. It explained why I'd seen so many men openly reaching down into their trousers and apparently rearranging themselves. At least, I hoped it did.

And then I saw another face I knew. It was Edouard, the Preston-based Frenchman I had met in Hastings. Back then, several lifetimes ago, he had seemed highly eccentric with his funny stance and his bag of different balls. But now the positions were reversed, and I felt considerably more eccentric than him. He struck me as possibly the only player here who understood what I was going through.

Edouard seemed delighted to see me. He asked after Peter and told me he was impressed to see me here. Since we had last met, Edouard had moved from Preston to Warsaw. He was a lecturer. He told me that he missed Preston dreadfully. 'English people don't like Preston, but I had the best year of my life in Preston. When I say I am going home, I am going to Preston.'

I told Edouard that so far I was finding this tournament very intimidating, what with the armed policemen, and the Germans, Austrians and Swedes, all of whom had large squads of players and coaches and who were obviously highly competitive.

'Well, don't be intimidated,' said Edouard dismissively. 'Have fun. If this was snooker, they wouldn't even let you watch these people play. We have a great opportunity here to play with the best.'

He walked over to the kiosk and bought a coffee. 'I have fifteen years and I am closer to you than to the Germans,' he said. 'They have sixteen thousand players! For the players here, getting here has been really intense. "Oh, your brother is getting married, oh, you have to bury your grandfather – oh, I'm sorry, you are out of the team!" Edouard took an exploratory sip of his coffee. 'In France, we select by "Hello, who's coming?"'

In line with the French selection procedure, their team was a strange mix of ages, shapes and personalities. Edouard introduced me to one of his colleagues, a middle-aged engineer from Dijon called Yannick, who had driven all the way to Latvia. Just outside Rīga, he had been pulled over by the police who, seeing his foreign number-plates, had claimed his vehicle was not roadworthy and threatened to impound it unless he paid them two hundred lati on the spot, a good old-fashioned backhander. He refused, so they towed his car away and Yannick spent his first day in Rīga at the police station filling in forms and trying to get his car back. Consequently, he was less than impressed with our armed guards. I wondered if I could bribe them to stop laughing and pointing at me.

I ploughed on with my training. It was miserable. Squads of players would work on particular lanes with their coach for an hour at a time. Barging in took considerable brass neck, but certain players thought nothing of pushing me out of the way when they needed to practise. Why would they? They were serious – and I was British. At the end of practice I realized I had been bitten by mosquitoes in about a dozen places. Perfect.

At lunchtime, after a thoroughly dispiriting morning's work, I went back to the hotel to look for Tina. She was sitting in the café area, reading a book. For a while, she had been joined by a group of local businessmen who were holding a breakfast meeting. All of them were dressed in black and a significant number had broken noses or cauliflower ears or both. Unlike nearly everyone else in Rīga, they also had mobile phones. After an hour or so the meeting broke up, and the local businessmen drove off in their expensive German cars without, Tina noted, having to pay anyone for their breakfast.

'Nearly blown up yesterday, coffee with the Mafia today. And how was your morning, darling?' asked Tina sweetly.

I informed her truthfully that I was going to come last, and by some considerable margin, and if she could see her way clear to accompanying me tomorrow morning I really would be terribly grateful, just for moral support, really, but if she was going to come with me, we should probably get some insect repellent this afternoon. OK?

She nodded and closed her book. I went up to our room to get changed. The dead cat was still lying in the neighbouring yard, only now someone had squashed it under a door. Lucky old cat, I thought.

In the afternoon, I went to the coaches' technical meeting, at which the positioning of windbreaks was debated, and it was decided that no country would be permitted to use measuring instruments to gauge the distance from ball to cup on the seventh hole, beton.

'Can we use hands?' asked the Dutch coach.

The imposing Leo Moik, elderly president of the Austrian Bahnengolf Association and one of the tournament invigilators, spoke emphatically, his words translated by Peter Soerensen.

'Leo's feeling is no,' said Peter. 'It's allowed to look on the plan, and point with fingers, but that's it.'

Leo's feeling tended to be no on most things and no one, I noticed, ever disagreed with him. His word was law. I sat mute throughout, a stranger in a very strange land. At the end of the meeting, Leo came up to me. 'You are Peter from British Association?' he asked. I almost said yes.

Over the following days, we learnt more about the different teams participating in the championships. There was a clear caste system at work. At the top were the developed nations of the minigolf world, Germany, Austria and Sweden, whose combined numbers constituted a third of the field, and who sent coaches to Latvia months prior to the tournament, for the purposes of mapping the lanes. They received funding from their governments. Then there was a broad middle band consisting of the Czechs, the Finns, the Swiss, the Danes, the Latvians, the Dutch, the French and possibly the Italians. There were the countries who had sent just a handful of representatives: Belgium, Estonia, Slovakia, Norway. And then there was us.[1]

The top tier was frighteningly well prepared. Germany in particular had brought a full team of seven men, a full team of four women, numerous substitutes, coaches, a cook and a physio. They had also brought four hundred balls, which they kept in temperature-controlled attaché cases. They stuck together

1. In terms of registered players, of the twenty current European members of the WMF, Britain ranks nineteenth, seven places behind Liechtenstein.

at mealtimes and were first on the course every morning. To compound the national stereotype, a couple of the German players were very kind, albeit in a rather rigid way.

'No, Andy,' said one, as I concluded another useless practice round, swinging my club jauntily like a cane. He grabbed my wrist and repositioned my hand. 'You hold it like this,' he said helpfully. 'Like a man.'

We became aware of grumbling among a few of the players. Facilities here in Latvia were not up to scratch. The eternit course in particular was very uneven. And why was the tournament taking place in August, and not June or September? Everyone knew that it rained heavily in Latvia in August. Practices were being missed; play would be delayed. No one played in the rain.

During one rain break, I got chatting with Al, one of the popular Italians.

'Do you like Rīga, Andy?' Al asked me. He was in his mid-twenties with a stylishly trimmed beard.

I replied truthfully that we hadn't seen much of it, and the bit we had seen had been bombed soon afterwards.

'I think Rīga is beautiful city,' said Al. 'So many beautiful girls.'

'Absolutely,' I said.

'The first night we are here,' Al told me conspiratorially, 'we go casino. We play blackjack. I meet girl. We do . . . the thing.' He winked and carried on. 'I come back here, have shower, come out here and play. The next night, I go into town, I do another girl, I come back and play. Then I sleep.' He yawned and stretched. 'It is a beautiful city . . .'

Al and Rudy managed to find time in their packed schedule to offer me advice, as did Finn. The Swiss, too, were very kind. After a couple of days, one of their team quietly approached me with copies of their notes on both the beton and eternit courses. There were diagrams of every hole, with dotted lines showing the exact path to the cup. 'These are for you,' said the Swiss team member. 'But please – do not show to Germans, Austrians or Sweden.'

The Swiss even donated one of their coaches to the British

effort, an elderly professorial type called Hans, who spoke very little English. Hans was genial enough in the bar but rather stern in training. He would point to a particular brick or small stretch of rail. 'No!' he would cry, when I missed it, a look of deep dissatisfaction crossing his face. 'Again!' He was used to tutoring fluent, confident players, but I just didn't have the chops; it was like teaching the classics to someone who couldn't read.

Gradually, Tina started to fulfil the role of coach. It was not what either of us intended or wanted, but I was drowning. I needed help. 'Have fun!' said Edouard every morning, but it was no longer about fun, it was about survival. The feelings of wretchedness and failure were almost overwhelming. Tina kept me company. She started giving me pep talks. She reminded me that this wasn't actually our life, that we had friends and family we would see again soon, that this was only a passing phase. But it was hard to keep everything in perspective when there was no one to whom we could turn, and wink, and smirk about it. We were through the looking-glass.

So the practice days passed, each country exhibiting one or more of its national characteristics. The Germans *were* ruthlessly efficient. The French bickered among themselves. The Latvians were dour, and who could blame them? The Italians were randy and feckless. The Swiss were resolutely neutral.

And the British were jolly but crap. They never gave up. Their upper lips remained stiff. To survive, I became a caricature of the Great British Loser, who bears the most terrible humiliations with good humour and boundless optimism. I was Eddie the Eagle. But I didn't do it for Britain. I did it for me.

At the opening ceremony, we were expected to process through Rīga behind our national flags to a town square, where we would be treated to some kind of local pageant. I had attended practice in jeans and my QPR away shirt; for the tournament I had planned to wear my official British Minigolf Association polo shirt. But all the other teams had matching tracksuits in their national colours. The Swiss strip incorporated a map of Switzerland; Slovakia's had their homeland bisected by an eternit hole. I was conscious of the fact that Britain was confirming another national stereotype by being the scruffiest team at the championships.

There was another problem with the BMGA polo shirt.

The crest depicted a reverse sphinx, with the head of a lion and the body of a minigolfer. The lion was roaring, which seemed both needlessly belligerent and, under the circumstances, daft. I didn't feel like a lion. Besides which, he was leaning on his putter, hand on hip, with the ball still two feet from the cup. He had nothing to roar about. He had missed an easy putt.

So, on the morning of the opening ceremony, we went into Rīga to look for something more suitable to wear in the parade.

First of all we tried the markets down by the railway station. They were housed in and around several First World War Zeppelin hangars, full of fish, cheeses, flowers and, on the outskirts, imitation watches, hi-fis and sportsgear. There were plenty of tracksuits and they were stupidly cheap, but I couldn't see anything in red, white and blue, and it wasn't as if I wanted a tracksuit. I hadn't worn one since I was ten, so God alone knew what constituted a smart one. I was operating on colour alone.

We walked into the built-up area of Rīga, the offices and boutiques. We tried the sportswear department of a dingy department store, but all six of their tracksuits were olive-green and for children. Nike had a store in Rīga, and so did Adidas, but neither was currently making British colours kit for the clueless thirtysomething. Both places were empty. I tried on a swooshed blue outfit in Nike*ciemats*. Staring at myself in the changing-room mirror, I couldn't tell if I looked ridiculous or not. I mean, I felt ridiculous, but that might just have been the sight of myself in a tracksuit in an empty sportswear shop in Latvia.

'Does it look OK?' I asked Tina. 'I'm lost.'

'It looks OK. I think,' said Tina, who was almost as disorientated as me.

Miraculously, in a shop called 100% Sport, we finally found what we were probably looking for. It was a red, white and blue tracksuit. There was even a Union Jack on the reverse of the jacket; the manufacturer had used the flag as a trademark. The tracksuit was in the 100% Sport sale. It was too big for me, but it was the right colour with the right flag stuck on it, so I told myself that the bagginess lent it some hip-hop style and bought it. I felt a bit queasy. Even reduced, to the average Latvian the tracksuit represented nearly a month's wages.

Later that day, some average Latvians got to see the tracksuit in action. My self-consciousness at wearing it in public was diminished only by the greater self-consciousness I felt at wearing it while marching in a big parade. We were all bussed into Old Rīga's town square, before processing through the municipal gardens to the opening ceremony. Each flag was carried by a boy and girl dressed in traditional Latvian garb; waistcoat and breeches for the boy, long plaid skirt and a crown of oak leaves for the girl. I asked my flag-bearers if they knew which country they were representing. They didn't.

We had been lined up in alphabetical order, so behind me were Rudy and Al and in front of me were an awful lot of Germans. When we arrived at the piazza in front of the Congress Centre, there was a small ensemble of accordion, bass and tambourine waiting. The boys and girls performed some synchronized country dancing and there were speeches in German, Latvian and English from Klaus Engels of the WMF and also a representative of the Latvian Sports Authority. During Klaus Engels' speech, one of the German team farted loudly, to the great amusement of his colleagues. 'Best success and good results and good health,' concluded the Latvian speaker, mindful of his governmental responsibilities. 'Also success not just in this competition but in life, and in other competitions,' he added, and then, just to make sure: 'And good success to the Latvian team!'

I learnt later that the square was adjacent to the British Embassy, and that the British ambassador, wondering where the music was coming from, had ambled down to watch the opening ceremony. 'I didn't notice any of my diplomatic colleagues there,' the ambassador told me. 'I have to say that we weren't actually sent a letter saying do come and attend the opening ceremony. Had we known there was a British delegation we might have arrived earlier. Do tell us when we can come and cheer!'

The following morning, standing around waiting to start, I was glad I hadn't told him. I was extremely nervous, and also rather uncomfortable with the sock full of balls stuffed down the front of my voluminous trousers. I noticed that a few players were listening to personal stereos to psych themselves up. I got Tina to fetch mine from the hotel room. The tape in the machine was by Latvia's biggest pop group, BrainStorm. We had tickets to see them play a concert on Friday night. Their big hit was called 'My Star'.

> If my star would fall
> Or disappear at all
> I will follow my star till the end of my days . . .

It was a good record. Earlier in the year 'My Star' finished third in the Eurovision Song Contest, the first time Latvia had ever entered the competition. No one told them they didn't have to send their very best band.

The music helped, but whatever small hope remained in my mind that I might not end the tournament in last place was quickly extinguished once I started playing. I had been drawn in the first round with Rudy the Italian. I was so nervous my hands were shaking. Over seventeen holes of eternit, I shot forty-one. Rudy took seventeen.

At the eighteenth lane, the labyrinth, Rudy was looking at a perfect round of eighteen. I played first and aced it. But so what? I had a total of forty-two on eternit, a huge score; I could see spectators, including our police guard and Hans my so-called coach, tittering behind their hands. Catastrophically, Rudy then took three shots to sink his ball. He fell to his knees and wept. Al gripped his friend's shoulder in consolation. I felt more sorry for Rudy than for myself.

Now the tournament was under way, the pressure was intense. The slightly antisocial behaviour of some competitors became positively sociopathic. They had even less time for the plucky Brit. They shuddered and growled when they missed a shot and howled in triumph when they aced one. I was reminded of something Kirsten Barnes had said about the sometimes erratic behaviour of top sportsmen: 'Some people are driven to succeed by personal improvement,' she had told me before I went to Denmark, 'while others are driven to succeed by beating other people, especially at international level. I'm not saying wanting to beat somebody else is a bad thing – come on, that's good. But you've got to maintain a balance of behaviour, so it doesn't bleed over into all areas of your personality.'

Many competitors here were noticeably failing to maintain that healthy balance. When they weren't playing, they shuffled round at the edge of the course, tutting and muttering to themselves. But there was no denying that they were good at minigolf.

The pressure was getting to me too, the pressure of losing, the pressure to be a Good Sport. I became irritable and unreasonably demanding. We abandoned all pretence that Tina was there to enjoy herself. She was now my trainer, my gofer, my shrink. She was the British Coach.

'All right, mate,' she said indignantly, after I asked her to skip lunch and spend half an hour working with me on the tunnel, 'I don't care that much.'

But she stuck with me.

In the middle of my first beton round, it started to rain. Play was halted while we waited for the shower to blow over. When we returned to the course, the putting surface was slick with water and dotted with clumps of sodden leaves. Someone had to clean it and dry it and that someone was the coach. While my fellow minigolfers and I tried to get back into the Zone, Tina mopped the lanes with a hotel towel. I left her to it. It wasn't my job.

Early that evening, we attended a meeting called by the presidents of the Austrian, Swedish and German minigolf associations. They were proposing the foundation of a separate European minigolf association. For miniature golf to grow on the international stage, it needed to gain recognition from a body called AGFIS/GAISF – the General Association of International Sports Federations. Recognition from AGFIS would lead to miniature golf being accepted as an event at the next World Games, which in turn would pave the way to the Olympic Games. But AGFIS/ GAISF only recognizes sports federations that have constituent organizations in at least three continents; the WMF, despite its name, no longer spoke for the world.[2] There was a US association, and an Asian association had been established in the last year. This was a historic opportunity, said Leo Moik forcefully, to guarantee the further development of minigolf as a sport. The motion was passed unanimously.

At the end of the first day, the scores were posted on a board outside the compound. There was my name and the Union Jack,

2. The WMF was formed in 1980, at which time its members were Germany, Austria and Sweden, the countries in which the game was most popular and where the miniature golf/eternit (Germany) and felt (Sweden) systems originated. (The minigolf/beton system was first built in Locarno, Switzerland by Paul Bongni in 1953.) Those wishing to know more about the various associations and federations that have come and gone during the game's brief lifetime, as well as the less popular Sterngolf (Star golf) and Dutch felt systems, are pointed to Michael Seiz's comprehensive *Minigolfwelt: vom Freizeitspass zum Leistungssport* ('*The World of Minigolf: from Pastime to Powersport*').

adrift by fifteen strokes already. It attracted the attention of a Czech film crew, who followed me round on the second morning until they had the footage they wanted, a dreadful seven on the straight run with target window. At my request, Tina asked them to leave us alone, but the cameraman just shrugged and said something in Czechoslovakian, which was almost certainly, 'I'm only doing my job.' I wanted to weep – no, bawl, but I held my features in check; I gave them *nothing*.

During a break in play, I confessed to Edouard how hard I was finding it playing on my own.

Edouard snorted. 'I would rather be on my own than with arseholes,' he said. The French team had had a fight over whether or not to go to the casino the night before. Edouard had stayed behind at the hotel. He mooted the idea of defecting to the UK mid-tournament. 'I think I will call Peter and ask for minigolf asylum,' he said. 'Have fun!'

'Life is first boredom, then fear,' wrote Philip Larkin in *Dockery and Son*, but the reverse is true of an international minigolf tournament. First comes the fear: the sleepless nights, lying awake, running through your shots, over and over; the pre-round jitters as you wait for them to announce and mispronounce your name and number – 'ONE, ONE, FOUR. ANDY MÜLLER.' And after playing, the boredom: sitting around by the drinks kiosk, sheltering from the interminable rain, waiting anxiously for your name to be called again.

Every morning I listened to the BrainStorm tape ('I will follow my star till the end of my days . . .') and Tina tried to help me remain positive and focused. But we both knew it was pointless. However hard I tried to play my own game, or have fun, I didn't have the experience not to blow up once or twice in every round. Some of the holes, like the tunnel, were just too difficult, even with an SV 27. I might get lucky and ace it, sure. But I might just as easily take seven.

I reached my lowest ebb at the eighteenth on the eternit, the labyrinth, on the third day. The ball kept bouncing off the metal maze. Clang! Clang! On the third rebound, it ricocheted deep into the mud of the flowerbed behind me. In full sight of twenty or so spectators, I had to get down on my hands and knees and dig it out. I was fourteen again, on the hockey pitch, humiliated. I straightened up to putt and, yes, there was dirt under my fingernails and, I noted with grim satisfaction, actual dog shit this time.

I took a six. Clang! Clang! Clang!

As lunchtime approached, the rain got worse and it was decided to abandon play entirely for the afternoon. I began to fantasize that I wouldn't have to complete all eight rounds and I could go home early. But the following morning the sun was out and it was announced that we would play until all rounds were concluded.

In fact, as the tournament progressed I did improve. On one spectacular circuit of the eternit, I scored nine holes-in-one. And I achieved a new personal best of thirty-six on beton, equalling Peter's score in Papendal and therefore becoming joint British record-holder, an achievement that might not impress the Danes but was good enough for me. It was a straw, and I clutched it gratefully.

In my final round I even beat someone, a grumpy Belgian called Pascal whose mood was not enhanced by being outplayed by me. I had five aces, a couple of which were lucky, but I was owed some luck, and Pascal's teammates laughed and applauded every one. He grew increasingly irate and, when signing my card, seemed unable to look at it or me.

But I didn't care. We had done it. It was over. Tina and I crossed back to the hotel, both of us feeling a massive sense of relief. As if to celebrate, someone had finally disposed of the dead cat from next door.

Statistics, then. I didn't make the cut. I did come last. Over eight rounds Player Number One One Four amassed a grand total of 310 strokes, a full twenty-eight behind the nearest competitor, Jürgen Pelt of Estonia, who must have been overjoyed that once again a useless Britisher had kept him off the bottom of the table. The bullish German girl who had ordered me off the eternit played her first eight rounds in exactly 200, a mere 110 shots better than me. She went on to win the overall women's competition, twelve rounds, in 295 – still fifteen less than my glorious tally.

'She is a man,' said Al dismissively. He had no plans to 'do' her.

On the final day's play, quite a crowd had gathered to watch the remaining competitors – about two hundred locals, plus WMF officials and regional camera crews and journalists. I spotted a small boy in a Manchester United shirt. After the tenth round, there was another cut, leaving just six women and nine men to battle it out in the individual and aggregate team competitions. They were all German, Austrian or Swedish.

As we were watching the penultimate round, the Czech cameraman came over to speak to us. I thought for a minute he was going to apologize for hounding me during the tournament, but he just tapped the badge of my QPR shirt. 'Queens Park Rangers?' he asked uncertainly.

I nodded.

The cameraman smiled broadly. 'Gerry Francis!' he said with satisfaction, and clapped me on the back. What a very strange trip this had been.

My 310 was still posted on the scoreboard by the entrance. Based on this, a couple of journalists sought me out for quotes for pieces they were writing about the championships.

'Aha!' said the man from the *Baltic Times*. 'You are the Eagle!'

'Well, respect to him,' I replied, 'he still has to jump off the bloody thing, doesn't he?'

The Germans won nearly everything. When the medals were handed out, the national anthem was played over the Tannoy and not one but three German flags were hoisted above the rostrum. They had come prepared.

'Do you think anyone bothered with "God Save The Queen"?' said Tina.

The closing ceremony was held at a restaurant called Lido on the outskirts of Rīga, which was like a Latvian-themed Harvester. It was the largest wooden loghouse in Europe, apparently, and had a stream trickling through the middle of it. We sat near the Danes, who were soon as drunk as only Danes can be. The Dutch and French and Belgians gave us shirts. We toasted one another with Balzām, the treacly black local liquor, and said our thanks and farewells to the friends we'd made: Rudy and Al, Hans and Finn. Edouard offered his services as national coach the next time Great Britain came to the championships. We left the restaurant to find a taxi. Above the entrance was a giant neon windmill.

The previous evening, still giddy from having completed the tournament, we drove up to Jūrmala to see BrainStorm play at the Dzintari concert hall. Jūrmala is the name given to the string of small towns stretching along the coast west of Rīga. It took us about half an hour to get there. Lining the Jūrmala road were several incongruous pieces of American architecture; Soviet filmmakers shot propaganda reels here about the perils of life in the capitalist USA.

Dzintari was rather lovely. In the Soviet era, up to half a million visitors from all over the USSR came to Jūrmala for their holidays. Élite Soviet retirees were inclined to make their home in the area, and many still lived there in *dachas* and bungalows. It was a gorgeous place, with white sand dunes and pinewoods and long, wide avenues of carved wooden buildings with stained-glass windows; it was conspicuously more picturesque than any-where Latvians had to live.

We joined the excited crowd in front of the Dzintari concert hall and pushed our way in. The concert was a sell-out, a celebration of BrainStorm's tenth anniversary and the release of a greatest-hits album.

The group's lifespan coincided with that of the independent Latvia. That initial period of independence in the Baltic States had been known in Estonia as the Singing Revolution. There was a great tradition in these countries of huge national song festivals. In 1988, nearly three hundred thousand people, approximately one in three of all Estonians, attended one such festival. They sang outlawed folksongs, breathing life back into their national identity.

The Dzintari concert hall had been built between the wars, during the country's first period of independence, but BrainStorm were playing tonight in the open-air hall added by the Soviets in 1960. Live, they were a better than an average Beatle-y pop band. But watching them in these surroundings, with these people, was rather like watching the Beatles themselves. The crowd adored them. There were screams, real screams, every time the singer Renārs – who described himself in one song as 'a horny little elf' – approached the microphone. And everyone knew the words. And everyone sang along.

When they played 'My Star' – in Latvian, of course – I thought, What an amazing thing this is. To most of the world, a Latvian pop group, like a British minigolfer, would have novelty value and nothing else. But tell that to the people gathered in this hall. They were celebrating music and community and freedom. The band belonged to them, like a football team belongs to its supporters. Or should.

> *My heart's gonna lead me through so many ways,*
> *And if you gonna join me I'll be your guide,*
> *Baby, 'never say never', be my 'Runaway Bride'.*

After the concert, we went down to the sea and walked hand in hand along the silver sands. The stars were out. I felt peaceful for the first time in months. I knew I was nearing the end of my sporting life. Coming to Latvia had taught me a simple lesson. Try to do the things you enjoy. Be with the people you love. Everyone should have the freedom to play, and I should have the freedom not to.

I told the British Coach how much I loved her.

'Good,' said Tina, 'because we are never, never going to do this again.'

15

Kreisplateau – circular plateau

It is international sport that helps kick the world
downhill. Started by foolish athletes, who thought it
would promote understanding, it is supported today by
the desire for political prestige and by the interests
involved in gate monies. It is completely harmful.
E. M. FORSTER, 1957

I can say I love England. I can't say I love my country. I
don't know what that means.
Guy Burgess, in ALAN BENNETT, *An Englishman Abroad*

When we got home, the eternit course in my local park had
gone. All that remained were shadows; no grass grew where the
lightning had struck, just a brown muddy flash surrounded by
weeds.

I telephoned the local council parks department, explained
who I was and got put through to the official who had authorized
the course's removal. He sounded nervous. It was posing a health
risk, he told me. Additionally, funds weren't available to refurbish
the course or, indeed, to staff it. The metal sidings had been sent
to the dump; the base, because there was a possibility that asbestos

had been mixed with the concrete when it was manufactured, had been disposed of safely.

'But that was a valuable national training resource!' I said.

'I had an uncle who died of asbestosis, sir,' he replied. 'Once you've seen what that can do to someone, you don't want to take the risk.'

The man from the parks department wasn't all doom and gloom, though. 'There's a really good one on the seafront at Lowestoft,' he said helpfully, 'with a manufactured landscape. They've really gone to town on it. That one's terrific.'

'Thanks,' I said, 'but I don't think I'll bother.'

I hadn't enjoyed representing my country. Adopting the guise of the Olympic village idiot had not been good for my self-esteem. On the second day of the tournament, we had had a visit from a British engineer called Pete. He was in Rīga to oversee the modernization of a sewage plant. Walking past the minigolf course on his day off, Pete had noticed the Union Jack among the clubhouse flags. Intrigued, he came in.

Pete appeared unconcerned with which sport was being played or Britain's lowly ranking in the international table. 'Representing your country,' he said to us, 'that's a real honour. Did you have to beat a lot of people to get here?'

'No,' said Tina truthfully. 'No one else wanted to come.'

'Well, anyway, good luck,' said Pete, and gave us the thumbs-up. 'Fly the flag!'

He was off to do some sightseeing. Across the park from the minigolf course stood an enormous Soviet war memorial marking the Communist 'liberation' of Rīga, three soldiers more than thirty feet high. Old Communists used the statue as a rallying point on Soviet anniversaries. Latvian nationalists had tried to dynamite it. It was a symbol of glorious unity or colonial oppression, depending on which flag you were flying at the time.

The tussle between the old and new Latvias was evident at the Latvian Sports Museum, a dilapidated four-storey house in old Rīga not far from Centrs. The museum is a large photographic exhibition, divided unambiguously between Latvian sporting life before and after the Soviets. In the early photographs members of the Rīga Gymnastic Club and the Rīga Bicycle Society pose for studio portraits and holiday snaps; the boxers and wrestlers look like circus strongmen. Until the Second World War, sports clubs and societies thrive. Posters in the museum extol the virtues of fresh-air and exercise.

Then everything changes. Clubs and unions are banned. The Latvian standard bears a hammer and sickle and CCCP appears on the breasts of the athletes. Incorporated into the USSR as one of the fifteen Soviet Socialist Republics, Latvia's sports system is reorganized according to the Soviet centralized model and the country's athletes now strive for the greater glory of the Soviet Union. The photographs take on the familiar character of Soviet iconography, but the exhibition is at pains to emphasize that these are Latvian champions, that Latvian athletes won a total of twenty gold, twenty-eight silver and fifteen bronze Olympic medals from the beginning of the century until independence in 1991. Using sport, a continuous national identity is being traced for Latvians from the Tsarists to the Soviets and beyond.

One of the great Latvian heroes celebrated in the exhibition was Uljana Semjonova, the six-foot-ten-and-a-half inch basketball player who helped win gold for the USSR in Montreal in 1976 and again in 1980 in Moscow. From 1970 to 1985, she was voted the most popular athlete in Latvia twelve times. In eighteen seasons of international competition, Semjonova was never on a losing team. More importantly, she never defected. She was a boon to the Soviets. In 1993, she was inducted into the Basketball Hall of Fame, at which point she was given to the world, or at least to the world of basketball and its sponsors. And here at the Sports Museum she was Latvian again.

I left the exhibition feeling not that sport had been restored to the Latvian people but that it had been passed into the hands of a new and hopefully more beneficent regime. But the lesson of the museum was that there were never any guarantees.

Governments love sport. In the words of Tony Blair, sport is 'a pro-education policy, a pro-health policy, an anti-crime and anti-drugs policy'. It keeps hospital waiting lists down. It keeps you out of trouble. It manages your antisocial tendencies. And it maintains your patriotism in case there's a war. As the then sports minister Kate Hoey put it in the House of Commons, 'Sport is a vehicle that can deliver so many government policies.'

For the Cold War superpowers, sport was the next best thing to dropping H-bombs on one another. East and West went at it with manic zeal. President John F. Kennedy used to say that the world's problems could be solved by stockpiling quantities of just two things – missiles and gold medals. It was, in George Orwell's much misappropriated phrase, 'war minus the shooting'.[1]

The expression appears in a piece Orwell wrote for the *Tribune* newspaper in December 1945, shortly after a tour of British clubs by the Moscow Dynamos, a Russian football team. The matches had seen considerable ill will and crowd trouble, and 'If such a visit as this had any effect at all on Anglo-Soviet relations, it could only be to make them slightly worse than before.' He goes on to say, 'There cannot be much doubt that the whole thing is bound up with the rise of nationalism – that is, with the lunatic modern habit of identifying oneself with large power units and seeing everything in terms of competitive prestige.'

When the Cold War ended, so did this high-stakes form of international rivalry. I think it's possible to see the sports mania of the 1990s as a displacement of all that frustrated nationalism. In the absence of old oppositional certainties, people began to identify with alternative 'large power units', superbrands like Nike, superteams like Manchester United, the great mass of sport itself.

'Nationalism is the easiest political emotion to gather people around,' said Tony Blair, in May 2001, shortly before the general

1. This quote is often cited by the 'much more than a matter of life and death' mob as evidence of the drama of sport, but the full quote is rather different: 'Serious sport has nothing to do with fair play. It is bound up with hatred, jealousy, boastfulness, disregard of all rules and sadistic pleasure in witnessing violence: in other words it is war minus the shooting.'

election. 'People tend to want to stick to their tribe. None of that is very positive.' But that has not prevented his government attempting to ally itself with an ongoing national obsession that it follows, not leads. The obsession is football.

I was increasingly aware of the split between football and sport. When Tony Blair sacked Kate Hoey, she said, 'To this government, football *is* sport. You *mustn't* upset football.' I thought of Sue Campbell at the Youth Sport Trust and what she'd said about the pernicious influence of football on coaching practices; and how she had expressed the hope that sport was more 'egalitarian, empowering, exciting' than the football culture that swamped it in the public imagination.

The chaos surrounding the closure of Wembley and the creation of a new national stadium is a dramatization of the conflict between football and sport. We would have a different national scandal on our hands had Hoey not done her job and pointed out that the proposed new Wembley had little or no provision for athletics. 'All my instincts told me things were wrong,' she said. 'I love football. I've even worked in the game. But they'd just taken over. That's not why the Lottery money was given for a new stadium, so that football could do what it liked.' In June 2001, she paid for her conscientiousness with her job.

The fact is that Kate Hoey was popular with sport and unpopular with the football establishment. In this, she was the polar opposite of her predecessor Tony Banks.[2] She was outspoken too – an advocate of foxhunting and terracing in football stadia, for which she received the approval of the Football Supporters Association; she was, they said, 'the first sports minister who took football supporters seriously'. Sue Campbell thought highly of her too, describing her as passionate and directly honest about what she believed. 'It's ironic,' Sue told me. 'These are the qualities we want from politicians, then when we get them we condemn them for having the clarity of view we want them to have.'

2. During his term in office Banks was frequently referred to, not entirely flatteringly, as 'the Minister for football'.

It's hard to avoid the conclusion that Hoey ran into problems because she stood up to football's old alliance of money and men. Tony Banks was thick with Ken Bates, the chairman of Chelsea FC, and the FA allowed Bates 'more or less total control of the Wembley project. When I started to ask questions he used his newspaper column to attack me. Then he asked me to lunch. I declined. I don't do those kind of lunches.'

Hoey was replaced by Richard Caborn, a seemingly clueless bumbler whose appointment was pure vanilla fudge on the part of the government. It was like asking me to be sports minister. In his first significant media appearance, Caborn was unable to answer even one of five simple sports questions. He described himself as a keen golfer, but couldn't name three Europeans playing in the US Open ('I haven't been watching the golf at all'). Even I could do better than that. Still, at least he wouldn't rock the governmental boat.

'I'm more bothered about getting young kids off the estates,' claimed Caborn afterwards, 'kids who are kicking cans around at the moment, and actually into sport. That's what I'm about.' Of course you are, Richard.

The tragedy of this is that Hoey genuinely loves sport. In her youth, she was a champion high jumper. She is still a regular runner, rock-climber and caver. Like Sue Campbell, she believes kids should be cheered on to achievement through participation. Plus, in the words of Rob Bonnet from BBC Sport, 'She resented football's gluttonous wealth and swaggering power, plus the passive couch potato culture that feeds it.' (Phew! Watch Rob's eyes the next time he reads you the football results. He hates you.)

Kate Hoey has said her happiest time as sports minister was in the Team GB training camp before the Sydney Olympics. The athletes picked up on it. Kirsten Barnes told me that she had met Hoey there. 'She seemed really genuine. She got stuck in, she knew what she was looking at. I thought she was great.' But Kate Hoey also understood the power of the Olympics to the government. 'We hope to be successful in the Olympic games,' she said beforehand, 'but, whatever the outcome, it will be an opportunity to sell sport to our young people.'

Ah, the Olympics. There is apparently something imperishable, untarnishable, about an Olympic medal. I had drawn inspiration from one before I went to Denmark. Never mind the Olympics' heritage of use and abuse by the superpowers, never mind the Nazi sympathies of Baron Pierre de Coubertin, founder of the modern games, never mind the staggering history of venality and corruption that surrounds the International Olympic Committee, never mind its inconsistency on drug-taking – publicly condemning it while apparently suppressing anything that might expose too many athletes and spook the sponsors – and never mind that, until recently, its president, Juan Antonio Samaranch, was an unrepentant Spanish Fascist who served under Franco and who, in the words of Andrew Jennings, co-author of *The Lords of the Rings: Power, Money and Drugs in the Modern Olympics*, 'gave the straight-arm salute until the very end'. That was all just 'politics'. The world still wants to believe in the Olympic Games.[3]

When I got back from Latvia, I tried assiduously to avoid the Olympics, not out of any sense of principle but because I was all sported out. I didn't need another international pageant, having just been in one. And at first it was easy. Given the time difference between Australia and the UK, television coverage was taking place overnight. You could sleep right through the worst of it and, provided you steered clear of news bulletins, newspapers and my father-in-law, you would be none the wiser.

But gradually it started to seep through. I found myself feeling uncommonly sympathetic to Eric 'The Eel' Moussambani, the twenty-two-year-old swimmer from Equatorial Guinea who

3. This is a paradox neatly expressed by Brian Eno in the July 2001 issue of *Q* magazine. In response to the question 'Do you like football?', Eno replied, 'I'm becoming increasingly anti-sport. I think sport is encouraged by governments to channel what would be male revolutionary energy into totally pointless activities. Sport is a great technique of social control. I always watch the Olympics, mind you.'

finished last in the 100m swimming heats with a time of one minute 52.72 seconds. Moussambani had never swum 100m before and nearly drowned in the process. At home, he trained in a twenty-metre pool with no lane markers. Good old Eric. However, my sympathy turned to envy when it was announced that, following his lionization by the world's media, Eric was poised to sign a series of lucrative sponsorship deals. All I'd got was a couple of shirts.

I was also rather proud of Igors Vihrovs, the Latvian gold medallist in callisthenics. It was the first gold medal an independent Latvia had ever won but that wasn't why I was impressed. My admiration for Igors was based on (a) his personal achievement from no doubt meagre resources, and (b) his obscure choice of sport.

The Games themselves were deemed to be a triumph and a credit to Australia, its sporting infrastructure and the enthusiasm of the Australian people. At the colourful closing ceremony, Juan Antonio Samaranch, who probably knows a good rally when he sees one, pronounced them 'the best Olympic Games ever'. The president usually says this anyway, but this time he appeared to mean it. After the fiasco of the Atlanta Games in 1996, the IOC must have been delighted that a renewed energy and integrity had accrued to the Olympic myth; it was all more gravy for the gravy train.

And then there were the British. You might not have heard but we did rather well, more medals than in any Games since Paris in 1924. Some of them were even in proper sports. We made stars out of Audley Harrison, Denise Lewis and Matthew Pinsent. And we made a saint out of Steve Redgrave.

Steve Redgrave seems like a decent man. His family loves him, he does his bit for charity and he has a healthy disdain for the media (not unconnected to his bit of bother with the Boat Race). He believes in sport and in the opportunities it gave him as a schoolboy. He was shortsighted and dyslexic. In his autobiography, he argues that he suffered in the classroom as much as any 'large child' on a cross-country run ('I'm scarred for life, in a sense, because I had to do English'). Redgrave thinks schools should have sports departments that offer all pupils a sport they can enjoy and perform well. Like Jarmo Sandelin, he also believes in destiny. 'I wanted to be a winner, not just a participant. Somehow, even at that age, I felt that my path was laid out for me.' He also records that he talked to himself and 'used to spend quite a lot of time on my own, by my own preference'.

Redgrave's single-minded determination to fulfil his destiny is legendary: in addition to a lifetime's rowing injuries, he has battled colitis and latterly diabetes. His record of five consecutive gold medals at five consecutive Olympic Games would be an amazing feat whenever and wherever it happened, but Sydney 2000 made him a superstar. When he left for the Games, he was respected; when he came back, he was loved. The knighthood followed shortly afterwards. But I can't help thinking that Redgrave is a rather peculiar role model. When we hold him up as a national hero and paragon of Olympic achievement, what exactly are we selling our young people?

For Steve Redgrave seems like a raving lunatic. He is the Ozzy Osbourne of British Sport. Like Ozzy, Steve Redgrave has ruined his health in the monomaniacal pursuit of glory, and the more he does it, the more his fans love him. Ozzy is managed by his wife, Sharon; Steve's doctor is his wife, Ann. Ozzy bites the heads off bats; Steve bites the heads off journalists. Like Ozzy, he shows little inclination to retire. Occasionally, both men get gold discs for their efforts. But Ozzy has yet to receive his knighthood, which in my view is a national disgrace on a par with Wembley.[4]

Success legitimizes bad behaviour, in our rock stars or our sporting heroes. The country loves Steve Redgrave because he is a winner. The manner of his winning may have been inspirational,

4. If we continue the Black Sabbath/Olympic boat analogy, Matthew Pinsent is Ozzy's sidekick and sparring partner Tony Iommi, the affable Tim Foster is bassist Geezer Butler and James Cracknell is solid drummer Bill Ward – though I suspect nobody ever called Black Sabbath 'a coxless four' and lived.

he may have triumphed with dignity, but had he spent twenty years doggedly finishing in fourth place, people would be more likely to think of him as a nutcase, albeit a dignified one, than a superhero.

Anyway, I liked the idea that this madman was now the nation's sporting figurehead and so, a few weeks after the athletes returned from Sydney, we drove up to Redgrave's home town of Marlow in Buckinghamshire to try to catch a glimpse of him. The local council had organized a parade in the conquering hero's honour and crowds were lining the streets, waiting to welcome him home. After riding in an open-top bus from his house in Marlow Bottom, Steve would be doing a walkabout in Higginson Park, so I took along my battered copy of Ozzy's *Bark At The Moon* album for him to sign, the one with Ozzy dressed as a werewolf on the cover. ⁂

(⁂ I didn't. Wish I had.)

The pubs and shop fronts of Marlow were hung with bunting, and bells tolled in church steeples, just like they were supposed to. 'WELL DONE 5TEVE!' shouted one banner. 'RED-GRAVE! JOB DONE!' exclaimed another. The Tourist Office had a Book of Congratulation for well-wishers to sign. 'Total respect!' averred one. 'An awesome performance from you and the lads!' beneath which someone called Fiona had added, 'Well done! It was worth staying up late for!' and a slightly suggestive X. In the window of a building society, somebody had created a display of four blue-blazered teddy bears sitting in a boat. The toyshop had run out of Union Jacks but the weasely-faced Cockney in the baseball cap still had plenty for sale from his holdall.

It was a cold morning but the expectant crowd was cheerful and patient. A one-man band hired by the council marched cacophonously up and down the high street, but no one seemed to mind. There were lots of children with their parents and, I thought, their grandparents too. I got chatting to one gentleman who had been to Steve's four previous homecoming parades. 'But this is a much bigger affair,' he said. He was leading a campaign to have a statue of Redgrave, or Steven as he called him, erected in Marlow.

'When all this media froth is over,' he told me, 'people are going to come from all over the world to see where Steven was born. I think a permanent tribute would be good for Marlow.' He had support for the idea of a statue from a former mayor and the *Bucks Free Press*. 'It's going to take off like a rocket,' said the man confidently.

Had he spoken to Steve about it?

'Oh, no,' said the man. 'I don't really think it matters what Steven thinks.'

When the bus finally appeared, nearly twenty thousand people had packed into the town and Higginson Park. The bus was accompanied by a truck bearing a brass band playing 'Congratulations'. They were cheered the length of the high street. Redgrave was with his wife Ann and his crewmate Tim Foster, and they all stood at the front of the bus and waved to the crowds. Redgrave and Foster had blazers on, like their teddy stand-ins. Behind them were assorted dignitaries and councillors, local hacks and several camera crews. On arrival, Steve Redgrave ignored the waiting press pack and got on with the job of meeting his public. And here, I had to admit, he was magnificent. He was courteous, friendly and made time for everyone who had turned out to see him. It meant that some people were in for a long wait but, again, no one seemed to mind. 'We want Steve! We want Steve!' they yelled happily. And Steve shook every hand, posed for every photo, and signed everything that was shoved in front of him – programmes, flags, the new Harry Potter.

When he got to me, I nervously handed over the album cover.

'Wow!' said Steve, taken aback. '*Bark At The Moon*! This is a fantastic album!' He flipped it over to study the track listing. '"Waiting For Darkness", that's wicked! Actually, we all listen to that one before we race!' And he played a little air guitar to demonstrate. ✱

(✱ He didn't say or do any of this, obviously.)

Over the next few months, Steve's career as a national institution really took off. He got his knighthood. He won the BBC Sports Personality of the Year. He ran the London Marathon and sold crisps and margarine. He was on *This Is Your Life*, *Ready Steady Cook* and *An Audience with Ricky Martin*. He even found time to appear at a few celebrity golf days and lower his handicap to sixteen (watch out, Tarby).

And he won a lot of awards. The readers of *Smash Hits* magazine voted him their Hero of the Year, ahead of Britney Spears and Stephen Gately from Boyzone. Redgrave appeared on stage at the *Smash Hits* Poll Winners Party at the Docklands Arena to collect his award, where he was introduced as 'Mr Five Gold Rings', which made him sound like a minor contributor to 'The Twelve Days of Christmas'. 'This is very special,' he said, holding up the hideous *Smash Hits* trophy in front of eight thousand screaming tweenagers. 'It makes this,' and he held up the gold medal in his other hand, 'look very small.' The girls screamed even louder. Redgrave looked like he wanted to bolt from the stage, but he stood his ground. If just one of these little girls got up tomorrow morning and thought about joining a rowing club . . .

Grace under pressure, that was what was special about Steve Redgrave. His life in sport had taught him to carry himself like a hero, even if at heart he was a compulsive obsessive. Even better for him (and his sponsors), he tended to win. The crowd in Marlow, and in the country at large, responded to Our Greatest Olympian™ with genuine respect and affection, which suited everyone.

Respect and affection were qualities notably absent from Wembley Stadium in the hours and minutes before the England football team's final game beneath the Twin Towers, on a damp and blasted afternoon in early October. England were playing Germany in a World Cup qualifying match. It was a truly obnoxious occasion. The first chorus of 'No Surrender to the IRA' at Baker Street, the first fan being bundled into a police van at Wembley Park. I traipsed up Wembley Way behind a straggly line of drunks in replica shirts, who were chanting some shite about bombers and world wars, and who sheltered from the heavy rain beneath their oversize flag.

And the match ... The misery of this England–Germany fixture is a matter of public record but let me reiterate it for you here. It was the most excruciating excuse for an afternoon's entertainment I have ever witnessed, and *not* because England lost 1–0. The result didn't matter. It was just a terrible, terrible game, played in the most abysmal setting and circumstances. It must have been bad. Afterwards, no one even tried to claim it had a good atmosphere.

It wasn't just a few fans bringing their jingoism to the occasion. The Wembley public-address system joined in by playing the 'Dam Busters March' and we had several group renditions of the theme from *The Great Escape*. Walking away, I turned to take one last look at our historic national stadium. Knock the fucker down, I thought.

Manager Kevin Keegan had been booed off the pitch after the match and promptly resigned. Keegan, it was widely felt, had a huge enthusiasm for the game, but no grasp of tactics. He was a footballing paradigm, the talented player hopelessly ill-equipped for coaching. Neither was he temperamentally suited to the job. Keegan had all of Steve Redgrave's passion but none of his self-control – under pressure, he displayed not grace, but peevishness and fear. The manner of his resignation, just four days before England's next qualifying game, was as self-regarding as his habit of referring to himself in the third person. 'I just feel for Kevin Keegan there is nothing more in football I want to do,' he said.

When it began to look like FA chief executive Adam Crozier (for the record, a Scot) was actively considering a foreign manager to replace Kevin Keegan, there was a predictable drizzle of protest. Alan Shearer said, 'It would be a sad reflection on us as a football nation if we went down that road.' David Beckham agreed: 'The England team should be managed by an England manager,' he said on MUTV. Former team captain Bryan Robson said, 'They should not appoint a foreigner. Terry Venables should never have been allowed to leave.'

What crap. No one cared that Jürgen Grobler, Steve Redgrave's coach and the architect of Britain's Olympic success, was German. But football was different.

Robson was not alone in calling for the return of El Tel. Many of the England squad, it was reported, wanted him back, as did the press and public. According to a poll in the *Mirror*, 81 per cent of those surveyed did not want the FA to appoint a foreign manager. The day after Keegan's resignation Tony Banks had said, 'The idea that only an English person can actually act as a coach for the English team is nonsense.' Two weeks later, though, ever the politician, he made a U-turn and publicly gave his backing to Venables.

Venables himself was circumspect but dutiful. 'I'm very English, very loyal,' he was reported as saying. 'I would want to see an Englishman do the job.'

The FA held firm. It was a decision that was more pragmatic than patriotic. They had already parted company with Venables once over his financial misdeeds; they didn't want to risk the same thing happening again. At the end of the month, it was announced that Sven-Goran Eriksson would be moving from Lazio to England on a five-year contract.

The following day, the drizzle became a downpour. Gordon Taylor, chief executive of the Professional Footballers' Association, called the decision 'a betrayal of our heritage'. John Barnwell, of the League Managers' Association, said it was 'another example of us giving away another of our family treasures to Europe'. Bobby and Jack Charlton put aside familial differences to say Eriksson's appointment was 'an insult to our national pride' and 'a terrible mistake' respectively (clearly Jack had forgotten the nine years he spent as manager of the Republic of Ireland). Jeff Powell of the *Daily Mail*, under the headline 'England Is Now A Third World Country', portrayed it as 'a black armband day when the FA lowered us into the ranks of football's banana republics', and Harry Redknapp, manager of

West Ham, said, 'You can't tell me we have no one in this country capable of being in charge of England. Ninety per cent of Premiership managers, including me, wanted Terry Venables.'

Eriksson's response? 'I know there are people who don't want me here,' he said, with a shrug, 'and I am sorry for them.'

A year later, much has changed. England, or 'Svengland', fell for the suave sophisticated Swede (sorry, it's catching).[5] England won their group and have qualified automatically for the World Cup. They beat Germany 5–1 in Munich, a result that still doesn't look right when I type it. Under Eriksson's guidance, players like Owen, Gerrard and Beckham have started playing as well for their country as previously they had for their clubs. Beckham has been hailed as the most inspirational England captain for a generation (not bad going for someone who not so long ago was being burnt in effigy). And England have started winning again.

But it's not just the winning. In his dealings with players and the media, Eriksson himself has been polite and unflappable. He has shown restraint, composure and equanimity in victory and defeat. England's renaissance, like Redgrave's knighthood, is contingent on success, but long may his England team continue to win. Sven-Goran Eriksson brings the values of sport back to English football.

Steve Redgrave was a winner. Sven-Goran Eriksson was a winner. I was a loser. But I like to think we all behaved with dignity on the international stage.

Flying the flag is more complicated than it used to be. At least George Orwell knew who to mistrust. These days, international sport is a coalition of interested parties that takes in not only

---

5. Not everyone agrees. After England's historic win in Munich, John Barnwell was quoted as saying, 'We at the League Managers' Association were not in favour of a foreign coach and that position still holds firm.' Harry Redknapp, now at Portsmouth so no longer a Premiership manager, said Eriksson had been lucky. 'I'm not anti-Swedish, but Eriksson took it at the right time. I know people who play for England, and, well, I don't know what he does, but, you know . . . he's a nice man.'

governments but bodies like FIFA and the IOC, and sponsors like Coke and Nike. It's war minus the shooting, with breaks for adverts and better camouflage. A thriving England football team, more than any other national sporting success story, is a powerful vehicle for whoever wishes to use it and whatever they wish to sell you. The World Cup will be a bandwagon, a swindle, a global clusterfuck, and almost none of it will be about sport.

If you're going to fly the flag, fly it for yourself. Let them follow you.

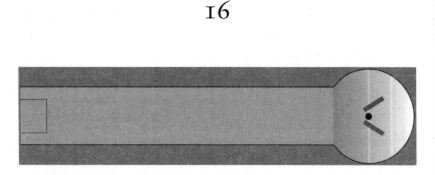

16

Schräger Kreis mit V Hindernis – sloping circle with V obstacle

The British minigolf season was drawing to a close. To date I had won nothing – no prize money, no prestige and precious few ranking points. I had yet to make a single cut. Time was running out.

The British Open was again taking place in Hastings. One year on, I returned to White Rock Gardens a changed man. I was at the course three days in advance of the competition with my balls and club. I scribbled notes about each hole in a spiral-bound exercise book I had bought in Denmark, drawing diagrams with dotted lines from tee to cup. I thought about my pre-putt routine. I rehearsed every stroke, legs far apart, crouched over the putter, swinging the club back and forth like a pendulum.

'Ha ha!' said Joe Vallory, when he saw me doing this. 'It's Edouard!'

He had a point. I felt closer in spirit to the European players than many of the British, whose lack of proper minigolf equipment and technique now seemed buffoonish to me. I realized I was looking forward to seeing Peter.

'How was Latvia?' he asked, when he appeared on Thursday morning.

'Hard,' I said.

Peter nodded. He had known it would be. I was grateful he hadn't told me quite how hard.

He had followed my faltering progress on the tournament's website. 'Did you have problems with eternit?' he asked. 'Theoretically it's an easier course than beton.'

'Not for me,' I said. 'I just don't have the skill.'

'Mm,' said Peter neutrally.

Steen and Morten were coming from Denmark to compete in the Open. I wanted them to enjoy themselves but Hastings in September wasn't quite as congenial as Odense in June. I saw the slightly tatty course through their eyes. The facilities seemed shabby now and some of the holes unacceptably irregular. They had been so generous to me; I felt the British players should offer them all the help we could.

'Up to a point,' said Tim Davies. Hastings was his home course and he didn't want to give too much away. Peter, too, was hopeful that Great Britain might at last have a contender who could give the Europeans a run for their money.

'Tim's best score here is thirty-four,' he said. 'Thomas Zeininger did score thirty-three last year in the final round, but that was exceptional. Tim has played this course every week for years.' Neither man wanted to squander that advantage.

When Steen and Morten arrived, I surreptitiously showed them the safe line I had plotted at the fifteenth hole, playing slightly left of centre from an onion-shaped nick in the felt. 'You do this,' I told them, 'you get over the bridge.'

They nodded.

'We gonna play for a few beers, *old boy*?' asked Steen.

'Later,' I said. I had to practise.

I continued my preparations, trying to let nothing distract me. Since I had last been here, this course had acquired a new and very particular notoriety. It had been used as the setting for Britain's, if not the world's, first crazy-golf-themed pornographic film. More specifically, the film had been made by a company that specialized in, ahem, 'the most daring pissing videos in the world'. The plot synopsis is as follows:

Ellie is sweet, innocent, absolutely stunning and just 18! During a game of crazy golf, Kellogg wets her jeans just yards from other players, Ellie pees her white cotton panties plus there's a spectacular double panty wetting scene as someone walks past.

I kept this information to myself. It was a bit of local knowledge no one needed to know. None the less, whenever I played the eighth hole, scene of the 'spectacular double', I did so gingerly, taking care never to touch the felt.

I chatted with the Austrian and German players. They were represented this year by Thomas, André Kuhn, Christian Freilach (no longer with Corinna but still smiling) and Heinz Weber. Heinz and I were old campaigners. We had been in Rīga together, although he had finished eighth in the men's individual standings and I had finished eighty-seventh.

'You can't play good minigolf if you have no fun playing minigolf,' he told me.

'Absolutely,' I said, mesmerized by the eighth hole. 'You've got to have fun, haven't you?'

The evening before the tournament Peter organized an informal competition between the British and the Europeans on the Arnold Palmer on Hastings seafront. We watched in awe as, without practice, in the wind and rain and never having played an Arnold Palmer before, Morten Rasmussen shot thirty-four. Tim, with his local knowledge and years of experience, shot forty-one. I shot forty-three and therefore nearly came last. I braced myself for another day down with the bottom feeders.

But in the tournament I spluttered into form. A summer in Europe had made me battle-hardened. Over two rounds I was a ruthless putting machine, not through skill – that was as lacking as ever – but because I was well prepared and disciplined. I really concentrated. In thirty-six holes, I only scored aces twice (Heinz had eleven) but, man, I had a *lot* of twos. I ground them out. By the time I finished, there was just one four on my card and nothing higher.

More importantly, I made the cut. Shit, I thought. This is when I blow it.

'I made the cut,' I said to Steen in disbelief. 'I'm worried.'

'Yeah, sometimes it's like you have a gun to your head,' said Steen, who trailed me by a couple of strokes. 'But not for you. You are playing well.'

Predictably, Morten, Thomas and Heinz led the field. Of the British players, Robert and Steve Vallory had both made it through, as had Tim's friends Ted and Mark. Tim himself had let his nerves get the better of him; he carded forty-three, a disaster, and thirty-seven, but he too was through. Peter, though, was nowhere. He even had the humiliation of a four at the bland eighteenth hole. 'I just couldn't concentrate,' he told me. 'There's too much to organize. I haven't had time to prepare.'

But I had. And having finally made a cut, I wasn't about to fold. My consistency deserted me on the last few holes (four, one, four, two) but too late to do any real damage to my final score. In his final round, Tim relaxed and produced an exceptional thirty-one, good enough to clinch the British top spot. It was a lifetime personal best for him. Heinz Weber, who had never played the course before Wednesday, scored thirty and won the tournament.

So, entirely without flair, I finished the British Open in tenth place. I was tied with Ted and Steen on 119 but ahead of them on stroke difference. I was the third highest placed British player. According to the rankings, Andy Miller was now the eleventh best minigolfer in the country. I couldn't quite believe it.

At the end of play, the Austrians insisted we join them for a drink. Yes, I said. That would be lovely. So we all stood by the course as the sun went down and toasted one another with cups of tea from the café, into which Thomas Zeininger decanted a bottle of Bacardi.

'Watch out! This gets you pissed *fast*,' said Steen approvingly.

'You nearly had me there,' said Steve Vallory, who had beaten me by one shot. 'Well done.'

'Well done, Andrew,' said Robert Vallory. 'You've worked hard. You deserved that.'

Joe Vallory didn't say anything. He had gone home after missing the cut.

Three weeks later, however, Joe was back on top. He won the English Open at a park just outside Oxford. This time I finished second, stealing it from Peter with an ace at the final hole.

'And in second place, it's Andy Miller,' announced Peter stoically when the game was over, 'who is just getting better all the time.'

The tournament was held on a scaled-down version of the WMF-approved Swedish 'felt run' course, which caused a bit of grumbling from the Vallorys, who thought it was both boring and too difficult. The elusive Martin Vallory turned up but after trying out a few holes announced he couldn't face it and went to the pub. But I didn't mind. It was a proper minigolf course, and I was fully equipped for it.

The course had been newly installed by tournament and BMGA sponsors Bishop Sports and Leisure, whose representative Gary Jenkins attended the event and handed over Joe's prize: £100 and a set of minigolf balls. Bishop Sports and Leisure, Gary told me, supplied sports and leisure equipment mainly to schools and local authorities. They had held the licence to distribute and sell both felt and eternit systems for many years, but obviously their market was not for the serious miniature-golf enthusiast 'like you guys'. Most of their business came from councils or seaside lease-holders like Jim in Clacton, and Bishop provided them with crazy golf for a fraction of the cost of building a course from scratch.

'When I've got a spare twenty grand,' I said lightheartedly to Gary, 'you can come and build a course in my back garden.' He didn't realize I was joking and gave me his card.

On 28 October, between the English Open and the final fixture of the season, a friendly in Sidcup, the General Association of International Sports Federations voted in Monte Carlo to admit the World Minigolf Sports Federation to its ranks. It was the culmination of ten years' work on the part of the WMF. The meeting I attended in Latvia had indeed been historic. Apart from the International Olympic Committee, AGFIS is the biggest sport association in the world. In the words of the WMF press release, 'Minigolf is now world-wide acknowledged as sport.' Minigolf could take its rightful place as an event at the World Games, and most national associations could expect to receive recognition and further funding from their governments. The WMF's bid was helped by the strong support of the German Sports Council.

'Do you think it'll make any difference here?' I asked Peter.

'I doubt it,' said Peter. He had already had an unsatisfactory exchange of letters with Sport England, whom he had approached with a view to obtaining funding. Not only had they refused, they had refused to give minigolf any recognition whatsoever. Sport England's view was that minigolf was a variation of golf; and it was Sport England's policy to recognize only one variant of any sport. Furthermore, they told Peter, they took a dim view of 'mini' variants. As they recognized just one governing body per sport, they suggested Peter seek recognition for minigolf from the English Golf Union instead. Not unreasonably, Peter found this position extremely frustrating.

'It's so inconsistent,' he said. 'Sport England recognize Rugby League *and* Rugby Union; those are variants of the same sport. They recognize the English Table Tennis Association, which you could say represents a mini variant of tennis, without the approval of the Lawn Tennis Association. None of the European minigolf associations is connected with their national golf associations. They get funding because their Sports Councils recognize minigolf as a sport in its own right. To be fair, the English Golf Union did at least make the effort to be helpful, but they told me they thought it was very unlikely that any formal application for membership would be endorsed. All the county golf unions would have to look upon it favourably.'

In other words, Sport England wouldn't recognize minigolf as a proper sport until the English Golf Union recognized minigolf as a variant of golf, which the English Golf Union had no intention of doing. And even if the English Golf Union had a change of heart and embraced our game, it wouldn't matter because Sport England didn't recognize variants anyway. Especially mini ones. Unless it was ping-pong. Peter was right. It was ridiculous.

Tim Davies had accumulated enough points with his Open triumph to be guaranteed the title of UK National Minigolf Champion. He had started up his own minigolf website, had made approaches to Sport England and the English Golf Union himself, and had received much the same response as Peter.

'We considered "minigolf" some years ago and concluded that we could not recognize this activity as a sport in its own right,' wrote Paul Baxter, of the English Golf Union. 'I assume by minigolf you refer to the organization of golf events played over crazy-golf courses, etc., usually found in play parks, the seaside and the like?'

The Sidcup friendly took place neither at a play park nor, for obvious reasons, the seaside. Instead, we were on the edge of a busy main road in Sidcup at a golf centre whose facilities included a minigolf course. It was mid-November, cold and very wet. There were seven of us – Peter, Tim, Scott, Lionel, Ted, Mark and me – just enough players to make a tournament (the WMF-approved minimum is six). I played confidently. Using my putter and a plain course ball, I had seven aces over two rounds. I deserved to do well in the competition and, for once, I did. I won it.

'I couldn't believe it,' said Tim. 'You were on fire!'

'Thanks,' I said. I was stunned.

'Well done,' said Scott, who had had another awful round.

'Well, you know, just lucky,' I said. I wasn't quite sure how to react. This was the first serious thing I'd ever won.

In addition to coming first, I scored extra ranking points for doing so on a course that had never hosted a tournament before and for setting a course record in the process. It was rather like getting bonus points in Scrabble for a well-placed Q or X.[1] As

1. Brian Eno again: 'I love Scrabble. My best ever score was the adjective "quixotic" over three triples. I think that was worth 292 points.'

a result I ended the season ranked fourth in the UK, behind Tim, Robert Vallory and Joe Vallory. My photograph appeared in the *BMGA Yearbook* with the caption 'Most Improved Player'.

After the game the seven of us sat in the golf centre's café and discussed ideas for attracting sponsorship. Given Sport England's apathy, it was felt that it might be best to look elsewhere for funding. Peter was reluctant to stray too far from serious miniature golf but several people, including me, expressed the view that the way forward was to find a sponsor for a wacky crazy-golf event and develop it from there. Ben and Jerry's ice cream sponsored a bog-snorkelling event and the world conker championships. Surely they could be persuaded to add us to their portfolio? As for recognition, a neighbour of Lionel's had been marketing manager for the old Sports Council. He was retired now but had suggested we apply for membership of the Central Council of Physical Recreation, which apparently lobbied for funding of minority sports. It was more likely we'd get somewhere if we took it one step at a time.

Yes, I thought, as the meeting broke up, still dizzy with triumph, yes. Someone's bound to run with this. Every other sport in the UK gets more coverage than we do, however violent or silly that sport may be. But the British love crazy golf. This is a fantastic opportunity for some far-sighted soul. This will be an Olympic event one day. We are pioneers.

But in the weeks that followed, my enthusiasm started to drain away. Now there were no tournaments to aim for, no more training weekends, I felt adrift. I started going out again. I saw the friends I'd neglected for most of the year and resumed doing the things I'd liked doing before minigolf came into my world. I wanted my life back.

Tim Davies settled into his role as British Number One and British Champion. He appeared on breakfast television and opened a new adventure course at a local wildlife park. He also extended his website into the most comprehensive collection of minigolf links on the web, which he described in an interview as 'an attempt to give something back'. In the event of a full British squad attending the next European Championships in Prague, Vicky was appointed as psychological coach. It was hoped that a German or Austrian player could be persuaded to help with the technical side of things.

Peter was thinking of stepping down as BMGA chairman after Prague. He had devoted almost five years and several thousand pounds of his own money to the cause, but seemed to spend all his time on administrative and organizational business. And his game was suffering. On tournament days, he was too busy liaising with the course owners or media to concentrate. He finished the season in tenth place. Next year, he was thinking about using self-hypnosis tapes to improve his chances.

Lionel was looking for a backer for a portable garden miniature-golf game he had devised. The Vallory family continued to attend and win events, although Joe's involvement was limited because he had taken on a Saturday job.

And me? I had achieved what I set out to achieve. I was officially one of the top five in the country at my chosen sport. I had won one tournament and been a runner-up in others. I had played at international level. Through sheer bloody-mindedness I had improved my physical technique and learnt to control the limitations of my temperament. I felt I understood the sporting life far better than I ever had before.

I no longer hated sport for the sake of it. And that was because of miniature golf.

But there was a trade-off. I couldn't shake the feeling that the experience had warped me. To prove a point, I had become the sort of person who not only knows there is crazy-golf porn in the world but, worse, knows where it's been filmed, to the nearest hole.

I really did want my life back.

I just felt for Andy Miller there was nothing more in minigolf I wanted to do.

17

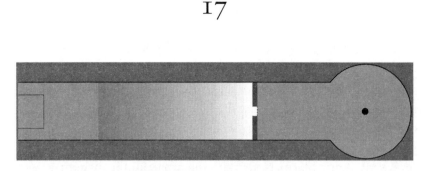

Favoritentöter – favourite killer

'People really care too much. It affects people's lives too much . . . And you think, crikey, should it really matter that much? Of course it shouldn't. But it seems to.'

GARY LINEKER

As part of my life reclamation project, I decided to call it a day with QPR. We'd had some laughs together, some good times, but over the summer break I started having second thoughts. It was never going to work in the long run. We were too different. It wasn't me, it was them.

They say you can change the manager, you can change the players, but the true fans will always be there. So long, suckers, I thought, as I bought the ticket for my final match.

My testimonial was the first home game of the new season, an archetypal goalless draw with Birmingham City. It was dire. There was a bit of excitement in injury time when Karl Ready elbowed someone in the face but that was about it. It seemed like a fitting farewell to the finest football team the world has ever seen.

And yet, inexplicably, I was back in the stands two weeks later. We beat Crewe 1–0. When Jude waved at me, I waved back. I'll stick it till Christmas, I thought. We might be going up.

In October, QPR played six matches and lost five of them. By Christmas, they had scraped just four wins out of twenty-five games. The good days had been brief and now they were over. How could the same squad be playing so much worse than last year? It was horrific but I kept going back for more. I couldn't take my eyes off what was happening to QPR. It was more than simply witnessing a car crash. It was like being involved in a multiple pile-up, with *QPR The Greatest* stuck in the tape deck and no prospect of anyone coming to cut you out of the wreckage.

Throughout this period, the club pressed ahead with a new marketing initiative called Real Fans Real Football. A First Division team was more authentic than a glitzy Premiership side, and so were its supporters. However, as the season degenerated, you could tell confidence was faltering. An advert for half-season tickets appeared on the club's website. 'Real Fans Real Football,' it said. '5000 Have Already Signed On.'

It was a small slip but there was obviously something badly wrong. I started to avoid the official website and bookmarked fan pages instead.

Back in August, there had been a mood of guarded optimism around the club. The previous season, everyone said, had been one of consolidation. Chris Kiwomya, Richard Langley and captain Gavin Peacock all signed new contracts. Ericsson continued to have their name displayed across the players' shirts. There was even a new sponsor for the Ellerslie Road stand, and a new name – the Alfred McAlpine Homes Stand.

'When I came back after being at Chelsea I wanted to achieve something here. I wanted to go up to the Premier League with Rangers. Now, I wouldn't have re-signed if I didn't believe that was possible,' said Gavin Peacock. 'I don't think Gerry would be here either if he didn't think we could go back to the Premier League.'

Gerry Francis agreed, in his usual downbeat way. 'This year our aim is to try and improve on last year,' he said, 'and hope that we may be in with a shout for the play-off positions.'

One year later, Gerry was gone and the club was in the hands of the administrators. Gavin Peacock was playing Premiership football, but on loan to Charlton as a matter of financial necessity. In an effort to cut the club's crippling wage bill, most of his teammates had gone too, sold or released on free transfers. Karl Ready was in Motherwell. Chris Kiwomya was in Denmark. Richard Langley had yet to recover from the cruciate knee ligament injury that had kept him out of action for nearly a year. QPR had not made the play-offs. In fact, they had been relegated to the Second Division (or the old Third Division) for the first time since 1967. The club's new manager was Ian Holloway, a former QPR player who had been part of Gerry's Premier League side just eight years ago, the season they had finished in fifth place as London's top team. Ericsson did not renew their sponsorship, and their 'Make Yourself Heard' banners were removed from around the pitch; after some uncertainty, it was announced that JD Sports, self-styled 'King of Trainers' would take their place.

In other words, one year later the oft-discussed scenario had come to pass. QPR were playing in a different league with a different sponsor and a different manager, having to make the best of an almost entirely new squad of young unseasoned players. Even Loftus Road Stadium was under threat. Rumours persisted that property developers wanted to buy the site and turn it into a supermarket or luxury flats. It was said that the new sponsor, Alfred McAlpine, had expressed an interest.

The only constant at the club were the fans, real or otherwise. Every week they came and watched the terrible football and shouted, 'WE! ARE! QPR! SAID WE ARE QPR!' and they were right, because nobody else was.

Tracy Stent has been a fan of Queens Park Rangers since she was seven years old. Her dad used to take her to stand on the terraces. She has two sisters and a brother, but she was the only one who loved Rangers. When she was a little girl, her hero was Gerry Francis. She has hazy memories of the 1976 season when the club so nearly won the First Division. 'I wasn't really old enough to take in all the implications of that. All I remember is

Dad going into a massive sulk. It must have lasted for months on end. I remember thinking, Silly old sod, what's the matter with him? I didn't understand at the time.' She laughed. 'I do now, obviously.'

Tracy met her husband Leon through the club. 'October 1987. It was an away fixture at Anfield. We were top of the league. We got beaten four–nil. And I met him on the train coming home.' Now they had two girls aged ten and seven. Both children had been mascots on match days and all the family were season-ticket holders. 'We've forced it on them, admittedly. When they're teenagers, they might not want to go any more. But I don't think that'll happen.'

The steady disappointments of this season had been hard on the family. In January, Arsenal came to Loftus Road in the FA Cup and destroyed QPR 6–0. Two of the goals were own goals. I was at the game. It was almost funny. The Rangers supporters were fantastic. After the third goal they started to sing '*FOUR–THREE! WE'RE GONNA BEAT YOU FOUR–THREE!*', adjusting the numbers upwards with every subsequent goal. But, really, it was a shambles. Tracy told me that her eldest hadn't wanted to go to school on Monday. Most of the other kids followed Premiership sides, including Arsenal. 'Just tell them, "At least I go and watch my team,"' said Tracy.

She had known in her heart Rangers were going to be relegated when, with nine games left to play, they lost at home to Grimsby by a solitary, scrappy goal. 'That was when I said to myself, "We're going down." It was one of the saddest days of my entire life. Not being dramatic, but it was almost like losing a close family member. I was totally devastated. I was glad we didn't have to go anywhere that evening. I made a cup of tea, read a few reports on the Internet. Did a little bit of crying.'

We'd met in a pub near Loftus Road. I bought Tracy another orange squash from the bar in case she started crying again. She believed there were three sorts of people who went to football matches: 'First you've got the people who might go to the occasional game,' she said. 'Sometimes they watch so-and-so, but occasionally they might go and watch the other lot down the road. Then in the middle you've got people who turn up to every game. They might have season tickets, might not. They watch their team, curse a couple of players – "Bloody hell, Ready!" that sort of thing – go to the pub, discuss the table and then they forget about it until the next game. And then you've got the third group, where football's all-consuming and it literally takes over their lives. And that's us.'

'Doesn't it ever get you down?' I asked her.

'I had my team chosen for me,' she replied. 'I could never change that. My dad was a Rangers fan for years. My grandfather used to see them play at White City. But if you're in that first group of people and you haven't particularly been shown one way or another to following a particular club, you differentiate. But we never would.'

This is how football fans hang themselves out to dry, of course. The worst thing you can do is change your club just because they aren't any good. The core value of the brand is knowing that you must never – *never* – betray the brand. To do so is to be Judas Iscariot or, worse, David Mellor. It's marketing nirvana.

The trick in the last ten years has been to convince those who do differentiate – i.e., the majority – that there is an easy way for them to feel like part of the devoted throng. Ten years ago Manchester United realized that four-fifths of the people who came to watch games at Old Trafford did so only once a season. If you sold each of them just one souvenir, you would get rich quick. 'I realized that the potential for the Manchester United brand was just beyond any expectations that I may have had,' Edward Freedman, the company's former head of merchandising, said recently. So, first, the company targeted the tourists, and then they went after the people who never even left the house. And it worked.

Manchester United became so good at doing this in the nineties, they started putting football fans off football. My dream of the Red Team and the Blue Team became a reality, only it turned out you only needed one team, the red one, for people to get bored and drift away. United's record of success, their relentless merchandising, the sheer cost of getting to see the team play, on television or in the flesh, all took their toll on the grass roots, leaving clubs like QPR to play the Real Fans Real Football card as a pragmatic alternative to United's mass-market dominance.

Manchester United then set their sights on the rest of the planet. Research from the polling agency Mori has suggested that the club has 50 million fans worldwide. 'The strategy is to turn those fans into customers,' said chief executive Peter Kenyon, 'Man United is more than a football club – it's a global football brand.'

Oh, but why stop at football? Man United's aspirations are as ambitious, and as messianic, as that abbreviation suggests. In the autumn of 2000, a film was released to cinemas, and subsequently on video and DVD (with extra material, of course), called *Manchester United: Beyond The Promised Land*. Its biblical title prepares the way for the dogma within. Although ostensibly a chronicle of United's season in the wake of winning 'the treble' – a holy trinity, be in no doubt – the film features fans from all over the world bearing witness to the miraculous power of the Red Devils (memo to press department: can we do something about that nickname? Very negative connotation). From New York ('It wasn't luck, it was belief. And belief will win you things when all hope is gone') to Northern Ireland ('We don't mix religion and football. Our religion is football') to China ('Two hundred million Chinese watched our game with Shanghai Shenhua'), the viewer is left in little doubt that the world would be a more peaceful and contented place if more of us dug deep and supported 'the biggest franchise in the world', united with our fellow man(cs).

For the Manchester United of *Beyond The Promised Land* is no mere football club. It's a red army that is deploying the forces of commerce to spread the values it believes in passionately: passion, belief and Manchester United. With Sir Alex Ferguson as its commander-in-chief, and Keane, Scholes and Beckham its generals, any mother would be proud to see her boy, or girl, enlist in its ranks. Sign up now! Artistically, the film compares unfavourably with Leni Riefenstahl's *Olympia*, but as an un-ambiguous hymn to power and unity, it probably has the edge. They should have called it *Manchester United: Strength Through Roy*.

Famously, the source of Manchester United's super power, the plutonium at its core, is the business's standing as a public limited company. Stock-market flotation is a route many football clubs went down in the nineties, but few had anything like the spectacular growth United did. And in QPR's case, the effect of plc status has been less like plutonium and more like Kryptonite.

When I briefly supported Liverpool, the only thing I knew about QPR was that they had a plastic pitch. Astroturf was installed in 1981, against the wishes of the rest of the league, because the club thought it might save on maintenance costs and bring in a bit of spare cash on non-match days.[1] Notwithstanding the advantage it gave the home side (FA Cup final in 1982, promoted in 1983), the new surface was never popular with players or supporters and grass was restored in 1988 – but only because the plastic wasn't wearing well and the extra revenue never materialized.

However, in the mid-nineties the plastic pitch made a slight return. The grass was relaid, and the base of each blade bound with plastic to toughen up the playing surface. QPR would be sharing the Loftus Road turf with a Rugby Union team, Wasps, whom new chairman Chris Wright had recently acquired at an estimated cost of £4 million (QPR cost him around £9 million). Both Rangers and Wasps were to be floated on the stock market as part of the newly formed Loftus Road plc. There would be 'synergy', said the 1996 prospectus; there would be 'significantly increased revenues'.

---

1. Interestingly, QPR's manager at this time, and one of the driving forces behind the plastic pitch, was Terry Venables. Throughout this period, he also had a lock-up in Ellerslie Road where he could be found on match days selling solid gold watches and perfume out of a suitcase. 🐜

(🐜 Lawyers, please note: this is a joke.)

It was a disaster. Like the plastic pitch, Loftus Road plc was a moneymaking scheme that enjoyed an initial flurry of publicity and success, but which subsequently became unpopular with fans, required constant maintenance and failed to deliver financially. But unlike the plastic pitch, the plc could not be uprooted without taking the rest of Loftus Road with it.

Chris Wright co-founded Chrysalis Records in 1968, finding success with artists as diverse as Jethro Tull, Spandau Ballet and Blondie. As chairman of the Chrysalis media group, Wright has a highly successful record of identifying pop-culture trends and profitably building them into his business – Chrysalis currently has interests in music publishing and recording, radio stations, book publishing, television production and the Internet. It must have made sense in the mid-nineties to add football to that portfolio, outside the Chrysalis umbrella, and to buffer the deal by taking on a rugby team too. 'At the time,' he says, 'there was a general perception that football was going to be a good business to be in because it was going to really grow, the revenues would really grow. And they have grown, but only for the likes of Manchester United.'

It was a cold day in late March when I met Chris Wright in his office suite at the top of Chrysalis's London headquarters. That morning, the Chrysalis Group share price stood at well over three pounds; a stake in Loftus Road plc meanwhile would cost you just seven pence.

Wright had stepped down as chairman some weeks previously after being barracked by Rangers fans (at – where else? – a Fulham game), three of whom had tried to get into the directors' box and were restrained by Security. It was a disastrous night for the club. They lost at home to their local, and much richer, rivals, and both Richard Langley and Clark Carlisle suffered chronic injuries that ruled them out for the rest of the season. Nevertheless, Wright was still paying the bills.

'If it wasn't for me QPR wouldn't exist at this point,' he told me. 'Until somebody can come in and stand in my place it's only me that's keeping the club alive.' The subsistence Wright was providing was in the form of a series of loans secured against the club's property, with interest.

Wright described the experience of being chairman as 'a nightmare'. At first, he told me, he had enjoyed being in charge. He had been a QPR fan for over thirty years, so actually running the club was 'very exciting. It was a big thrill.' But it didn't take long for the thrill to fade: 'Half of the second season was miserable. The whole of the third season was totally miserable. The fourth season, last year, was OK because we were safe. But the financial situation just got worse and worse. We couldn't sell players 'cause we didn't have any spare players that anyone wanted. Covering the losses was getting more and more difficult. The performance on the pitch . . .' He shook his head in disbelief. 'I mean, I haven't enjoyed it really . . . I quite enjoyed some of it last year, I enjoyed the first season, but I haven't really enjoyed it, to be honest with you, since half-way through the second season. Out of five.'

To be fair to Chris Wright, it wasn't the stock market alone that did for QPR. The club was already in trouble when he bought it. Previous chairman Richard Thompson had presided over the sale of many of the club's best, and most valuable, players, failed to invest the proceeds in its infrastructure, and had seen Rangers relegated from the Premiership to the First Division. Many fans loathed Thompson and there had been large and noisy protests against him outside Loftus Road. So Wright's arrival was widely greeted as good news – the club would be in the hands of a 'lifelong fan' (Wright has been a season-ticket holder since 1973) with apparently bottomless pockets and with the stated intention of restoring the club's fortunes, on and off the pitch.

But the decision to fund the project via flotation was, as the song says, like pouring water on a drowning man. Plc status by definition meant that any losses sustained were in the public domain, and their transparency ensured that once you started to lose money confidence faltered and you were likely to carry on losing money. More importantly, the initial funds released by the sale were

hopelessly mismanaged, as were subsequent deals and contracts –
a total of £27 million squandered between 1997 and 2000.[2]

When Wright stood down as chairman after the trouble at the
Fulham game, several newspapers ran pieces in which the tycoon
was presented as just another football fan, whose heart was
breaking at the sorry state of his club. 'In retrospect, buying into
QPR was not my best decision but it was for sale and I was
there,' Wright was quoted as saying. 'I let my heart rule my head.'
He called his decision to resign 'the saddest decision of my life.'
Elsewhere, he expressed forgiveness for the supporters who had
attacked him. 'They [the fans] are upset with the results, and I
understand that. I'm a fan and it hurts me just as much.'[3]

I asked Tracy how she felt about this expression of empathy
on the part of the former chairman.

'QPR fans don't want pity,' she said bluntly. 'We want it
sorted out.'

The business aspirations for Loftus Road plc had been straightforward. Rather than invest in the club's infrastructure, the company would spend the flotation money upfront. By doing this,
QPR would be returned to the Premiership, where they would
quickly reap the rewards of improved gates, television rights and
all the concomitant merchandising hoop-la. Wasps, too, could be
built up to fulfil their significant earning potential. West London
was crying out for a major new stadium and conference venue,
so in the mid- to long-term both clubs would relocate from Loftus
Road to a new purpose-built 35,000-seater stadium, maybe near
Heathrow. Paul Hart, the finance director of Loftus Road plc,

2. For a full account of QPR's spectacular but preventable decline, see
Suicide and a Team Called QPR by Sean Smith, soccernet, 27 February
2001, and *QPR Show How To Lose £27m In Four Years* by David Conn,
in the *Independent*, 28 September 2001.
3. This it-hurts-me-too PR strategy is perhaps best encapsulated by Everton
chairman Bill Kenwright's widely reported response to being heckled by
an irate supporter: 'I tried to calm him down but he would not listen. I just
told him, "I understand your pain."'

admitted in an interview that 'We're generally not investing in the stadium we currently have,' going on to say that 'The real future of the business is in its ability to unlock land in prime locations to build new facilities and to generate income from retail and corporate banqueting.'

We'd be back in the Premiership quicker than you could say Stadium of Light. The football club would underwrite the expansion plans of the business that, when successful, would inevitably benefit the football club. Easy.

But the plan failed. Football clubs, like shares, may go down as well as up. The business employed the wrong directors, who appointed the wrong managers, who selected the wrong expensive players on extravagant five-year salary deals. The flotation cash was frittered away, most infamously on bringing Vinnie Jones to QPR from Wimbledon for half a million pounds, on an ill-considered contract that allowed him to go on strike then insist that the club buy him out for roughly twice his original transfer fee. Promotion remained elusive, and the money started to run out. It was a saga of ruinous ineptitude.

'I don't think you have to be a fan to do those jobs, not necessarily,' Tracy Stent told me unsentimentally, 'but I think you have to understand the culture of football. They've had a lot of people at QPR who don't understand what makes football tick and what makes fans tick.'

When I saw Chris Wright, I asked him if, as a QPR fan, he had ever felt uneasy about these grand plans, particularly the idea of quitting Loftus Road. The stadium was, after all, the scene of the club's greatest triumphs, and a Shepherds Bush landmark. 'There was never a conflict between me as chairman and me as fan about something like that,' he told me bluntly. 'Clearly still it would be in the best interests of the club to do that. It would be in the best interests of every fan, there is no question at all about it. But it's not much of an option when you've got a team that's going to be in Division Two.'

In truth, while some fans would never sanction Rangers leaving Loftus Road, others could see the benefits of such a move. But

Wright's strong conviction that relocation was in every QPR fan's best interests stemmed from his being a very particular sort of fan – one who owned the club. Over five years he has sunk millions of pounds into Loftus Road with no return on his investment. His distress at QPR's decline is not simply that of a supporter whose team has under-performed, however much he says so. It's the frustration of a successful speculator whose latest venture has gone bafflingly, humiliatingly wrong and whose losses are fast approaching the point where simply liking football is not enough to compensate him.

Several people I spoke to felt that Wright had been looking to bail out of QPR for some time and that the minor skirmish at the Fulham game (and it was minor compared to some of the vitriol hurled at previous chairman Richard Thompson) had given him the perfect excuse. If the fans don't want me, I'll go. Wright was obviously disturbed by the abuse he had received, but when I asked him about it, the first thing he mentioned instead were the injuries to Richard Langley and Clark Carlisle. 'We lost our two best young players with anterior cruciate knee ligament injuries within a ten-minute period,' he said, 'our two most valuable players, in terms of having any saleable value.'

Wright had seen the writing on the wall. Without players like Langley and Carlisle, the team stood almost no chance of avoiding the drop to the Second Division, which in itself was going to be financially catastrophic; but their injuries also temporarily removed them from the transfer market, depriving both the club and Wright of the much-needed cash-flow their sale might deliver. If this were a Chrysalis business, he would have already pulled the plug. It was time to go.

I asked him if he felt he had failed at Loftus Road.

'Yes, definitely,' he replied. 'I've failed to bring success to the club, which was probably always going to be difficult, but I've also failed in that I've seriously endangered my own financial position and the club's financial position as well.'

So now Wright was in limbo, waiting for someone to come along who would take on what was left of the plc and, in his words, 'trying to keep the wheels on the cart'. He thought that Wasps and QPR would probably de-merge, as it would be easier to sell the constituent parts of the business piecemeal. For obvious reasons, attending games was not currently an option, so on match days he switched off his mobile and played tennis or went for long walks. 'I just tell them to call me after the match. Then I know it's over. It can be awful. You know, we've gone one up, then it's one all, then there's a penalty. It's just . . . I can't deal with that. At five o'clock, I turn the mobile back on and wait for it to ring. If I've got four new messages it's good news, and if there's no calls it's bad news.'

I felt rather sorry for him.

Two weeks later, on a day when Manchester United declared pre-tax profits of £17.3 million, Wright announced that Loftus Road plc was going into administration, with debts of approximately £11 million and estimated losses of £570,000 a month. He let it be known that he had put more than £20 million into Loftus Road over five years.

Later that week a tabloid newspaper ran a reassuring profile of Wright in its business pages, which emphasized the ongoing profitability of Wright's interests outside football. Of Loftus Road, he said, 'I had no magic ingredient but all I can say to the fans is that I care as much as they do. If QPR lose, my Saturday night is ruined just as much as theirs.' Accompanying the article were 'Chris's Top 10 Tips' for business success, the first of which will have struck a chord with many QPR fans.

'When choosing a career, make sure you do something you enjoy – you will have more chance of being successful.'

Why does this matter? Not so long ago, it wouldn't have mattered to me at all. But the slow demolition of QPR was troubling for several reasons, only one of which was the enduringly crappy football.

When Rangers was floated on the stock market as part of Loftus Road plc, many supporters were encouraged to buy shares in the club. Most only acquired a handful, a symbolic interest, like planting a square of the sacred turf in your own back garden. This being QPR, of course, that square was plastic and refused to grow, but comparatively little harm was done. However, some fans sought to invest in Loftus Road, believing like Chris Wright that it was time to join the football gold rush; and like Chris Wright, they were wrong. Tracy knew of one man, a pensioner, who had bought £30,000-worth of Loftus Road shares, the majority of his life savings. He stood to lose all of it. It was little comfort to him to recall that the value of shares could go down as well as up.

After the business was put in the hands of the administrators, the board of Loftus Road regularly deflected fans' questions about their plans for its constituent parts by telling them that it was all very complicated and convoluted, and wrapped up in a financial milieu that was probably beyond them, and they should try not to worry. When I met Chris Wright, he told me, 'I think in general people can't be expected to understand all the ramifications of share prices and public companies.' But the plc still took their money.

On a more prosaic level, there was the effect on the club. Every week, or thereabouts, the dwindling fan base came to their uncared-for stadium and persistently stood (although it contravened the QPR Behaviour Policy) and chanted and watched the team they loved get steadily worse and worse, and sink lower and lower. They gave QPR their loyalty; they got nothing back that they hadn't put in themselves.

A football club belongs to its fans, or ought to. At best, Chris Wright was a well-meaning Saturday fan who, like so many, came to believe that by buying something, you could be part of the great sports nation – if only he'd stopped at a replica shirt. But at worst, he and the board had been as selfish as their predecessors. They had borrowed the club, and by the time they tried to pass it on, it was ruined beyond repair. In the week Loftus Road went into administration, one source near the club was quoted as saying, 'A lot of tyre-kickers have come round, looked at it and walked away without making an offer.' Next stop, the scrap heap. And all the fans could do was watch.

Six months later, things looked much, much worse. After a strong start to the season, Ian Holloway's young side was struggling. For the first time in decades, Rangers were dumped out of the FA Cup in the first round, in a 4–0 rout by Third Division Swansea City, who themselves were on the brink of administration. No buyer could be found for QPR, although several options had come and gone – a Knightsbridge property developer, a proposed merger with Wimbledon FC, a preferred bid from a mystery consortium with excellent media contacts, fronted by 'a lifelong fan' who nobody had ever heard of. Rumours spiralled out of control; fans were blamed for jeopardizing bids by gossiping about them on the Internet. Former chairman Richard Thompson was believed to have expressed an interest in repurchasing the club. The Reverend Sun Myung Moon's Unification Church, which owns football clubs in Brazil and South Korea, made inquiries about acquiring Loftus Road. 'They wanted to know the costs involved,' said club spokesman Mike Hartwell, confirming that a meeting had taken place. But even the Moonies kicked the tyre and walked away.

Chris Wright's head was firmly in control of his heart once more. One week before Loftus Road plc went into administration, a new company was formed called London Wasps Holdings Ltd, which subsequently purchased Wasps from the administrators for £2.5 million. The rugby club would continue to play their matches at Loftus Road with Wright as chairman. More significantly for QPR, Wasps Holdings purchased both clubs' training ground in Twyford Avenue for the same sum, potentially worth a fortune in prime West London real estate should it ever be sold. So Loftus Road plc as a company now consisted of QPR, the Loftus Road stadium, the reduced debt to Wright plus a further £4 million to the taxman and various other creditors. Wright hoped that this would facilitate a sale of QPR to new owners. But still no one came to the rescue.

Meanwhile, the administrators were only guaranteeing limited funds until the end of the season, after which time . . .

When Wright bought the club from Richard Thompson, fans

chanted the new chairman's name around the ground. Five years on they still did, but with somewhat less affection. '*FUCK OFF, AND TAKE THE WASPS WITH YOU*' was one. '*WE'RE SHIT AND WE'RE SICK OF IT*' was another. People remembered that Thompson had written off his losses, which Wright apparently had no intention of doing. Potential bidders were finding it difficult to raise the money: neither banks nor wealthy individuals believed football represented the sound investment it had in the mid-nineties.

The spring saw the formation of a supporters' trust called QPR 1st, a group of fans including Tracy and her husband, whose purpose was to provide a unified voice for QPR fans and improve communication both with the club and the media. They hoped to encourage Loftus Road shareholders to join them. If the trust accumulated enough shares, fans would have the right, for the first time, to be heard at board level.[4]

Although QPR 1st was not universally popular – they were a thorn in the side of the club, and some fans perceived the trust's members as cliquey or unprofessional, or both – they provided a focus for concern and protest, and along with the older Loyal Supporters Association, scored some genuine victories, notably at the Extraordinary General Meeting at Loftus Road in May to ratify the sale of Wasps and the training ground to Chris Wright. One QPR 1st member, a commercial banking expert, forced an amendment to the deal so that a proportion of any future profits from the sale of the training ground would go to QPR, a potentially lucrative bit of quick thinking.

'It's really enjoyable, really exciting,' Tracy told me. 'It's helping us to cope with a lot of what's going on on the pitch. The fans that I really feel for at the moment are the ones that just want to watch the football. The message we're trying to get

4. QPR 1st, like supporters' trusts around the country, is backed by a government initiative called Supporters Direct, the very existence of which seems to acknowledge the essential cupidity and untrustworthiness of football clubs.

across is join us, get involved. Participate in whatever way you can.'

When I first went to see QPR play, I was a sports atheist. I didn't believe in sport and I ridiculed those who did. But minigolf changed that, if only a little. It taught me to give others the respect I craved for my chosen sport.

So now I subscribe to a sort of queasy agnosticism. I think I understand the worth of sport itself but, if anything, my dislike for the culture around it has grown. One seems almost irreconcilably opposed to the other. Sport should be about freedom, self-expression, participation, but sport culture has become oppressive, exclusive and destructively commercial. Make Yourself Heard, Just Do It – these are phrases that mimic the essence of sport, its sense of liberation, in an attempt to privatize it.

Some people love sport, really love it. I'm not one of them. But they don't deserve to be ripped off for it.

So I joined the QPR supporters' trust. I admit it's just a gesture but I'm hoping that when the time comes and we march on Downing Street, demanding equal rights for minigolfers, there'll be a few blue and white hooped shirts marching with us, in a show of solidarity and mutual respect.

I'm not a proper football fan but that's OK. Maybe you are. Maybe you hate football. Or maybe you support Manchester United. But we should all remember one thing, chairman, fanzine writer or armchair fanatic, atheist, agnostic or true believer:

For evil to triumph it requires only that good people go shopping.

18

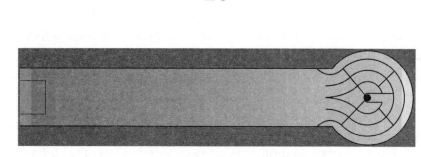

Labyrinth – labyrinth

In Myrtle Beach, South Carolina, USA, at the junction of the North Kings Highway and 7th Avenue North, there dwells a minotaur:

This fearsome beast guards the entrance to Mount Atlanticus Minotaur Goff, a pun nearly as tortuous as the thirty-six crafty holes of miniature golf that lie within his dominion. In Greek mythology, Theseus entered the Minotaur's lair with a ball of twine to help him find his way back to the light. But I'd happily lost the thread ages ago. I liked it in here. It was brilliant.

According to the dramatic back-story sketched on my scorecard, it was on 29 March 1998, just after lunch, when a land mass suddenly appeared two miles out to sea from the Myrtle Beach Pavilion. The land mass was nothing less than a miniature golf resort, some fifty thousand years old, which had broken away from the sunken continent of Atlantis and inched its way to the United States over thousands of years. Cor! As if this weren't incredible enough, the inhabitants of Myrtle Beach woke up two days later to discover that the resort had mysteriously transplanted itself atop the old Chapin Company department store a full two blocks from the ocean. It was a yarn that made the Lost World in Croydon appear both plausible and dull.

It was another beautiful day on the Grand Strand. The sun was out and the wind blew the smell of gasoline and ozone up from the beach. The centrepiece of Minotaur Goff is a series of interconnected huts with thatched roofs, supported on stilts, through which players conclude their tour of this historic site, and which offers a perfect view of the course, its waterfalls and rolling acres of Astroturf, the lions and giraffes that roam across its plains, the plesiosaur that basks in its crystal blue lagoon; and beyond, the skyline of Myrtle Beach itself, its roller-coaster, its surf shops, seafood diners and night spots. It was neither charming nor peaceful but as I stood in my treetop vantage-point, with the wind in my hair and a week of minigolf ahead of me, I thought, I have come home. When I die, scatter my ashes on the slopes of Mount Atlanticus.

I was in Myrtle Beach for a holiday. After eighteen months, I wanted to revive the childhood love I'd felt for miniature golf, a love that had absolutely nothing to do with sport. I wanted some fun. It took only a few hours for Myrtle Beach to deliver this on an epic scale. It was utterly fantastic, in both senses.

Myrtle Beach is the miniature-golf capital of the world. When you fly in, you can spot the courses from the air, bursts of bright blue and green between the parking lots. There are almost fifty of them, spread across thirty locations from Murrells Inlet in the south, along Highway 17 and up to the North Carolina border. Most of the courses are as barmy and as fabulous as Mount Atlanticus and when we were there, they were building still more of them. They have the acreage, the ambition, the inclination and the weather. The sea looks lifeless next to the frothing dyed blue lakes and streams of the miniature golf courses; the threadbare grass at the roadside compares unfavourably with the evergreen felt a few yards away; the fake buildings, the giant skulls, castles and fibreglass caverns are far more appealing than the squat, functional boxes that line the autoroutes.

To be honest, apart from the miniature-golf courses, Myrtle Beach is an ugly place: two strips of highway running parallel to the ocean and a lot of motels, condos and non-specific urban blight. Fortunately this isn't an issue. Myrtle Beach wasn't built to be looked at, it was meant to be used. As the east coast's number-one party town, it's exactly like Skegness, while being nothing like Skegness at all.

On TV 33, the local visitor-information channel, they show interviews with young, excited clubgoers, queuing on the sidewalk outside the Freaky Tiki.

'What did your mom tell you not to do when you came to Myrtle Beach?' presenter Andrea Kersee asks a group of excited teenage girls.

'She just told us to behave!' squeals one.

'And not to drink!' snickers her friend.

'Don't get arrested,' drawls a third girl, with the thousand-yard stare of one who knows what it means to go downtown.

I was here for a week with an old friend called Mark. Myrtle Beach is where they invented the shag, the enduring beach-music craze, and every time a local radio station played 'Shaggin' the Night Away' or 'There Ain't Nothing Like Shaggin'' or 'My Baby Sure Can Shag', we had to pull the car over because we were giggling like eight-year-olds. It wasn't just the miniature golf that was putting me back in touch with my inner child.

'Y'all still got that fog in London?' asked the woman at Alamo Rent-A-Car kindly, when we first picked up our blue Toyota. 'Boy, that must be real depressing for you.'

You got the feeling that they don't see many British people in Myrtle Beach.

'Are you from Austria?' enquired the girl at Mount Atlanticus, when we handed back our clubs.

'I'm afraid not,' I said regretfully, looking at the fifty-two on my scorecard. Later, I realized she probably meant Australia but at that moment I was more concerned with my useless score. Whatever skill I had scraped together the previous year had completely vanished over the winter break. Mark had never played competitively before and beat me easily. It didn't bother me too much. To be bothered would be to let sport in, and this trip wasn't about sport. It was about having a good time, without getting arrested.

On our way to the next course, we stopped to fill up the car. 'Y'all from England?' asked the woman behind the desk, when I went inside to pay. 'Y'all still got that foot-and-mouth disease?'

Back home, the epidemic was at its height. 'Yes, that's still going on,' I said.

'My daughter gets e-mail from one of your soldiers,' explained the woman.

'Yes,' I said, 'they're having to do quite a lot of tidying up.'

'He pretty much said they was just burnin' cattle,' said the woman flatly.

Pea-soupers and cow extermination, I thought, as I walked back to the car. It made you proud to be Austrian.

Just before I left home, the English Tourism Council had enlisted crazy golf in the campaign against foot-and-mouth. Before the Easter break, adverts were placed in national newspapers urging people out to the coast or into the country, the bits of it that were open. The adverts chose quintessential family pursuits – cycling in the countryside, nosing around a stately home or playing crazy golf by the sea – to try to prompt an economic upturn. If our crazy-golf courses were as spectacular as the giant adventure-golf courses of Myrtle Beach, it might have worked.

There are seven pirate courses in Myrtle Beach; there are also four jungles, a Wild West frontier town, a Jurassic dinosaur park,

Gilligan's Island, some Hawaiian caverns, a bone-shaking train ride through a gold mine, a dragon-infested medieval castle incongruously located at the heart of a New England fishing village (actually a themed outdoor mall), and a tropical island whose natives worship miniature golf as a god. An aeroplane has crashed on the island. Its crew is missing. Every ten minutes, the steel-drum tape fades and the crew's distress call is broadcast. Their cries of mounting terror drift across the greens and fairways, the ponds and the wreckage of their plane. The name of the course is MAYDAY! Golf. You get the impression that no one ever says: 'Is this too much?'

The only thing they appeared not to have in Myrtle Beach were windmills. After a few days, I realized we hadn't seen a single one. A rampaging Tyrannosaurus Rex. Enough pirate galleons for an armada. But no windmills.

The biggest and brashest course on the Grand Strand is probably the Hawaiian Rumble, rated by *Golf Magazine* the number-one miniature-golf course in America. At start of play, each minigolfer receives a complementary *lei* along with their putter, scorecard and balls. To the accompaniment of a lilting Hawaiian guitar, or the hits of the Beach Boys, the player tours a landscape that is both imaginative and challenging. The course is overshadowed by an enormous dormant volcano, which erupts noisily and smokily every twenty minutes. They even have parrots living in the clubhouse.

Hawaiian Rumble is one of three courses owned by Bob Detwiler, an avuncular local businessman who is also president of the US ProMiniGolf Association. After I'd complimented Bob on the sheer excitement of the Rumble, I asked if there were any windmills in the area.

'Well, son,' replied Bob, 'there used to be. Wacky Golf had one, but that disappeared about ten years ago. They're kind of old-fashioned. But you never know, fashions change.'

'Do you think windmills might make a comeback?' I asked.

'Sure,' said Bob. 'But they'll have to be twenty feet high and blow fire out of their ass!'

Of course, they invented miniature golf in America.[1] It was a fad that enjoyed brief and massive popularity during the Depression, becoming known as 'The Madness of 1930'. According to John Margolies, Nina Garfinkel and Maria Reidelbach in their book *Miniature Golf*, at the start of the decade there were up to fifty thousand courses in the USA, 'providing much needed stimulus to such diverse interests as cotton, lumber, concrete, steel, roofing, and lighting'. The authors estimate the craze saved a hundred thousand workers from soup kitchens and bread lines. It was lucrative and addictive. Golfers played all night. In Chicago and New York, there were rumours of Mob involvement in a mini-golf racket. Politicians expressed concern that miniature golf's

---

1. Arguably.

The accepted version of events is as follows. In 1916, James Barber of Pinehurst, North Carolina, employed amateur architect Edward H. Wiswell to construct a miniature golf course in the grounds of his estate. However, the course was not open to the public. In 1926 Garnet and Frieda Carter built their own miniature golf course, with obstacles, as part of Fairyland Inn, a resort located on Lookout Mountain, on the border between Georgia and Tennessee. In 1929, Garnet Carter patented the course template under the name Tom Thumb Golf, although there are indications that it was his wife who originally designed it. Two years later, Garnet Carter was a millionaire several times over. In 2001, a postage stamp was issued commemorating him as 'the inventor of miniature golf.'

But Tim Davies has brought to my attention an article that appeared in the *Illustrated London News* on 8 June 1912, entitled 'Bridge, Stick, Tunnel and Box: A Golf Game for Putters' with an illustration by 'our special artist A. C. Michael', entitled 'At the Garden Party: An Exciting Moment of Gofstacle'. The illustration shows a group of flannelled young chaps enjoying a game that looks suspiciously like crazy golf, with the following caption: 'Gofstacle is played with golf balls and putters. Four balls go to the set and these are coloured like croquet balls. The obstacles to be negotiated include hoops, rings, a tunnel, a bridge and a box which has to be entered up an incline. It is played like golf croquet, and may also be played as is golf, the obstacles taking the place of holes. It is claimed for it that it is calculated to improve putting. Its popularity is undoubted.'

Or, to put it another way: in your face, Garnet Carter.

popularity presented a threat to social order. The lyricist Mitchell Parish, fresh from co-writing 'Stardust' with Hoagy Carmichael, contributed to a hit tune entitled 'I've Gone Goofy Over Miniature Golf'. There were others, notably 'Since My Wife Took Up Miniature Golf' and 'Since They're All Playing Miniature Golf' by the entertainer Eddie Cantor:

> *The bankers, the beggars, reformers and bootleggers*
> *Are all playing Miniature Golf.*
> *Why talk of unemployment and that times are hard*
> *When a guy can make a fortune in his own back yard?*
> *The tough eggs, the killers, the gangsters and guerrillas,*
> *It seems that the world has turned pansy.*
> *We've got to look the matter squarely in the face,*
> *With babies swinging putters all around the place,*
> *America'll be bringing up a humpbacked race*
> *If we keep playing Miniature Golf.*

The craze blew itself out fast, but by the 1950s miniature golf had re-established itself as a family activity for baby-boomers, or the perfect venue for a first date. This ritual achieved celluloid immortality in Martin Scorsese's *Raging Bull*. The movie is routinely praised for the verisimilitude of its fight scenes but the episode at the miniature-golf course is so unrealistic it looks like a parody of the rest of the film. Jake La Motta (Robert De Niro) takes Vickie (Cathy Moriarty) on a date to a miniature-golf course where, implausibly, her ball gets lost beneath one of the obstacles. With deep meaningfulness, both Jake and Vickie are dressed in white. The obstacle is a church.

Vickie: 'What does that mean?'

Jake: 'It means the game is over.'

It was in the 1950s that miniature golf turned into a real business. In 1954 a former insurance executive called Don Clayton built his first Putt-Putt course in Fayetteville, North Carolina, as a test of skill rather than a display of novelty. There were no windmills in Putt-Putt. 'Our putters are great athletes and great men,' said Clayton. 'We have made competition out of a thing that was recreational. I believe this is the type of drive and commerce that made this country great.' The business quickly grew into one of the great American roadside franchises, like McDonald's or Holiday Inn. There are currently 260 Putt-Putt courses in nine countries, including South Africa and China.

In the early 1960s, Arnold Palmer Enterprises started up their own miniature golf franchise, which is where we came in. Arnold Palmer and his agent Mark McCormack, the future head of IMG, were pioneers of the kind of personality sports branding so ubiquitous today. Some of the products to which they lent the Palmer name were obvious, golf balls, golf schools, and some less so: Arnold Palmer Foot Detergent, for instance, or a chain of 110 Arnold Palmer Dry Cleaning Centers. 'I must confess I didn't originally see the point,' says Palmer candidly, in his autobiography.

The point was to make hay while the sun was shining, and bales of it. Palmer and McCormack were wildly successful and Palmer deserves his place in the histories of both golf and the modern sports business. The Arnold Palmer Putting Courses were one small part of the bid for total global Palmerization. By 1964, there were 125 courses across America. The first British course opened in 1965, as part of an Arnold Palmer Driving Range in Coventry and, as we know, more followed, mostly at the seaside. Palmer was involved in the design of the courses, hoping to achieve 'a country club atmosphere', and several of the fairways and greens are scaled-down versions of international championship holes – the sixteenth at Augusta, Georgia, and the eleventh at Troon in Scotland. However, to preserve the novelty of miniature golf, and to ensure the courses did not appeal only to golfers, tasteful and symbolic obstacles were incorporated into the design. There was a windmill, of course, but also a water-wheel (industry), a rocketship (the space race) and a replica of the Washington Monument (America).

On our second night in Myrtle Beach, Mark and I went out to Coastal Federal Field to see the Myrtle Beach Pelicans, the local baseball team, take on the Lynchburg Hillcats in the Carolina League. Before the game, Andrea Kersee from TV 33 appeared on the field to sing 'The Star Spangled Banner'. As she emoted and enunciated every word, the crowd stood in complete silence and, at the song's close, cheered wildly and sincerely.

During the game, for something to do, I reflected on the paradox of the Arnold Palmer Putting Courses' success in Britain. Compared with other miniature-golf franchises, they were intended to be relatively sophisticated and urbane places. Additionally, the courses were nifty pieces of integrated corporate and national brand work, before such work was commonplace. Arnold Palmer Enterprises took a sport, shrank it and put it to the service of international commerce. And how did the British respond? We made crazy golf out of them. At last, I thought, something to be proud of.

The following day, Jon Drexler flew in from Houston. The last time I'd seen him had been over that disconsolate final meal in Denmark after he had missed the cut by a single stroke. I was really looking forward to telling him my war stories from Latvia. Jon wanted to get some practice on the Hawaiian Rumble. The US Open was a month away, and once again Bob Detwiler was hosting and organizing the tournament across all three of his courses. As head of the US ProMiniGolf Association, Bob had also installed an eighteen-hole eternit course next to the parking lot of the Hawaiian Rumble. The USPMGA is affiliated to the World Minigolf Sport Federation. Qualification for the US team at the World Championships in Finland would take place on the eternit, and I knew that Jon would like a few rounds just to make sure he was ready.

On the drive up to the courses, we stopped at Buccaneer Bay ('Arrr, Mateys, Family Fun For Everyone'), just for the hell of it.

'You know,' smiled Jon, 'this is kind of weird for me. I never do this for fun.'

Since I'd last seen him, Jon had run into difficulties with his miniature golf, but not because of any failure of technique. He had become embroiled in a row that, as he told me about it, seemed to offer final, definitive proof that miniature golf could be considered a legitimate sport, and that we should resist the temptation to turn it into one.

There are currently two miniature-golf tours in the States where putters can compete for prize money. No one gets rich playing minigolf but ten-thousand-dollar purses are not uncommon. Bob Detwiler's USPMGA runs one tour, including the US Open and US Masters, both of which take place on Bob's courses in Myrtle Beach. The rival, and larger, organization is the Professional Putters Association, which co-ordinates tournaments in six states and a national tour as well. The PPA is affiliated to Putt-Putt Golf Courses of America Inc., and PPA tournaments may only take place on Putt-Putt courses. Jon usually played on the PPA Texas state tour.

The Professional Putters Association takes a dim view of its members participating in rival competitions, so much so that anyone found competing in one runs the risk of having their PPA membership revoked; PPA officials have been known to attend rival USPMGA events to see if they can identify anyone putting under an assumed name. Putt-Putt Inc. is also highly concerned with its public image. When a story entitled 'This Ain't No Minigolf! Hide Your Liquor And Lock Up Your Wives And Daughters – The Putt-Putt Tour's In Town!' appeared in a golf magazine, at least one player profiled in the article was suspended from the PPA for misconduct. Drinking, gambling and topless bars do not fit the Putt-Putt family picture.

When Jon applied for a waiver that would allow him to represent the USA at the World Championships in Finland without being thrown off the Texas tour, the PPA refused. Bob Detwiler manages the US team, and as such the World Championships are seen by Putt-Putt Inc. as a USPMGA event. And PPA members may not play in USPMGA events under any circumstances, even global ones.

'I want to go to the World Championships,' said Jon ruefully, 'so I said to the PPA, "If you don't give me a waiver, I won't sign up for your organization until September when I come back from the World Championships, and I'll finish up the tour then." But because there were other people who were planning to play in a non-PPA tournament in Florida in March, they rewrote the membership rules to prevent their members playing in other tournaments before the PPA season began. They essentially said that anybody who plays in a non-PPA event this year and is not a member, and who applies for membership later, will not be accepted. Including me.'

Which meant that, to all intents and purposes, Jon had been dismissed from the tour, and without even visiting a topless bar once.

'I haven't actually been suspended,' said Jon, 'but they have told me they will not accept my application, and they will not give me a waiver. So effectively I have been suspended for this year.'

'But why?' I asked.

'Because Putt-Putt consider the tour to be a marketing tool and not something to promote the sport,' said Jon. 'Anything that supports other brands is against their organization. The ironic thing is that if I didn't say anything to the PPA, I probably would have gotten away with it.'

In other words, Jon Drexler was being penalized for wanting to represent his country – for wanting to play – because it conflicted with Putt-Putt's ambitions for their brand.

Up at the Hawaiian Rumble, I asked Bob Detwiler what he thought Putt-Putt stood to gain by excluding people. 'I don't know,' he said. 'What they're doing is alienating all the guys that play in their tournaments. Because those players feel like they're being prohibited or limited, which they are, and denied a chance to win some money on our tournaments, which doesn't seem right. One of our guys is thinking of suing them right now. He believes he has a solid case. The Federal Trade Commission is really upset over the fact that they are limiting them from participating in other tournaments.'

This conflict reminded me of the legal battles that flared up occasionally in snooker or boxing, or rival cricket tours.

'All I'm trying to do is promote miniature golf,' claimed Bob Detwiler. 'I'd be promoting theirs too! If their guys play well here, they could go to the World Championships, to the World Games, maybe even to the Olympics, all through the US ProMiniGolf Association. But all they can do at the moment is play in PPA tournaments. Which is fine, but they're missing the boat.'

He might simply be trying to promote miniature golf, but affiliating with the WMF had been a smart move on Bob Detwiler's part. If the game took off again in America, he was perfectly positioned to capitalize on it. The PPA would be left behind.

'They're so stupid, I can't believe it,' he said. 'The potential is huge. And you know what it would do for their business?' Bob Detwiler leant back in his chair, flung his arms wide and made a noise like an exploding volcano.

Outside on the eternit course, Jon and I attempted a few of the holes that had tortured me at the European Championships. Beach music floated across from the Hawaiian Rumble. As I lined up my putt on the Blitz, a small grey lizard darted across the surface that I had played in Rīga and Odense and Clacton-on-Sea. This might be the last time I ever do this, I thought. There was no amount of money you could pay me to go to Finland in Jon's place. I didn't even really want to play the eternit now, not when there were so many mind-bending wonderlands nearby. Standing here felt like an unwelcome acid flashback, especially with the lizard. But Jon wanted to play and I didn't want to stop him.

We drove back to the hotel. Just round the corner, across the way from the sportswear store with an enormous picture of Roy Keane in its window, former Olympic figure skater Nancy Kerrigan was appearing at the Ice Castle Theater in an ice-dance version of the 1980s movie *Footloose*. The show was called, as you might expect, *Footloose On Ice*. In 1994, Nancy Kerrigan was the victim of one of the most famous rivalries in sports history when Shane Stant, an associate of her fellow US team member Tonya Harding, attacked her during the Olympic trials in Detroit, clubbing her viciously on the knee with a metal baton while she practised.

I asked Jon Drexler if he ever felt like taking a baton to any PPA members or, worse, buying them tickets to see *Footloose On Ice*.

'I don't hate them that much,' said Jon.

Jon's troubles with the PPA were causing him to be more disillusioned than angry. 'When my not-a-suspension is over, I don't know if I'll go back on the PPA tour,' he said sadly. 'I'll make my decision next year. At the moment I feel, what's the point, if I'm going to get suspended every other year when I want to play for Team USA, you know? Why do I want to play in an organization that doesn't want me as a continuous member? And these are my friends that I play with in Texas. I could go take the legal avenue, file injunctions, start making them waste money. Would I win? I don't know. Could I possibly jeopardize the tour over this? Maybe. But these are the people I hang out with. I can't get too crazy about this because either I won't get a chance to play with them any more, or I'll just ruin it for everybody.'

I could only begin to imagine how frustrated he must feel with this situation.

He gave a resigned smile. 'I just think it's stupid,' he said. 'But what's the point of winning an argument if you lose everything else in the process?'

I was reminded of Jon's generous words when, in August, Gilbert Felli, the Director of Sport for the International Olympic Committee, ignoring minigolf's recent acceptance by AGFIS, briskly dismissed miniature golf's chances of ever making it as an Olympic event. He was quoted in *USA Today* as saying that miniature golf 'is not recognized by us at any level'.

When I read Gilbert Felli's comment, I thought, I don't recognize the International Olympic Committee at any level, so piss off Gilbert Felli.

But then I thought: Who needs the IOC anyway? When sports get too big, they get hijacked, souped-up, ruined. Me and a few thousand other people understand the uniqueness of miniature golf. We know it's a sport. We'd like others to join us. But how would we feel if, as a result, it got taken away from us?

What's the point of winning an argument if you lose everything else in the process?

So the campaign to have minigolf recognized as a real sport is going to be a gentle one. We want a quiet revolution. Through us, people will rediscover sport on their own terms. And we'll keep the windmills. It would be a pity if we banished all the craziness from crazy golf.

On our last morning in Myrtle Beach, it rained for the first time, a torrential rain that lashed the sails of the pirate ships and turned the crystal blue lagoons the colour of water. On the way to drop off the car, and after spending an hour in a second-hand record store, we stopped at Mount Atlanticus for one last round of Minotaur Goff. There were no people on the sidewalks and no people in the lobby of the miniature golf course. The girl behind the desk looked surprised to see us, dressed in our wet-weather gear and ready to play.

'The Austrian guys, right?' she said.

Leaving Mark at the first tee, I walked right through the labyrinth and climbed the steps to one of the treetop huts. The view of Myrtle Beach was much reduced, with mist draped around the roller-coaster. The course was almost empty, but down by the giant ostrich in the far corner, a small boy was trying to finish his round. Although he was soaked, he was biting his lip in concentration. He looked to have five or six feet to cover, it was difficult to tell from this distance. But the putt was good and as the ball rolled safely to the cup, the boy launched his putter into the air in triumph. It spun above his head and, rather than try to catch it, he stepped to one side, laughing as it fell to the ground.

And then his friends called for him, and he picked up the club, fetched his ball from the cup and ran inside.

'O my goodness!' cried Sancho. 'Didn't I tell your worship to look what you were doing, for they were only windmills? Nobody could mistake them, unless he had windmills on the brain.'

'Silence, friend Sancho,' replied Don Quixote. 'Matters of war are more subject than most to continual change.'

The Adventures of Don Quixote
MIGUEL DE CERVANTES SAAVEDRA

WIN A
FREE GO

The Seven Pillars of
Crazy Golf Wisdom

I • II • III • IV • V • VI • VII

I

⚑ Crazy Golf Brings People Together

Yes. People who like crazy golf.

II

⚑ Crazy Golf Builds Character

Yes. If you want.

III

⚑ Crazy Golf Is A Beautiful Game

Well . . . no, probably not. But I think it is.

IV

⚑ Crazy Golf Is A Universal Language

No sport is a universal language but miniature golf comes closer
than most. British people speak crazy golf, which is a corruption of
the original. But that might change.

V

⚐ Crazy Golf Is The New Religion

Absolutely not. Let's not make that mistake again.

VI

⚐ It's Not Whether You Win Or Lose, It's How You Play The Game

Yes. We should all try harder to remember this.

VII

⚐ 'Some People Think Crazy Golf Is A Matter Of Life And Death'

I can assure them it isn't. But it might be one day. If you want.

Scorecard

This book couldn't have been written without the considerable help of the following people:

David Aaronovitch; Anne-Liese Badyan; Liam Bailey; June Baker; Kirsten Barnes; Victoria Barnsley; Lionel Bender; Steve Beswick; Alan Bishop; Michael Bracewell; David Browne; Gareth Burchmore; Sue Campbell at the Youth Sport Trust; Dick Copperwaite; Rachel Cugnoni; Tim Davies; Bob Detwiler of the USPMGA; Mark Devlin at QPR; Jon Drexler; Joanna Ellis; Don Faircloth; Edouard Faure; Simon Garfield; Joanne Glasbey at *Esquire*; John Hadman; Steen Handberg; Dave Haslam; Rupert Heath; Kjell Henriksson and Alfred Schrod of the WMF; Sorrel Hershberg; Philip Hoare; Tom Hodgkinson at the *Idler*; Leo Hollis; David Hooper; Mark Hutchinson; Dave Jacobs; Gary Jenkins; Jude the Stadium Cat; Michael Keane; Gordon Kerr; Shawn Levy; Mark Luffman; Tony Lyons; Ian MacDonald; Dominic Maxwell; Carol Miller; Neil Mudd; Stephen Nash; Peter Neumann of the PPA; Mike Newman; Stephen and Caroline Page; Alex Parker; Geoff Parmiter; Martin Parr; Peter Parr; Nicholas Pearson; Steven Poole; Christopher Potter; Clive Priddle; Nick Rennison; Dan Rhodes; Jarmo Sandelin; Jon Savage; Jenny Searle; Lindsay Seers; Sportspages Bookshop; Catherine Stead; Tracy Stent; Harold Swash; Mark Taylor; Ben Thompson; the Vallory family; Tina Varsani; Georgia Viehbeck at Arnold Palmer Enterprises; Heinz Weber; Tony White; Chris Wright; Paul Wright; Duncan Youel.

Special thanks to everyone at the BMGA, especially Peter and Tim, for their patience and support. Find the BMGA on the web at *http://members.aol.com/MiniGolf98/* or via *www.miniature golfer.com*.

At Curtis Brown, my agent Jonny Geller, and also Doug Kean.

At Penguin, my editor Tony Lacey, and also Zelda Turner, Hazel Orme and Keith Taylor; John Bond, Carol Baker, Charlotte Greig, Tom Weldon, Peter Bowron and Joanna Prior; John Hamilton, and Jon Gray at gray 318 for the cover.

All my colleagues at 4ᵗʰ Estate.

Thanks, Mum and Dad.

God save the Kinks.

Finally, I would like to thank my wife Tina for everything. She wrote this book almost as much as I did – paid the bills, did the driving, kept me sane and thought of the best jokes. More than anyone, she knows the score.

The publishers are grateful to the following for permission to reproduce extracts from their work:

Excerpt from *How to Travel with a Salmon and Other Essays* by Umberto Eco, published by Martin Secker & Warburg. Reprinted by permission of The Random House Group Ltd.

Excerpt from *Perfect Tense* by Michael Bracewell, published by Jonathan Cape. Copyright © Michael Bracewell, 2001. Reprinted by kind permission of the author.

Excerpts from *Revolution in the Head* by Ian MacDonald, published by 4ᵗʰ Estate, 1994, Copyright © 1994 Ian MacDonald. Reprinted by kind permission of the author.

Sport (The Odd Boy). Words and Music by Vivian Stanshall. Copyright © 1969. Reproduced by permission of EMI Music Publishing Ltd, London WC2H 0QY.

My Star. Words and Music by Renars Kaupers. Copyright © 2000, Micrec Publishing Ltd, Latvia. Reproduced by permission of EMI Music Publishing Ltd, London WC2H 0QY.

E. M. Forster quotation reprinted by permission of the Provost and Scholars of King's College, Cambridge, and the Society of Authors as the Literary Representatives of the E. M. Forster Estate.

Excerpts from *The Sporting Spirit* by George Orwell (Copyright George Orwell), by permission of Bill Hamilton as the Literary Executor of the Estate of the Late Sonia Brownell Orwell and Secker & Warburg Ltd.

Every effort has been made to contact copyright-holders. Any errors or omissions will be corrected in future editions.